RAISING THE FLOOR

RAISING
THE
FLOOR

HOW A UNIVERSAL BASIC INCOME
CAN RENEW OUR ECONOMY AND
REBUILD THE AMERICAN DREAM

ANDY STERN

WITH LEE KRAVITZ

PUBLICAFFAIRS
New York

Library of Congress Control Number: 2016931951
ISBN 978-1-61039-625-7 (hardcover)
ISBN 978-1-61039-626-4 (e-book)

First Edition

10 9 8 7 6 5 4 3 2 1

To Matt, Kaitlyn, and Cassie . . . and to a new American Dream where each of our children has the freedom and security to choose the life they want for themselves and their family

CONTENTS

MY INVITATION

SIXTEEN YEARS INTO the twenty-first century we are trying to find solutions to its unique problems—especially those that are challenging the way we work, earn a living, and support our families—with ideas and methods that worked in the twentieth.

Most Americans—working or not—have lived through a very tough period, especially since the financial crash of 2008. What I have found from speaking with thousands of people from every economic strata is that they often blame themselves for not finding a permanent or good-paying job; for getting laid off or working inconsistent hours; for taking multiple low-wage jobs or contingent work just to make ends meet; for, especially in the case of recent college graduates, needing to move back into their parents' house; for not building a nest egg or enough savings to retire; for working tirelessly so that their kids could go to college—and now their children can't get a job.

What I want to say to each and every one is: This should not be about personal blame because the changes that are causing this jobless, wage-less recovery are structural. You worked hard. You played by the rules. You did exactly what you were supposed to do to fulfill your part of America's social contract.

There is hope for our economy and future, but only if we come to terms with how the current explosion in technology is likely to create a shortage of jobs, a surplus of labor, and a bigger and bigger gap between the rich and poor over the next twenty years.

When I left my job as president of the Service Employees International Union (SEIU) in 2010, I undertook a five-year journey to better understand the way technology is changing the economy and workplace, and to find a way to revive the American Dream. I have structured this book around many of the people I met on this journey, their assessment of the problem, my observations about whether I think they are on the money or just plain wrong, and then the solution of a universal basic income. That solution is a work-in-progress. I invite you to join me in debating it, refining it, and building a constituency for it, so that we can help America fulfill its historical promise to future generations of our children.

Andy Stern
Washington, DC
June 2016

RAISING THE FLOOR

CAN WE INVENT A BETTER FUTURE?

"There's something happening here. What it is
ain't exactly clear."

—Buffalo Springfield

CAMBRIDGE, MA. NOVEMBER 17, 2014

I am walking around one of the most out-of-this-world places on earth—the MIT Media Lab in Cambridge, Massachusetts. There is a huge amount of brainpower here: more than twenty groups of MIT faculty, students, and researchers working on 350 projects that range from smart prostheses and sociable robots to advanced sensor networks and electronic ink. The Media Lab is famous for its emphasis on creative collaboration between the best and the brightest in disparate fields: scientists and engineers here work alongside artists, designers, philosophers, neurobiologists, and communications experts. Their mission is "to go beyond known boundaries and disciplines" and "beyond the obvious to the questions not yet asked—questions whose answers could radically improve the way people live, learn, express themselves, work, and play." Their motto—"inventing a better future"—conveys a forward-looking confidence that's been lacking in our nation since the 2008 financial crisis plunged us into a recession followed by a slow, anxiety-inducing recovery.

On this cloudy November day, it seems that all the sunlight in Cambridge is streaming through the glass and metallic screens that cloak the Media Lab, rendering it a luminous bubble, or a glowing alternative universe. Architect Fumihiko Mako designed the building around a central atrium that rises six floors—"a kind of vertical street," he called it, with spacious labs branching off on each floor. Walking up the atrium, you look through the glass walls and see groups of (mainly) young geniuses at work.

Or are they playing? I am struck by how casual and unhurried they seem. Whether they are lounging on couches, gathered around a computer screen, drawing equations on a wall, these inventors of the future seem to be having a whole lot of fun. That's not how the thirty people who are leaders in the labor movement and the foundation world who accompanied me here would characterize their own workplaces. They have been grappling with growing income inequality, stagnant wages, and increasing poverty in the communities they serve, and also with political gridlock on Capitol Hill. It's been harder for them to get funding and resources for the important work they do.

They have come here, as I have, to get a glimpse of how MIT's wizards and their technologies will impact the millions of middle- and lower-income Americans whose lives are already being disrupted and diminished in the new digital economy. Will these emerging technologies create jobs or destroy them? Will they give lower- and middle-income families more or less access to the American Dream? Will they make my generation's definition of a "job" obsolete for my kids and grandkids?

For the past five years, I've been on a personal journey to understand an issue that should be at the heart of our nation's economic and social policies: the future of work. I have been interviewing CEOs, labor leaders, futurists, politicians, entrepreneurs, and historians to find answers to the following questions: After decades of globalization and technology-driven growth, what will America's workplaces look like in twenty years? Which job categories will be gone forever in the age of robotics and artificial intelligence? Which new ones, if any, will take their place?

The MIT Media Lab is one stop on that journey; since the early 1990s, it has been in the forefront of wireless communication, 3D printing, and digital computing. Looking around at my colleagues, I think: People like us—labor organizers, community activists, people at the helm of small foundations that work for social and economic justice—don't usually visit places like this. We spend our time in factories and on farms, in fast-food restaurants and in hospitals advocating for higher wages and better working conditions. While we refer to our organizations by acronyms—SEIU (Service Employees International Union), OSF (Open Society Foundations), and NDWA (National Domestic Workers Alliance)—there is one acronym most of us would never use to describe ourselves personally: STEM. Most of today's discussion will involve science, technology, engineering, and mathematics—the STEM subjects—and it will go way over our heads. Instead, we'll be filtering what we see through our "progressive" justice, engagement, and empowerment lenses, and how we experience technology in our own lives.

Personally I am of two minds about technology. On the one hand, I want it to work well and make my life easier and more enjoyable. On the other, I'm afraid of the consequences if all of the futuristic promises of technology come to fruition.

As I wait for the first session to begin, I take out my iPhone and begin reading about the Media Lab's CE 2.0 project. CE stands for consumer electronics, and CE 2.0 is "a collaboration with member companies to formulate the principles for a new generation of consumer electronics that are highly connected, seamlessly interoperable, situation-aware, and radically simpler to use," according to the Media Lab's website.

CE 2.0 sounds really, really great to me. Then I realize that I'm reading about it on the same iPhone that keeps dropping conference calls in my New York apartment to my partners and clients in other parts of the city. So how can I ever expect CE 2.0 to live up to the Media Lab's hype? And then I find myself thinking: What if it does? What if CE 2.0 exceeds all the hype and disrupts a whole bunch of industries? Which jobs will become obsolete as a result of this new generation of consumer electronics? Electricians? The people who make batteries, plugs, and electrical wiring? I keep going back and forth between the promise and the hype and everything in between. Even though CE 2.0 is basically an abstraction to me, it conjures up all sorts of expectations and fears. And I think that many of my friends and colleagues have similar longings, doubts, and fears when it comes to technology.

All of the projects at the MIT Media Lab are supported by corporations. Twitter, for instance, has committed $10 million to the Laboratory for Social Machines, which is developing technologies that "make sense of semantic and social patterns across the broad span of public mass media, social media, data streams, and digital content." Google Education is funding the Center for Mobile Learning, which seeks to innovate education through mobile computing. The corporations have no say in the direction of the research, or ownership of what the MIT researchers patent or produce; they simply have a front-row seat as the researchers take the emerging technologies wherever their curiosity and the technology takes them.

Clearly, there is a counter-cultural ethos to the Media Lab. Its nine governing principles are: "Resilience over strength. Pull over push. Risk over safety. Systems over objects. Compasses over maps. Practice over theory. Disobedience over compliance. Emergence over authority. Learning over education." For me, that's a welcome invitation to imagine, explore new frontiers, and dream.

Before we tour the various labs, Peter Cohen, the Media Lab's Director of Development, tells us that there is an artistic or design component to most of the Media Lab's projects. "Much of our work is displayed in museums," he says. "And some are performed in concert halls." One I particularly like is the brainchild of Tod Machover, who heads the Hyperinstruments/Opera of the Future group. Machover, who co-created the popular Guitar Hero and Rock Band music video games, is composing a series of urban symphonies that attempt to capture the spirit of cities around the world. Using technology he's developed that can collect and translate sounds into music, he enlists people who live, work, and make use of each city to help create a collective musical portrait of their town. To date, he's captured the spirits of Toronto, Edinburgh, Perth, and Lucerne through his new technology. Now he is turning his attention to Detroit. I love this idea of getting factory workers, teachers, taxi cab drivers, police officers, and other people who live and work in Detroit involved in the creation of an urban symphony that can be performed so that the entire city can enjoy and take pride in it.

We head to the Biomechatronics Lab on the second floor. Luke Mooney, our guide to this lab, is pursuing a PhD in mechanical engineering at MIT. Only twenty-four, he has already designed and developed an energy-efficient powered knee prosthesis. He shows us the prototype, a gleaming exoskeleton enveloping the knee of a sleek mannequin. Mooney created the prosthesis with an expert team of biophysicists, neuroscientists, and mechanical, biomedical, and tissue engineers. It will reduce the "metabolic cost of walking," he tells us, making it easier for a sixty-four-year-old with worn-out knees and a regularly sore back like me to maybe run again and lift far more weight than I could ever have dreamed of lifting.

Looking around, I'm struck by the mess—coffee cups and Red Bull cans, plaster molds of ankles, knees, and feet, discarded tools and motors, lying all over the place, like the morning after a month of all-nighters.

The founder of the Biomechatronics Lab, Hugh Herr, is out of town this day, but his life mission clearly animates the Lab. When he was seventeen, a rock-climbing accident resulted in the amputation of both his legs below his knees. Frustrated with the prosthetic devices on the market, he got a master's degree in mechanical engineering and a PhD in biophysics, and used that knowledge to design a prosthesis that enabled him to compete as an elite rock-climber again. In 2013, after the Boston Marathon bombings, he designed a special prosthesis for one of the victims: ballroom dancer Adrianne Haslet-Davis, who had lost her lower left leg in the blast. Seven months later, at a TED talk Herr was giving, Haslet-Davis walked out on the stage with her partner and danced a rumba. "In 3.5 seconds, the criminals and cowards took Adrianne off the dance floor," Herr said. "In 200 days, we put her back."

At our next stop, the Personal Robotics Lab, Indian-born researcher Palash Nandy tells us the key to his human-friendly robots: their eyes. By manipulating a robot's eyes and eyebrows, Nandy and his colleagues can make the robot appear sad, mad, confused, excited, attentive, or bored. Hospitals are beginning to deploy human-friendly robots as helpmates to terminally ill kids. "Unlike the staff and other patients, who are constantly changing," Nandy says, "the robot is always there for the child, asking him how he's doing, which reduces stress."

With the help of sophisticated sensors, the Personal Robotics Lab is building robots that are increasingly responsive to the emotional states of humans. Says Nandy: "Leo the Robot might not understand what you need or mean by the words you say, but he can pick up the emotional tone of your voice." In a video he shows us, a researcher warns Leo, "Cookie Monster is bad. He wants to eat your cookies." In response, Leo narrows his eyes, as if to say: "I get your message. I'll keep my distance from that greedy Cookie Monster."

Nandy also sings the praises of a robot who helps children learn French, and one that's been programmed to help keep adults motivated as they lose weight.

My colleagues are full of questions and also objections:

"Can't people do most of these tasks as well or better than the robots?"

"If every child grows up with their own personal robot friend, how will they ever learn to negotiate a real human relationship?"

"If you can create a robot friend, can't you also create a robot torturer? Ever thought of that?"

"Yeah," Nandy says, seeming to make light of the question. "But it's hard to imagine evil robots when I'm around robots that say 'I love you' all day long."

As awestruck and exhilarated as we are by what we see, my colleagues and I are getting frustrated by the long pauses and glib answers that greet so many of our concerns about the long-term impact of the technologies being developed here on the job market, human relationships, and our political rights and freedoms. As they invent the future, are these brilliant and passionate innovators alert to the societal risks and ramifications of what they're doing?

On our way into the Mediated Matter Lab, we encounter a chaise lounge and a grouping of truly stunning bowls and sculptures that have been created using 3D printers. Markus Kayser, our guide through the Mediated Matter Lab, is a thirty-one-year-old grad student from northern Germany. A few years ago he received considerable acclaim and media attention for a device he created called the Sun Sinter.

Kayser shows us a video of a bearded hipster—himself—carrying a metallic suitcase over a sand dune in Egypt's Saharan Desert. It's like a scene in a Buster Keaton movie. He stops and pulls several photovoltaic batteries and four large lenses from the suitcase. Then he focuses the lenses—at a heat of 1,600 degrees centigrade—onto a bed of sand. Within seconds, the concentrated heat of the sun has melted the sand and transformed it into glass. What happens next on the video gives us a glimpse into the future of manufacturing. Kayser takes his laptop out of the suitcase and spends a few minutes designing a bowl on the computer. Then, with a makeshift 3D printer powered by solar energy, he prints out the bowl in layers of plywood. He places the plywood prototype of the bowl on a small patch of desert. Then he focuses the lenses of the battery-charged Solar Sinter on the sand. And then, layer after layer, he melts the sand into glass until he's manufactured a glass bowl out of the desert's abundant supplies of sun and sand.

"My whole goal is to explore hybrid solutions that link technology and natural energy to test new scenarios for production," Kayser tells us. But the glass bowl only hints at the possibilities. Engineers from NASA and the US Army have already talked to him about the potential of using his technology to build emergency shelters after hurricanes and housing in hazardous environments—for example, the desert regions of Iran and Iraq.

"How about detention centers for alleged terrorists?" one of my colleagues asks slyly. "I bet the Army is licking its chops to build a glass Guantanamo in the desert only miles from the Syrian border."

Another asks: "Has anyone talked to you about using this technology to create urban housing for the poor?"

Kayser pauses before shaking his head no. The questions that consume our group most—how can we use this powerful technology for good rather than evil and to remedy the world's inequities and suffering—do not seem of consequence to Kayser. This is by design: the Media Lab encourages the researchers to follow the technology wherever it leads them, without the pressure of developing a big-bucks commercial product, or an application that will save the world.

If they focus on the end results and specific commercial and social outcomes, they will be less attuned to the technology, to the materials, and to nature itself, which would impede their creative process. I understand that perspective, but it also worries me.

As I watch Kayser and his Solar Sinter turn sand into glass, another image comes to mind: Nearly 4,700 years ago, in the same Egyptian desert where Kayser made his video, more than 30,000 slaves, some of them probably my ancestors, and citizen-volunteers spent seven years quarrying, cutting, and transporting thousands of tons of stone to create Pharaoh Khufu's Great Pyramid, one of the Seven Wonders of the Ancient World. That's a lot of labor compared with what it will take to build a modern-day community of glass houses in the vicinity of the Pyramid, or in Palm Springs, using the next iteration of the Sun Sinter. I'm concerned about the Sun Sinter's impact on construction jobs.

Employment issues are at best a distant concern for the wizards who are inventing the future. Press them and they'll say that technological disruption always produces new jobs and industries: Isn't that what happened after Gutenberg invented the printing press and Ford automated the assembly line?

It was. But, as I reflect on this day, I remember a conversation I had with Steven Berkenfeld, an investment banker at Barclay's Capital. Berkenfeld has a unique and important perspective on the relationship between technology and jobs. Day in, day out, he is pitched proposals by entrepreneurs looking to take their companies public. Most of the companies are developing technologies that will help businesses become more productive and efficient. That means fewer and fewer workers, according to Berkenfeld.

"Every company is trying to do more with less," he explained. "Industry by industry, and sector by sector, every company is looking to drive out labor." And very few policy makers are aware of the repercussions. "They convince themselves that technology will create new jobs when, in fact, it will displace them by the millions, spreading pain and suffering throughout the country. When you look at the future from that perspective, the single most important decisions we need to make are: How do we help people continue to make a living, and how do we keep them engaged?"

At the end of our visit to the Media Lab, my job, as convener of the group, is to summarize some of the day's lessons. I begin with an observation: "It's amazing how the only thing that doesn't work here is when these genius researchers try to project their PowerPoints onto the screen." The twenty or so people who remain in our group laugh knowingly. Just like us, the wizards at MIT can't seem to present a PowerPoint without encountering an embarrassing technological glitch.

I continue by quoting a line from a song by Buffalo Springfield, the 1960s American-Canadian rock band: "There's something's happening here. What it is ain't exactly clear." That's how I feel about our day at MIT; it has given us a preview of the future of work, which will be amazing if we can grapple with the critical ethical and social justice questions it elicits. "I've spent my whole life in the labor movement chasing the future," I tell my colleagues. "Now I'd like to catch up to it, or maybe even jump ahead of it, so I can see the future coming toward me."

Toward that end, I ask everyone in the group to answer "yes," "no," or "abstain" to two hypotheses.

Hypothesis number one: "The role of technology in the future of work will be so significant that current conceptions of a job may no longer reflect the relationship to work for most people. Even the idea of jobs as the best and most stable source of income will come into question."

Hypothesis number two: "The very real prospect in the United States is that twenty years from now most people will not receive a singular income from a single employer in a traditional employee-employer relationship. For some, such as those with substantial education, this might mean freedom. For others, those with a substandard education and a criminal record, the resulting structural inequality will likely increase vulnerability."

There are a number of groans ("Jesus, Andy, can you get any more long-winded or rhetorical?") but each member of the group writes their answers on a piece of paper, which I collect and tally. The first hypothesis gets eighteen yeses and two abstentions. The second gets sixteen yeses, three noes, and one abstention.

I am genuinely surprised by these results. Six months ago, at our last meeting of the OSF Future of Work inquiry, my colleagues had a much more varied response to these hypotheses. At least half of them did not agree with my premise that technology would have a disruptive impact on jobs, the workplace, and employer-employee relationships, and some of them disputed the premise quite angrily. ("What do you think we are, Andy—psychics?") Today's tally reflects their acknowledgment that something is happening at MIT and across the United States that will fundamentally change the way Americans live and work—what it is ain't exactly clear, but it merits our serious and immediate attention.

As they go about inventing the future, the scientists and researchers at the Media Lab aren't thinking about the consequences of their work on the millions of Americans who are laboring in factories, building our homes, guarding our streets, investing our money, computing our taxes, teaching our children and teenagers, staffing our hospitals, driving our buses, and taking care of our elders and disabled veterans.

They aren't thinking about the millions of parents who scrimped and saved to send their kids to college, because our country told them that college was the gateway to success, only to see those same kids underemployed or jobless when they graduate and move back home.

They aren't thinking about the dwindling fortunes of the millions of middle-class Americans who spent the money they earned on products and services that made our nation's economy and lifestyle the envy of the world.

They aren't thinking about the forty-seven million Americans who live in poverty, including a fifth of the nation's children.

Nor should they. That is my job, our job together, and the purpose of this book.

But I'm getting ahead of myself. The reason I am at the MIT Media Lab stems from a combination of personal and professional factors in what seemed to many to be my abrupt decision to step down as head of America's most successful union, the Service Employees International Union, or SEIU. To better understand where I am coming from and going with this book you need to understand my personal journey.

Chapter 1

MY JOURNEY

I N 2010, I seemed to be at the top of my game: leader of the country's largest and most influential union, a central player in the most significant piece of social legislation since the establishment of Medicare, and appointed by President Barack Obama to sit on the bipartisan Simpson-Bowles Commission to propose an answer to the country's long-term deficit problems. Despite this, I stepped down that year as president of the Service Employees International Union (SEIU).

From the mainstream *Washington Post* to the conservative *Wall Street Journal,* the media speculated as to why I had decided to leave SEIU at the height of my power and influence. *RedState,* a conservative journal, claimed that I was resigning because I was bored with having to spend time on the day-to-day contract battles that are a union's bread and butter. "You'd probably be bored, too, if you had taken a relatively obscure union of janitors and doormen and turned it into the largest and most powerful private-sector union in America . . . put a president of the United States into the Oval Office . . . and fulfilled one of the union movement's main objectives: nationalized healthcare." It suggested that I was itching to conquer new frontiers: "Does hanging out with a bunch of janitors and nurses' aides and arguing with their employers sound like a challenge any more?"

RedState couldn't have been more wrong. Those janitors and window cleaners, those doormen and security guards, and those nurses' aides and home- and child-care workers were the people I care about most: nothing motivates them more than the American Dream—the promise, to anyone who works hard and plays by the rules, of a good and secure livelihood and a better future for their children. When I was elected president of SEIU in 1996, that sacred American Dream still seemed possible for the people I was privileged to serve; by 2010, it had been replaced by paralyzing anxiety.

My goal at SEIU had been to build a union that could win victories for workers in the twenty-first-century global economy. Unions as a whole moved glacially. They looked backward instead of forward for solutions, and they seldom took risks. I sought to make my own and other unions more relevant in an era of declining membership and laws that had made it harder for unions to organize. In order to do that, I rocked the boat and pursued new ways to organize workers and make their influence felt in the halls of Congress, where the laws restricting unions were made.

I didn't resign from SEIU because I was bored. Rather, after nearly fifteen years at the helm of SEIU, I had lost my ability to predict labor's future. To be an effective leader, you need to be able to look twenty, thirty, even forty years down the road. That way, you can envision the future you want to create and plan back from it, instead of simply reacting to events as they occur. John L. Lewis, president of the United Mine Workers, had been able to do that in the 1930s. Walter Reuther, head of the United Auto Workers, could do that in the 1950s and 1960s. And I could do that in the 1990s and early 2000s. But, by 2010, the economy was changing and fragmenting at such warp speed that I couldn't see where it—or labor—was headed. Without a clearer vision of the future—of the world in 2025 or 2040—I couldn't develop the inner compass needed by a leader who seeks to bring about major social change, and I was out of good ideas.

So I stepped away from SEIU and, aside from my work with Simpson-Bowles, I spent the next year healing, recharging, and thinking about new ways I might help the people I cared about. At the end of that year I embarked on what became a four-year journey to discover the future of jobs, work, and the American Dream. My journey coincided with significant economic trends—a jobless recovery and the concentration of more and more wealth in the hands of fewer and fewer people. It took place during an era of political gridlock that devastated the middle class and threatened the economy as a whole. Wages were stagnant. People had to work two or three jobs to stay afloat. Students were coming out of college thousands of dollars in debt and with no substantial job prospects. For them, the idea of owning their own home and creating a better future for their children had become the American Pipe Dream.

Early on, I saw that unions would play only a limited role in shaping the twenty-first-century economy. Not only because unions are typically slow to adapt, but also because the economy is being transformed by new technologies that will automate more tasks and require fewer full-time jobs and marginalize the role of collective bargaining, leaving a dearth of dues-paying union members. Already, the new landscape of work is populated by free agents and temporary workers who have more freedom and flexibility in their work life, but no job security and significantly less leverage with the people and companies who hire them.

My focus turned to larger questions: If there are significantly fewer jobs and less work available in the future, how will people make a living, spend their time, and find purpose in their lives? Also, how can we keep the income gap from growing so wide that it erupts into social discord and upheaval?

I began looking for an idea that could unite all Americans and call us to a higher national purpose. The old American Dream—the one that had spoken so deeply to my parents' generation, and my own—had been discredited by current events and decades of stagnating wages. We needed a new American Dream—one that offers a vision of the life we can genuinely aspire to, strive for, and pass on as a birthright and inspiration to our children and future generations of Americans.

And if I came upon that unifying idea, my question to myself and others would be, "How can we organize our economy and social institutions so that this new American Dream becomes achievable for everyone?"

Along the way, I came across a potential answer to these questions. I'll detail what a *universal basic income* (UBI) is later in this book. For now, imagine a check coming in the mail each month to every single American, whether they work or not, with sufficient money to eradicate poverty and give all Americans the opportunity to achieve their dreams.

But I'm getting ahead of myself again. To appreciate why a UBI may be the most practical solution to our economic problems, and one that most if not all of our country's political parties can potentially embrace, it will be helpful to know about the perspective I gained while attempting to create major social change during labor's most turbulent and transitional years.

SEVERAL YEARS AGO, in an interview with *Washington Post* reporter Ezra Klein, I called the labor movement "the greatest middle-class, job-creating mechanism that we have ever had in America that doesn't cost taxpayers a dime."

Here's what I meant:

There was nothing inherently valuable about taking a pickax, putting a light on your head, traveling down the depths of a coal shaft, and banging that ax against a wall to extract coal. And yet, in West Virginia, coal mining built a middle class. Not because the coal miners had unique skills or went to college, but because they belonged to a union. That was true in America's steel mills and on its assembly lines, on its railroads and on its loading docks. In the industries that made our economy the envy of the world, private-sector unions turned crappy jobs into ones that promised good pay, generous benefits, and enough job security to give working families the stable middle-class existence at the heart of the American Dream.

Union members weren't the only workers who benefited. Today, people hardly take notice when a Fortune 100 company like Ford or General Motors negotiates a contract. But in the 1950s and 1960s, labor negotiations were front-page news. If Ford's autoworkers got a three-percent raise, it set a standard for workers throughout the country that made it much more likely they'd receive an equivalent raise, even if they worked in a grocery store, gas station, or bank.

At the same time, unions exerted considerable political clout and helped to lessen inequality by pushing for a minimum wage, job-based health benefits, Social Security, high marginal tax rates, and other economic policies that ensured that America's prosperity would be shared.

In 1950, the year I was born, nearly 35 percent of the nation's workers were unionized. By 1972, when I graduated college, that number had fallen to 27 percent, but unions still represented a solid percentage of the nation's workers. Today, less than 12 percent of the nation's workers are unionized, including only 6.6 percent of the private-sector workforce.

My first job after college was as a caseworker for the Pennsylvania Department of Welfare. The social-service workers in our department had voted to become part of SEIU, and they had won the right to collective bargaining. One day, shortly after being hired, I saw a notice on the bulletin board announcing a membership meeting at SEIU Local 668's office. I went for the free pizza, but stayed because I was fascinated with the work the labor representatives did, and how committed they were to changing lives.

In 1977, I ran for president of Local 668. The woman who would later become my wife ran for secretary-treasurer—on the opposing slate. I was lucky enough to win. And, at twenty-six, I became the youngest president of my local and, I believe, of any major local in SEIU history. I spent the next thirty-three years organizing workers, negotiating contracts, and helping SEIU grow from 400,000 to 2.2 million members during a period when union membership nationally fell from 23 percent to less than 12 percent of the nation's workers.

What had happened to diminish labor's overall numbers and power?

In 1981, when three thousand members of the air traffic controllers union went out on strike, President Ronald Reagan dismissed them from their jobs, ushering in an era of anti-union activities by corporations that poured millions of dollars into union-busting practices while lobbying Congress to get rid of or weaken unions so they could reduce labor costs. As corporations stiffened their resolve, unions became more hesitant to strike. In 1970, two years before I joined SEIU, there were 371 strikes in the United States; in 2010, the year I retired from SEIU, there were only eleven.

The decline in manufacturing jobs, coupled with the emergence of globalized supply chains across every industry sector, contributed further to the downward trend in union membership. Heavy industries such as steel and auto had been labor's sweet spot since the 1930s, but now they represented a much smaller part of the US economy. And globalized supply chains meant that multinational corporations could search for the lowest-cost suppliers and outsource formerly American jobs to China, India, and other developing nations.

As illustrated in the chart below, the decades-long decline in union membership has followed the same trajectory as the decline in the middle-class share of the nation's aggregate income. In other words, as union membership has declined, income inequality has gotten worse.

In a speech he gave at the Greater Omaha Chamber of Commerce Conference in 2007, Ben Bernanke, the chairman of the Federal Reserve, attributed 10 to 20 percent of the rise in income inequality to the decline in unionization. In an econometric study of data from advanced economies during the years 1980 to 2010, the International Monetary Fund came to a similar conclusion: "On average, the decline in unionization explains about half of the five percentage point rise in the top 10 percent income share. Why? Because as unions weaken, workers have less influence on the size and structure of top executive compensations."

In 1965, CEOs earned twenty times as much as the average worker; today, they earn nearly three hundred times as much.

Ties that bind

As union membership decreases, middle class income shrinks

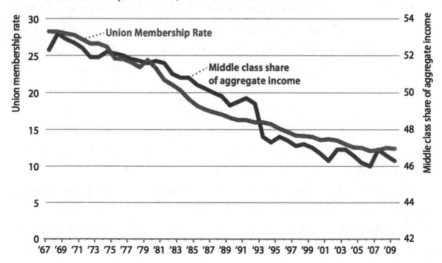

Historically, SEIU members made more than their nonunion counterparts, even for the same jobs in the same city. The union's strength made sure that our members working as janitors and nursing aides shared in their company's success—and that the executives and shareholders of their companies didn't get an even more outsized portion. And yet society-at-large seemed unaware of unions' role in leveling the playing field and keeping executive pay from going through the stratosphere. People who grew up during the Reagan years could be downright hostile to unions. As older workers retired with union-negotiated benefits, the younger workers who replaced them didn't understand or appreciate the history and purpose of unions; hence, there was less empathy and public support for our accomplishments.

In my twelve years as SEIU's organizing director, we became the nation's fastest-growing union; by the time I was elected president in 1996, we had 1.4 million members. During my acceptance speech that year at our convention in Chicago, I told the fifteen hundred delegates why I wanted to make SEIU even stronger: "I refuse to accept that our children will be the first generation in history to do worse than their parents. I want my kids to grow up and leave home able to support themselves—without having to work three jobs. I don't want them to be afraid to get sick because they don't have health insurance. Or to grow old because they don't have retirement security." Then I turned to my two children and said: "Matt and Cassie, I love you. For you—and for the sons, daughters, nieces, and nephews of everyone in this hall—this union is going to fight like hell."

I said these words with fierce optimism and hope. As the new century neared, SEIU was facing life-and-death challenges from the powerful forces arrayed against labor as a whole, including employers who were no longer local but regional, national, and even global in scope. "With every passing day, giant corporations—Kaiser, Hospital Corporation of America, ServiceMaster, and ABM—are growing bigger, more powerful, and more greedy," I told the crowd. "And unless we make the tough decisions to become smarter and stronger, they will eat us up and spit us out before we even know what's hit us."

By the time we gathered for our 2000 convention in Pittsburgh, SEIU had added more than 300,000 new members, including 74,000 home care workers in Los Angeles and 10,000 school workers in Puerto Rico. We had become the largest labor union in the AFL-CIO—larger than the Teamsters, the Steelworkers, the American Federation of Teachers, the United Auto Workers, and the American Federation of State, County and Municipal Employees.

We couldn't have chosen a more historic town to celebrate that achievement. It was here, in 1935, that United Mine Workers president John L. Lewis called for semiskilled workers in the automobile, rubber, glass, and steel industries to organize and join the Congress of Industrial Organizations (CIO). At the time, the American Federation of Labor (AFL) consisted mainly of small, craft-based unions that ignored and even looked down upon industrial workers. Lewis understood that the future of the labor movement lay in organizing these semiskilled industrial workers. Twenty years later, in 1955, the CIO would merge with the AFL, and together for the next two decades they would help raise the living standards of millions of American families and pave the way for blacks and women to enter the economy and middle class.

I asked the delegates in Pittsburgh to join me in writing the next great chapter in labor's history. The manufacturing economy of Lewis's time had given way to the service economy of our own. Instead of adhering to the outmoded practice of negotiating labor contracts one facility, one city, and one employer at a time, I urged them to work towards negotiating regional and national industry-wide contracts. I underscored our other historic goal—to gain the political power we'd need to elect a president of the United States who'd be pro-labor and work for significant healthcare and labor law reform.

By organizing entire industries—for instance, building services, healthcare, and child care workers—we could win fights that no local could ever win alone. And that was especially crucial in the emerging global economy. In New York City and elsewhere in the US, our janitors and security officers worked in buildings owned by global financial interests and foreign pension funds. The two largest security companies in North America—Securitas and Group 4—were based in Sweden and the UK. Two of the three largest school bus companies in North America were based in Great Britain. And the services industry worldwide was increasingly dominated by three multi-service outsourcing companies: Sodexho, based in France, operated in seventy-six countries; Compass, based in Great Britain, operated in ninety countries; and Aramark, based in the United States, operated in nineteen countries around the world.

"Today's global corporations have no permanent home, recognize no national borders, salute no flag but their own corporate logo, and take their money to anywhere where they can make the most—and pay the least," I said at our 2004 convention in San Francisco. "When you look at it and all the historic challenges before us, I'm sure some of you [will] join me in wishing we could go back—back to the days when unity in your local union was enough to win better contracts with a local employer, or when a single local union could elect the politicians that affected their jobs. Back to a slower time without global communications when our bosses were down the street and not in London or Paris, and when jobs in public service and healthcare were secure and not targeted for outsourcing and benefit cutting. But we all know that world is gone—it's gone forever—and any organization that fails to adapt will be gone forever as well."

As a loose trade association of sixty-five separate and autonomous unions, the AFL-CIO didn't have the organizational strength and unity to lead labor into this globalized future. For example, there were fourteen different unions trying to organize healthcare workers, and unions in disparate industries that dealt with the same employer didn't coordinate or cooperate, which undermined their efforts to win better contracts for their members. At my urging, SEIU and four other unions called on the AFL-CIO to consolidate the smaller unions into twenty larger ones that were each devoted to a single sector of the economy. "Can This Man Save Labor?" That was the question *BusinessWeek* asked on its September 13, 2004 cover, next to a photo of me. "Service Employees President Andy Stern has radical plans to remake the US labor movement," it said. "Will other union leaders go along?"

Five months later, the AFL-CIO rejected our plan. Along with six other unions, SEIU left to form our own federation, which we called "Change to Win." Our goals included much of what we had been trying to do at SEIU: consolidate smaller unions into a few large ones, encourage unions to organize on an industry-wide basis, put our members' interests, not parties or politicians, as the core of our political activities, and put the emphasis on organizing new members because there is power in numbers. We achieved many of our objectives, but ultimately we could not find the political will or shared strategy to execute some of our key principles. By 2014, only three of the founding unions remained in the federation.

WE HAD CONSIDERABLY more success achieving our goals in the political arena. SEIU supported Barack Obama in 1996 when he was a candidate for the Illinois State Senate, and in 2002 when he ran for the US Senate. In 2006, when he was considering running for the presidency, he asked if we'd consider supporting him again. "It depends," I told him. "Any candidate seeking our support needs to produce a universal healthcare plan and a way to pay for it. They also need to spend an entire day walking in the shoes of one of our members so that they can better understand the challenges facing workers and working families."

On August 9, 2007, Obama worked alongside SEIU home care worker Pauline Beck as she took care of eighty-six-year-old John Thornton, a former cement mason who lived in Alameda County, California. Obama prepared breakfast for Mr. Thornton, then mopped the floor, did the dishes and laundry, and made his bed. Mr. Thornton was an amputee, and throughout the day the senator helped him get into and out of his wheelchair. At the end of her workday, Pauline went home to take care of a grandnephew and two foster children who didn't have families of their own. Obama said that she helped him to realize the importance of paid sick leave for the entire workforce. "Heroic work, and hard work. That's what Pauline is all about," he would say four years later at the White House, with Pauline standing at his side as he announced his support for a law to extend overtime pay protections and a guaranteed minimum wage to the nation's home care workers.

SEIU became the first major union to endorse Obama in 2008. Our political action committee spent $71 million to elect him president, and we deployed an "army" of 100,000 SEIU volunteers to knock on doors and make phone calls on his behalf.

Between January and July of 2009, the logs of the Obama Administration show that I visited the White House twenty-two times, the most of any person who didn't work on the White House staff. I was there to help the Administration devise a strategy for healthcare reform, SEIU's key issue. For me, the battle was personal. My daughter Cassie had died eight years earlier after complications from spinal surgery. She was thirteen years old. If we had had a better healthcare system, "Cassie might still be here with me," I told friends. In my most despairing moments, I imagined her standing by my side, with a sign that said "Healthcare for All."

In September of 2009, we set up a "war room" in Washington to push for the president's legislation as it worked its way through Congress. SEIU locals across the nation pushed hard for healthcare reform. On March 23, 2010, following the historic bill signing, the president came over and hugged me and said: "Without SEIU members and your stories and your lobbying and your demonstrations, this would not have happened."

BECAUSE OF SEIU'S successes and my role in creating the Change to Win Federation, I had become an increasingly polarizing figure within the labor movement. The leaders of other labor unions didn't like that SEIU was bucking the tide and growing so fast or that I had more access to President Obama than they did. I also faced a revolt within my own union from leaders who wanted to hold on to their independence and traditions despite evidence that workers who worked for the same employer or in the same industry were stronger together.

Our best shot at strengthening labor nationally was the Employee Free Choice Act, which would have made it easier for workers to join and organize unions by eliminating the waiting period and secret ballot (which favored management) and allowing workers to organize a union simply through a majority sign-up. After working so hard to get President Obama elected, I was disappointed that he didn't fight harder for the Employee Free Choice Act. (Healthcare reform was clearly a higher priority for him.) In an ideologically divided Congress, the bill was doomed without his vocal support.

I had watched too many labor leaders stay far too long. When I announced my resignation as president two years before the end of my term, I said on video to SEIU's 2.2 million members: "There's a time to learn, a time to lead, and then there's a time to leave. And shortly, it will be time to retire . . . and to end my SEIU journey." I was fifty-nine years old—and tired. I kept thinking about my father. When he was sixty-four, he learned he had cancer; four years later he was dead. His death still weighed on me. So did the realization that I hadn't fully mourned the losses of my daughter and marriage. Instead, I had thrown myself into my work—into fighting to win for workers. I needed to stop running—to take stock of my life, and do the even harder work of healing. I was burnt out and, as I noted earlier, I had run out of new ideas, I had lost my feel for the future.

President Obama had just appointed me to the National Commission on Fiscal Responsibility and Reform, which would become better known in the media as Simpson-Bowles, after the names of its co-chairs, former US Senator Alan Simpson of Wyoming and former White House Chief of Staff Erskine Bowles. The other presidential appointees were David M. Cote, the CEO of Honeywell International; Alice Rivlin, the former director of the Office of Management and Budget; and Ann Fudge, who had been CEO of Young & Rubicam. The Executive Director was Bruce Reed, who later became the Chief of Staff to Vice President Biden. There were six members of the House and six members of the Senate on the Commission, divided evenly between Republicans and Democrats.

We were instructed to identify policies that might "improve the fiscal situation in the medium term and to achieve fiscal sustainability in the long run." In eight months of public hearings and deliberations, I received a graduate school-level education in macroeconomics and got a chance to work with Senator Judd Gregg (R-NH) on alternatives to the employer-based retirement system, which was leaving more and more Americans without a pension as companies used the recession to reduce head count and cut benefits. Working on the Commission with Republican Congressmen Jeb

Hensarling from Texas and Paul Ryan from Wisconsin, now Speaker of the House, I learned how conservatives view the economy and the world, a lesson that would prove especially useful to me four years later when I considered whether it would be possible to build a coalition to support a universal basic income.

That next journey—the one at the core of this book—would begin with a trip to Silicon Valley to have a conversation about technology and the economy with the visionary entrepreneur who had helped launch the computer and information technology revolutions. How did Intel co-founder Andy Grove see the future?

Chapter 2

ARE WE AT A STRATEGIC INFLECTION POINT?

THE SUMMER AFTER I left the presidency of SEIU in 2010, I read an article in *Business Week* by Andy Grove, the former chairman and CEO of Intel Corporation, suggesting that America's leaders might learn some important lessons from China and other Asian countries when it comes to job creation. Grove argued that "these countries seem to understand that job creation must be the number one objective of state economic policy." He noted how America's formerly great job-creation machine was sputtering as companies sent manufacturing and even engineering jobs to other countries where they could be done more cheaply. Management and shareholders were happy with the result, as growth and profitability improved, but companies no longer "scaled" in America, leading to a troubling long-term loss of middle-class jobs.

Grove, who passed away as this book was going to press, argued that Americans needed to plan long-term for more job creation; otherwise we'd become a volatile society consisting of a few "highly paid people doing high-value-added work" with "masses of unemployed." He noted how "our fundamental economic belief" that "the free market is the best of all economic systems—the freer the better," has limits. "Our generation has seen the decisive victory of free-market principles over planned economies. So we stick with this belief largely oblivious to emerging evidence that while free markets beat planned economies, there may be room for a modification that is even better."

That Andy Grove, one of America's most venerated capitalists, had argued in *Business Week* for a "modification" in free-market principles made an impression on me. So much so that, a year later, I recalled his comments in a *Wall Street Journal* op-ed I wrote after meeting in Beijing with high-ranking officials in the Chinese government. I had traveled to China to help forge a better dialogue between the two countries concerning economic and trade issues. I was particularly impressed with China's willingness to plan for the future by investing in renewable energy, the construction of millions of homes, expansion of next-generation IT, clean-energy vehicles, biotechnology, and high-end manufacturing, even as it pursued more short-term economic growth. I referenced Grove at the beginning and end of my column and repeated his warning about Americans sticking with old beliefs: "If we want to remain a leading economy," I quoted him as saying, "we change on our own, or change will continue to be forced upon us."

After my op-ed appeared, I sent a copy of it to Grove with a note asking if he'd be willing to meet with me to talk about the future of the US economy, and especially how technology would affect job creation. In fact, the visionary business leader had wanted to meet me for an altogether different reason, as I discovered during our meeting.

We met on August 20, 2012, at his office in Los Altos, an affluent town on the southern end of the San Francisco Peninsula. The building was on an unassuming side street. There wasn't anything futuristic or even contemporary about it, nothing to give even the slightest hint that a man who had recently been one of the world's most powerful and influential business leaders had set up shop there. To the contrary, it reminded me of the type of building that used to house travel agents and accountants in the days when those jobs were the work of people and not software. I rang the bell once, then again, before being let in. The sign on the door said SARUS. Later I would learn that SARUS stands for "Strategic Advisors Are Us," that "Us" is really just Andy Grove, and that everybody who is anybody in Silicon Valley, including Apple co-founder Steve Jobs, had, at one time or another, sought his strategic advice.

Andrew Grove (nee Andrew Istvn Grof) was born in Budapest, Hungary, in 1936. He survived scarlet fever, the Nazis, and a repressive

Communist government by the time he was a teenager. In 1956, when the Soviets invaded Hungary, he fled to the United States, where he changed his name and taught himself English. After earning a PhD in chemical engineering from the University of California, Berkeley, Grove spent five years working as a researcher at Fairchild Semiconductor. In 1968, Fairchild executives Gordon Moore and Robert Noyce left to start the company that eventually became Intel. Grove joined them, and over the next two decades he and the company he presided over would become key players in sparking the computer revolution that gave birth to Silicon Valley.

Moore predicted that the power of the computer chip would continue doubling every eighteen months—an observation that would prove consistently true and eventually be codified into Moore's Law. Grove came up with his own theory of change, basing it on lessons he had learned when Intel lost ground to Japanese memory chipmakers in the early 1980s. He tells the story of Intel's rise, fall, then rise again in his 1996 book *Only the Paranoid Survive: How to Identify and Exploit the Crisis Points that Challenge Every Business.*

Intel dominated the memory chip business in the 1970s, but by the end of the decade couldn't see where the business was heading and stopped making major investments in it. Meanwhile, the Japanese, anticipating a huge future market for memory, built new plants and increased their manufacturing capacity. When the demand for computers exploded in the United States in the early 1980s, the Japanese were ready to rush in with high-quality product priced far lower than Intel's memory chips.

Grove sets the scene in 1985 as he and Moore sit in Grove's office contemplating their options: "Our mood was downbeat. I looked out the window at the Ferris wheel of the Great America amusement park revolving in the distance, then I turned back to Gordon and I asked, 'If we got kicked out and the board brought in a new CEO, what do you think he would do?' Gordon answered without hesitation, 'He would get us out of memories.' I stared at him, numb, then said, 'Why shouldn't you and I walk out the door, come back, and do it ourselves?'"

That's exactly what the two men did. They left the memory chip market and over the next several years they focused their R&D

efforts on microprocessors. They also spent billions of dollars build-ing plants to manufacture the new product. In the early 1990s, Intel microprocessors were used in IBM's personal computers, the hottest product around, and Intel far exceeded its former success as a memory chipmaker.

Grove was forty-five minutes late to my meeting with him. After explaining why—he had taken his grandson to the movies—he told me why he had agreed to see me. He hated Obamacare. It's "wimpy," he explained in his heavily accented English. "It doesn't deal with the real problem—the irrational system for payments and price setting" that keep healthcare costs so high.

Grove's opinions had been colored by his own healthcare problems: He suffers from Parkinson's disease, a degenerative disorder of the central nervous system that makes it difficult for him to talk. I detected urgency in his voice. He was particularly interested in data-driven analysis and how electronic medical records might curb healthcare costs. "How viable is the technology for doctors and insurance carriers?" he said he'd been wondering. To help him answer that question, I agreed to introduce him to people I knew who administered large health insurance plans.

I spent most of the meeting listening to his views on healthcare and then technology, the government, and their implications for jobs and work. But I could not resist before I left asking for his advice on the troubles plaguing America's labor unions. I ticked some of them off: the decline in private-sector union membership, the war on public-sector unions, and the recent failure of Congress to pass the Employee Free Choice Act. "If you were in my shoes," I asked. "How would you fix labor and focus it on the future?"

Grove paused for a few seconds. "I am not arrogant enough to think that I can solve your problems," he said. "But I can tell you what I have learned: Figure out what the outcomes are, what you care about achieving, and scrap everything else." He also advised: "Fund the projects that everyone else wants to bury." In a sense, he was telling me to do what he had done at the critical juncture he and Moore faced when Intel was getting beaten so badly by the Japanese: Don't look back, look forward and imagine the future, picture real outcomes, then go about achieving them, no matter what the naysayers say.

In the cab to the airport, I replayed our conversation in my head. It wasn't hard for me to figure out what I cared about achieving: I wanted to help working Americans lead better lives and the middle class to survive and thrive. For most of my career, I could envision only one way to achieve that outcome: through the labor movement. In the 1990s, when my own and other unions resisted the change needed to shape the future, I tried to fix the labor movement. I even tried upending many of its practices and core beliefs. But toward what end? Twenty-five years from now, if my colleagues and I had done nothing more than strengthen labor unions, would the American worker be better off? Would future generations be poised to lead better lives than their parents? Would more low-income workers be confident that they could achieve the American Dream? Grove had reinforced what my gut said: unions, as important as they had been, were no longer the only or even best way to achieve what would matter most to American workers in twenty-five years. The deal was sealed—it was time for me to look beyond unions for answers.

When I got back to Washington, I dipped into *Only the Paranoid Survive* again to see if it offered additional insights. I was particularly intrigued by this definition:

> *Strategic Inflection Point (n)—An event, development, or confluence of events and developments over time that result(s) in a significant change in the progress of a company, industry, sector, economy or geopolitical situation. An inflection point can be considered a turning point after which a dramatic change, with either positive or negative results, is expected to result. Most strategic inflection points appear slowly, and are often not clear until events are viewed in retrospect. Denial is often present in the early stages.*

I was amazed at how well this definition described the US economy as a whole and the unease I'd been sensing lately in almost everyone I met. For example, more and more young people who had graduated high school and then college with good grades couldn't find an entry-level job in an area that could blossom into a career. At age twenty-five or even thirty, they were still working in unpaid internships or low-paying retail or barista jobs, or, frustrated, they were going back to school and accumulating even more debt. To make ends meet, more and more of these young people seemed to be moving back home and living with their parents.

My unemployed older friends, in their forties, fifties, and sixties, were struggling to find new jobs or cobble together enough sources of income to support their families. Almost everyone I knew was worried about the future of their health, finances, children, friends, parents, neighborhood, and city—and also our country. I joked to a friend that the initials USA now stood for the "United States of Anxiety." "No kidding!" he said, a reaction I received many times over. He looked like he was about to cry.

At the time politicians and pundits kept saying that the economy was fundamentally healthy—witness the strength of the stock market and the strong balance sheets of so many US companies. They kept saying that we were in the recovery phase of the 2008–09 recession—and that everything would be "back to normal" soon. Meanwhile, the United States of Anxiety was on fire with blame. Some of that blame was aimed at China or globalization or at US government regulations inhibiting businesses from hiring more people, but much of it was leveled at American workers for not working hard enough or being skilled enough to compete. Pompously, many in the elite claimed that if America's workers were better educated, more productive, and willing to take steeper pay cuts, we'd be losing less ground to the Chinese.

Listening to my friends and their children talk, I realized how easy it was for hardworking Americans who'd played by the rules to internalize and personalize that blame. To say, for instance, that their kids would have gotten better jobs if they'd only taken more science, technology, engineering, and math (STEM) courses, or gone to a better college. Some of my older peers held out hope that they'd get their old job or at least a decent one back when the economy improved. Fact is, most of them had stopped hoping or looking. They knew that few, if any, companies would consider hiring anyone over fifty-five—or anyone who had been unemployed for more than a year.

When economists and politicians repeatedly tell you that we are in the middle of a recovery and that more good jobs are on the way—but you see no new job in sight—it's easy to blame your personal downturn on bad luck or what you perceive as your own "deficit" of talent, will, and effort.

But what if the US economy had been going through a major *structural* shift over the past three or four decades? What if we'd reached one of Grove's strategic inflection points—and our personal horizons were being narrowed by forces that we couldn't control?

Look at the chart below. The "golden age" of America's industrial economy lasted from 1945 until the mid-1970s. During those thirty years, the four major indicators of economic health—employment, productivity, GDP, and median wages—grew in lockstep, and the rising tide of American prosperity lifted all ships. While the income of the wealthiest Americans grew by 8 percent, the wages of the poorest Americans rose by 42 percent. Between 1959 and 1973, the number of Americans living in poverty dropped from a high of 23 percent to a low of 11 percent, raising the expectations of lower-income workers that they, too, would move up the social and economic ladder into the middle class.

Then, as now, the American Dream was built on a foundation of good jobs for anyone who was willing to work. If you graduated

The Great Decoupling of Wages and Jobs from Growth

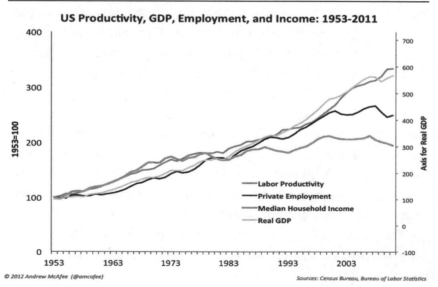

US Productivity, GDP, Employment, and Income: 1953-2011

Labor Productivity
Private Employment
Median Household Income
Real GDP

© 2012 Andrew McAfee (@amcafee)   Sources: Census Bureau, Bureau of Labor Statistics

college and worked hard, you could expect to be rewarded with a steady job, even lifetime employment, typically with the same company. If you didn't get the chance to go to college, you could still gain entry into the middle class through a union job at a construction site or in a factory. Whatever your route to the middle class, a steady job (with its employer-disbursed paycheck) gave you the wherewithal to send your children to college and maybe even graduate or medical school so that they, too, could achieve a better life.

In our postwar industrial economy, there was a national consensus amongst workers, economists, and policy makers that jobs were the central delivery system for income, healthcare, and retirement benefits. Both symbolically and in fact, an employer-disbursed paycheck was your ticket to a secure and comfortable future. In aggregate, those paychecks gave us the consumer spending that made our economy the envy of the world. Take them away—or lessen their value—and the theme of social mobility loses its marquee role in the narrative of the American Dream. Which is exactly what happened—a strategic inflection point that, in Grove's analysis, appears slowly and is often "not clear until events are viewed in retrospect."

When economists referred to growth during the "golden age" of the postwar American economy, they meant that *all four* indicators (US productivity, GDP, employment, and income) were growing. But look at what happened in the mid-1970s. Wages fell. Then, for the next forty years, they stagnated. In 2014, the median household income of $53,657 was $2,423 lower than it had been in 1999 when adjusted for inflation. According to the Brookings Institution, "Almost two-thirds of American households earn less money today than they did in 2002." Of particular note: young people who entered the workforce in 1991 and 2001 aren't seeing the same pattern of lifetime wage gains that workers who joined the job market in the 1970s and 1980s experienced; also, older workers are now losing income at a much faster pace. Brookings' Rob Shapiro, the author of the report, told the *Washington Post* that he blames these trends on two structural shifts in the economy: globalization, which has pushed US companies to cut jobs and wages in order to compete with foreign competitors; and advances in labor-saving technology, which have hurt the market value of lower-skill workers.

We can see a similar trend-line for employment. In 2000, jobs broke off from GDP and productivity. As the latter two indicators have continued to grow, the economy has not created jobs at anywhere near the same pace. Both employment and wages are stagnating. In their book *Race Against the Machine,* MIT professors Andrew McAfee and Eric Brynjolfsson described this trend as "The Great Decoupling" of jobs and wages from growth.

Whenever I look at the chart on page 30, it reminds me of a snake—a ravenous snake. Notice the long tail and gaping mouth. In presentations to members of Congress, I've used the snake analogy to suggest what happens when Congressional laws and/or inaction weaken unions: The jaws of corporate greed grow wider and wider. When I use that analogy, some people chuckle but even more look as though a light bulb has gone off in their heads—they really get the connection between Wall Street's greed and how Congressional inaction hurts unions and also Main Street.

Typically I'll pair the "snake" chart with a second one (page 33) showing how corporate profits and the stock market reached new highs following the recession, while median household income fell by four percent. My point is that corporations are chomping down on a bigger share of the profits and making their executives and shareholders richer at a time when most Americans are struggling harder than ever before to stay afloat.

Democrats and Republicans alike tend to dismiss these claims. They say that the sorry state of the economy is an aberration, the result of a recession brought on by an unregulated housing market. Also, that it's temporary.Witness the falling unemployment rate, a sign of good times to come, they say.

This job-less, wage-less growth isn't an aberration; nor is it temporary. It marks a strategic inflection point that merits our immediate and serious attention. Here's why:

The cracks in the US economy are getting wider: The Great Recession of 2008–09 exposed the shanty scaffolding that many Americans were using to support themselves: two incomes, student and credit card debt, home equity, intergenerational housing, and a second or third job. It pushed companies to rethink their staffing needs, deploy new technologies, globalize production, use more part-time

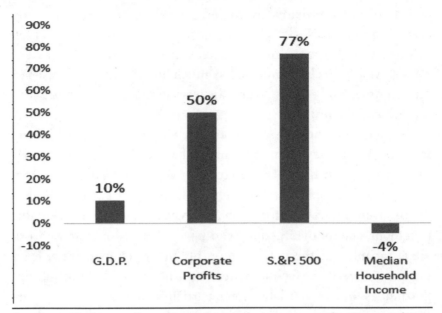

SOURCES: Real gross domestic product and corporate profits, Bureau of Economic Analysis (Q2 2009 to Q3 2013); Standard & Poor's 500-stock index, S.&P. Dow Jones Indices (June 2009 to November 2013); median household income, *Sentier Research* (June 2009 to October 2013).

and contingent/consultant work, and cut wages and benefits. Politicians and the Federal Reserve proclaim that the economy is officially on the way to "recovery," but to the 75 percent of Americans who don't believe the hype according to polls, the cracks in the US economy seem more gaping, since the post-recession economy has been delivering most of its rewards back to executives, shareholders, and the already rich.

The gap in job opportunities has increased the income divide: British economist Alan Manning coined the term "job polarization" to describe the gap between job opportunities at the top and bottom of the wage scale at a time when middle-income jobs are disappearing. In the US, job polarization has led to top earners in the US claiming a huge share of the productivity gains of the broader economy. In 2014 the top 10 percent of income earners accounted for a disturbing 46 percent of America's income. The top one percent took home almost half of that, while the top one-tenth of one percent ended up with approximately 10 percent of total income. These top earners are the ones who gain the most from a rising stock market, record corporate profits, and the increase in housing prices. The richest 400 Americans have amassed as much wealth as the poorest 155 million Americans—dramatizing the obscenely growing gap between the rich and the rest of us.

Too few working-age Americans are either working or looking for a job: While the unemployment rate has slowly ticked down from its post-recession high of 9.6 percent, a significant portion of that drop is due to people who have left the labor force, gone on disability, or given up looking for a job. For reasons I've never been able to fathom, able-bodied people who have stopped looking for work aren't included in the nation's monthly unemployment rate, leaving most Americans feeling better than they should about job opportunities. In fact, our labor force participation rate, a statistic that measures the percentage of working-age Americans that are either working or looking for a job, is at a thirty-eight-year low and has barely recovered from the nosedive it took during the 2009 recession. In August 2015, only 62.6 percent of our nation's working-age population was either working or looking for work; the other 37 percent weren't working or even looking. And the number of men in the workforce is at its lowest level since 1948, according to the Bureau of Labor Statistics (BLS).

In the late 1960s, when I was in college, almost every man between the ages of twenty-five and fifty-four went to work. The number who didn't have a job in any given week has gone up from 5 out of 100 in 1970, to 11 out of 100 at the turn of the century, to 16 out of 100 as I now write.

Why is this drop in the labor force participation rate—from a high of 67.3 percent in 2001—so troubling? "Because there are a lot of people who have useful and productive skills that could really contribute to the economy, and we're just failing to find ways to get them involved," says labor economist Betsey Stevenson. Also, workers who leave the labor force have a really hard time returning. Companies shun them in favor of younger workers who may seem more dynamic; their skills become outdated, they lose motivation, and their ability to find another job diminishes.

Untangling what has driven the continued drop and stagnation of the labor force participation rate, whether it is due to structural or cyclical factors, is a hotly debated topic amongst economists. While causes matter, and economists will hopefully sort them out, what we do know is that the low labor-market participation rate suggests that the falling unemployment rate vastly overstates the health of our labor market. Since each percentage point represents 1.5 million Americans between the ages of twenty-five and fifty-four, as I write, a staggering fifty-six million potential workers aren't in the workforce. The economy has a better chance of growing, according to economists, if we have more working-age men and women in the workforce, taking home a paycheck and spending money.

The plight of the long-term unemployed can be heartbreaking. Too often, these proud Americans are forced to turn to friends and family to cover the rent, find a temporary place to crash, or simply eat a healthy meal. Over time, this reliance on others can strain relationships and damage self-esteem. Ironically, when stressful efforts to find employment fail and workers finally give up, they are erased from the official unemployment statistics, leaving them uncounted and unsupported, and feeling as though they are invisible to policy makers.

This is not what we want for the American people—or for our nation's economy.

College is no longer considered as good an investment: Although policy makers still tout college as a ticket to higher wages and a middle- or upper-middle-class lifestyle, more and more parents are questioning its value, especially as the cost of tuition continues to skyrocket. (At this writing, the cost of a four-year private college had risen to a high of $63,000 per year for tuition, room and board at some elite schools, more than most families earn.) As for the return on that investment, the BLS indicates that more than 15 percent of men and 11 percent of women under the age of twenty-nine with a bachelor's degree are unemployed. In 2012, a record 21.6 million young adults, age eighteen to thirty-one, moved back in with their parents—typically to make ends meet in a tough job market.

Another big problem is underemployment—debt-ridden college graduates are taking low-paying jobs that have nothing to do with their education level or career goals. In the process, they have been displacing other young workers who are less educated and skilled.

Only 40 percent of Americans think that college is a good investment, according to numerous polls, and they are right. Analysis by the Economic Policy Institute (EPI) found that in 2001 workers with undergraduate (but not graduate) degrees earned on average $30.05 an hour; in 2014, they earned $29.55 an hour. That is a decline of 27 percent when inflation is taken into account. Real hourly wages for the bottom 70 percent of all college-educated workers in the workforce have declined. And so, increasingly, parents debate whether four-year colleges make any financial sense at all. A growing number of websites and magazines, including *Forbes* and *Kiplinger's*, now rank colleges according to their comparative value or return on a family's investment (ROI). And, according to the forty-sixth annual PDK-Gallup poll, in 2014 only 44 percent of Americans were convinced that going to college is "very important." That's a marked turnaround from the forty-second annual poll, in 2010, when a full 75 percent of Americans polled said it was very important. According to the newest data from an ongoing Gallup-Purdue University study of college graduates, just half of recent college alumni "strongly agree" that their education was worth what they paid for it.

We have become a low-wage nation: For the lucky Americans who do have jobs, too many of them work for shockingly low pay. Almost eight million working Americans live below the poverty line despite collecting a steady paycheck. Wages, as a share of the country's gross domestic product, are at an all-time low. Since 2000, one place where the new economy has not discriminated is that whether you are a high-school dropout, high-school graduate, an individual with some college, a college graduate, or have a nonprofessional master's degree, in every category average incomes have been falling.

Low pay, even with a steady paycheck, creates a boatload of concerns for workers, but lower-paid workers, those that make less than $35,000 a year, are among the most anxious of Americans. Eighty-five percent of lower-paid workers fear that they won't even meet expenses, up from 60 percent in 1971. Almost half of those polled felt less secure financially than just a few years ago.

Most new jobs created in today's economy are concentrated in the retail, food service, and home healthcare sectors, which rarely include benefits, and often leave workers scrounging to pay the bills and without a clear path to the middle class. To make matters worse, a 2010 report from the US Department of Commerce found it is harder to maintain a middle-class lifestyle than ever before as prices for critical goods such as healthcare, college, and housing outpace income growth, leaving families to turn to debt financing and other stopgap measures to hang on.

Part of this trend of low-wage work is a result of the shift from manufacturing to service. In 1978, 28 percent of American workers labored in factories and 72 percent worked in services; today, 14 percent work in factories and 86 percent in services. In 1960, the three largest employers, GM, AT&T, and Ford, were unionized companies with wages that you could raise a family on. Today's top three employers are Wal-Mart, McDonald's, and Yum! Brands (KFC, Taco Bell, Pizza Hut). Median pay for the more than 15 million retail workers is less than $20,000 a year ($9.60 an hour), and for the 3.4 million fast-food workers it is only $8.80 an hour. Today's job-rich companies offer poverty-level wages. As noted in a *New York Times* expose, even the "high-skilled" Genius Bar techies at Apple make on average just $11.25 an hour despite selling on average $472,000 of goods per employee per year. "You go into an Apple store and you see the future," says Jeff Faux, founder of the Economic Policy Institute. "The future of the labor force is all in those smart college-educated people with the T-shirts whose job is to be a retail clerk."

Another part of this trend toward low-wage work has been our failure to keep the minimum wage pegged to inflation. The falling value of the minimum-wage has left families, who are supported by individuals on a minimum-wage salary, well below the poverty line. Exacerbated by the shift to service, the effects of a low minimum wage include pushing workers into shadow labor markets and teaching workers that their work is simply not valuable—a wrong and disastrous message to be sending to American workers.

Sadly, the Great Recession only hastened this low-wage job transition. A study by the National Employment Law Project showed that

Jobs lost in the recession   Jobs gained in the recovery

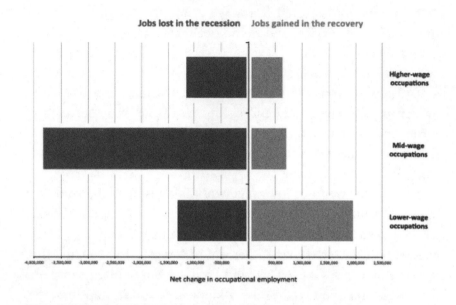

Net change in occupational employment

Source: National Employment Law Project

while the majority of jobs lost during the recession were middle-wage jobs, the majority of those added since the recession have been low-wage, accelerating the trend that gained force in the recession.

My earlier book, *A Country That Works: Getting America Back on Track,* analyzed the impact of globalization and offshoring on the economy. I noted the roles played by privatization, deregulation, tax policy, and corporate greed in "un-leveling" the playing field. I talked about the weakening of labor unions, how it was hurting the creation of good middle-class jobs. And I pulled back the veil on what was then the elephant in the room: the oversized influence of corporate money in politics.

I wrote that book two years before the Great Recession of 2008–09, four years before I served on the Simpson-Bowles Commission with its focus on cutting the deficit, five years before I visited Andy Grove at Strategic Advisors Are Us, and seven years before the Supreme Court ruled on *Citizens United,* allowing corporate and union money to flow unencumbered into politics. Much of what I wrote then is even more relevant today, as the middle class is even more under siege. Without job and wage growth, it has become harder for people who aren't wealthy to envision and achieve the American Dream for their families. "The middle class was always synonymous with economic security and stability," notes social researcher Tamara Draut, vice president of policy and research at Demos, a liberal think tank based in New York City. "Now it's synonymous with economic anxiety." The factor now exacerbating these trends—the new elephant in the room—is technology's impact on jobs and work. Technology, in fact, has become the most important factor in "the confluence of events and developments" that makes this a strategic inflection point for the US economy. We are in the midst of fundamental economic change. For many people, including myself, the change seems personal: it's as if our own shortcomings have brought us to this terrifying level of uncertainty and unease. But, as I learned from my visit to see Andy Grove, and even more from his writing, the change we're experiencing is structural. We didn't see it coming because it appeared slowly, over decades, and only became clearer when we looked back.

What about hope for the future? According to the Bureau of Labor Statistics, two-thirds of the new jobs projected to be created by 2020 will be low-wage and most will only require a high-school diploma or less: office support, food prep, child care, personal care aides, home health aides, janitors and cleaners, teacher assistants, non-construction laborers, security guards, and construction laborers. In 2009, 24 percent of American workers were employed in low-wage jobs, as compared to 76 percent in middle- or upper-income jobs. In 2020, 48 percent are projected to work in low-wage jobs, with only 52 percent projected to work in middle- or upper-income jobs. Any solution to our growing anxiety cannot overlook the need for good jobs. We can't confuse the difference between job growth offering poverty employment, and jobs growth that offers family supporting wages. Only one will restore dignity and security to the American people.

Grove calls it a "10X" force—"When a change in how some element of one's business is conducted becomes an order of magnitude larger than what that business is accustomed to, then all bets are off. There's wind and then there's a typhoon, there are waves and then there's a tsunami. There are competitive forces and then there are super-competitive forces . . . In the face of such '10X' forces, you can lose control of your destiny. Things happen to your business that didn't before, your business no longer responds to your actions as it used to. It is at times like this that the telling phrase 'Something has changed' is apt to come up." (What was that Buffalo Springfield song I mentioned at MIT?)

"Denial is often present in the early stages," Grove writes. In the later stages, too, I'd guess. For years, when union membership kept falling, from 35 percent of the private-sector workforce, to 20 percent, to 10 percent and lower, there were some labor leaders, including AFL-CIO's John Sweeney, who kept denying we had a problem. Everyone in the labor movement, myself included, was slow to see the impact of globalization on American jobs. Sometimes denial is just a failure of imagination. Or it's a form of not seeing the forest through the trees. When I was on the Simpson-Bowles Commission, I was amazed at some members' insistence that our multi-trillion-dollar debt problem could be solved by a simple change in budget procedures—for example, spending caps, or a line-item veto for the president, or having a biennial rather than annual budgeting schedule. If the discussion ventured beyond the budget process—for example, to the consequences of our proposals on income inequality or economic growth—they'd bring it back to the budget calendar, to the trees.

"The ability to recognize that the winds have shifted and to take appropriate action before you wreck your boat is crucial to the future of an enterprise," Grove writes.

And so it also goes with nations and their economies. In our own nation, do enough Americans (and especially our leaders) have the ability to recognize that the winds have shifted? Are we capable of taking appropriate action before we wreck our boat?

There are signs that give me hope.

While our country is arguably as divided and polarized politically as it has been since the Civil War, anxiety about the economy may be the great equalizer. A November 25, 2013 *Washington Post*-Miller Center poll revealed that more than 60 percent of workers worry that they will lose their job due to the economy, with nearly a third saying they worry "a lot." The poll found no significant partisan divide, racial divide, gender divide, or geographic difference in its findings on anxiety about jobs, income, and the future. Some 71 percent of adults think the country is on the wrong track, and 60 percent believe the US is in a state of decline.

As I write these words, I am reminded of one of my favorite pieces of music: Aaron Copland's "Lincoln Portrait." It always inspires patriotic feelings in me. Many orchestras have played this symphony, and various politicians, actors, and other celebrities have read the narration that accompanies it. In my favorite version, played by the Chicago Symphony Orchestra, actor James Earl Jones narrates from Lincoln's speeches and letters. About eight minutes into the piece, Jones says, "Fellow Citizens, We cannot escape history." He pauses, then says, in his deep voice: "That is what he said, that is what Abraham Lincoln said."

The words that follow are taken from Lincoln's Annual Message to Congress, delivered on December 1, 1862, just a month before he planned to sign the Emancipation Proclamation freeing the slaves. "The dogmas of the quiet past are inadequate to the stormy present . . . The occasion is piled high with difficulty, and we must rise with the occasion . . . As our case is new, so we must think anew and act anew." That is what Abe Lincoln said. He said: "We must disenthrall ourselves, and then we shall save our country."

The combination of Jones's voice and Lincoln's words, punctuated by the orchestra's brass section, always emboldens me. At this strategic inflection point in our nation's economy, we must rise with the occasion and think and act anew. Only then can we save our country from the anxiety that engulfs and cripples us.

THAT WE ARE at a strategic inflection point was again vividly brought home to me in early 2014 over the huge buzz in the world of economics—indeed, the world at large—caused by the 687-page book titled *Capital in the Twenty-First Century* by the French economist Thomas Piketty. Translated from French into English, it rose to number one on the *New York Times* Best-Seller List—an extraordinary achievement for such a weighty tome.

Like most of the people who purchased the book, I read very little of it—the first sixty pages and parts of the rest. So why did *Capital in the Twenty-First Century* inspire so many op-ed pieces and debates on radio, the Internet, and TV? Because it gave credence to a phenomenon that millions of Americans have been wrestling with since the 2008 recession—the growing gap between their own incomes and those of the wealthiest one percent who've been getting richer and richer despite the economic downturn. That unease had found earlier expression in Occupy Wall Street, the spontaneous and almost anarchistic protest movement that took over Zuccotti Park in New York's financial district on September 17, 2011. I visited the park several times to lend the protestors my support. Their slogan—"We are the 99 percent!"—struck a chord with people who felt disenfranchised by social and economic inequality around the world. Over the next few years, their disgruntlement was borne out by a slew of disturbing statistics, which fueled further interest in Piketty. The facts behind the disgruntlement speak for themselves and were widely reported in the news media:

- The richest one percent in the United States now own more wealth than the bottom 90 percent.
- The wealthiest 160,000 families in the United States have as much wealth as the poorest 145 million families.
- The richest 85 people in the world own as much wealth as the bottom half of humanity.
- If you are born poor in America, you have a much greater chance of staying poor than if you were born into the same class in countries such as Canada or Denmark.

On April 16, 2014, I attended a presentation by Piketty at the Graduate Center of the City University of New York. It was followed by a discussion of his work by two Nobel Prize–winning economists: Joseph Stiglitz, my colleague at Columbia, and Paul Krugman, who was about to leave Princeton to join the faculty of CUNY's Graduate Center. The other two commentators were Steven Durlauf, an economist at the University of Wisconsin-Madison, and Branko Milanovic of the Luxembourg Income Study Center at CUNY.

The auditorium was packed. Piketty, forty-four, was academia's newest rock star. He taught at the Paris School of Economics. He was clean-shaven, with a boyishly full head of dark hair. He wore an elegant gray suit and white dress shirt, with no tie, and left the top two buttons of his shirt undone. By contrast, the others on stage looked tweedy, tenured, and a bit smug.

In a lilting French accent, Piketty said, "Like everybody else, I'm better at analyzing the past than predicting the future." That's the standard disclaimer all economists seem to make before they trumpet the importance of their latest earth-shattering theory or criticize those of us who believe that the best way to predict the future is to create it.

Piketty's theory rests on a formula he devised for measuring economic inequality: $r > g$. What do r and g mean? r is the rate of return on capital, which Piketty defines as real estate, stock, and other financial assets; g is the rate of growth in the economy. There are two basic types of income: income produced by capital, which tends to be concentrated in the hands of a small group of wealthy people. And income from labor, which is disbursed broadly through the entire population. Wage growth is directly dependent on the growth of the economy. So when $r > g$, the earnings from capital increase faster than wages. Hence, the people who own capital accumulate a higher proportion of the nation's total income and inequality gets worse, as is happening in Europe, Japan, and the United States according to Piketty. The rate of growth of capital in these countries is rising at 4 to 5 percent a year, whereas their economies are growing at a rate of only 1 to 1.5 percent a year—a trend he sees as continuing well into the future.

During his talk at the Graduate Center, Piketty showed half a dozen charts and graphs to illustrate why the rich keep getting richer in Europe and the United States. The chart on page 44 is one of them: It shows the share of the national income accumulated by the top 10 percent of earners in the United States between 1910 and 2010. Another similar chart showed the share of the top 1 percent of earners in Britain, Canada, and Australia during this same period.

What's fascinating is not just the decline in income inequality between 1945 and 1979 in the US and a similar period in the other Anglo-Saxon countries, but also that the resulting equality stabilized. Why did this occur?

According to Piketty, the owners of capital took a particularly big beating during and between the two world wars. In Europe, many

physical assets—including factories and plants and the infrastructure needed to move products—were destroyed. Assets were appropriated to finance the wars and higher income taxes were levied. There was rampant inflation and, in some cases, economic collapse. During this forty-five-year period, g was either the equivalent or higher than r, closing the historical gap between workers and the wealthy.

There was a similar trajectory in the United States, where the great fortunes of the Gilded Age, and later the Roaring Twenties, were devoured by the Great Depression. That unforeseen and devastating collapse of the US economy closed the wealth gap, as it had in Europe. It also led to the New Deal and its social safety net programs, creating a floor, which aimed to keep the poor and vulnerable from falling dangerously below the poverty line again.

Another response to the Great Depression that was significant in lessening income inequality was the National Labor Relations Act, also known as the Wagner Act, which President Franklin D. Roosevelt signed into law in 1935. It guaranteed the basic rights of private-sector employees to organize into trade unions, to engage in collective bargaining for better terms and conditions at work, and to take collective action including strike if necessary. The US economy prospered after World War II, and unions (backed by the Democratic Party) developed tactics and policies that made it possible for working Americans to share in their company's success and live the American Dream.

And so, from the end of World War II until 1973, there was substantial economic growth and broadly shared prosperity in the United States. The gap between the income of high earners and middle and low earners barely changed. Up and down the ladder, incomes for all income groups—those at the top and bottom as well as those in the middle—stabilized and basically grew at the same rate, doubling (when adjusted for inflation) for almost thirty years.

And then, something equally unforeseen occurred. The economy took a sharp turn in the direction of ever-increasing inequality.

Since 1979, r (the rate of return on capital) has been greater than g (the rate of economic growth), leading to more inequality. And in 2010, a whopping 93 percent of the new wealth created in the United States went to the top one percent of earners. What's most disturbing is that economic inequality has been rising to the level of the Gilded Age of the late nineteenth and early twentieth centuries, when a small number of bankers and industrialists (labeled "the robber barons" by critics) controlled the US economy.

Earlier I discussed the various factors that led to the structural changes in the US economy. Among them: the decoupling of wages and jobs from growth; the decline in unions and worker power; the deregulation of banks and financial institutions, and the disruptive impact of emerging technologies. Piketty gathers these factors under the umbrella of a powerful new storyline: the return of patrimonial capitalism, where the economic elites inherit their wealth instead of working for it. "Unless drastic measures are taken, the future belongs to people who simply own stuff they've inherited from their parents," says Piketty. How do we stop wealth and power from concentrating in the hands of the one-tenth of one percent? Piketty suggests a global wealth tax—in effect, an annual progressive tax on stocks and bonds, property, and other assets that usually aren't taxed until they are sold.

"The study of history is important because a lot of what is happening now has happened in the past," Piketty emphasized in his presentation at the Graduate Center. He noted how the inventions of the automobile, airplane, and radio in the early 1900s brought a huge concentration of wealth, just as Facebook and Google are doing today. "That doesn't imply that wealth and inequality will rise indefinitely, there will be some mobility," he said. "But the large wealth concentration will restrict economic growth and keep our democratic institutions from functioning properly."

And then it was time for other experts to chime in, beginning with Stiglitz, who noted how he and the others on stage (aside from Piketty) went to graduate school in the 1960s and 1970s—"a time of relative equality." Stiglitz praised Piketty for providing economists with "an organizing framework" for thinking about wealth inequality and for "refocusing our attention" on the role of inheritance in inequality. He also underscored how "the extremes of economic inequality get translated into political inequality," with more power accruing to a smaller and smaller number of wealthy individuals and families. Witness the election of policy makers who make it easier for rich people to accumulate capital. And the phenomenon of "assortative mating"—when offspring of the wealthy attend the same elite universities and marry members of the same self-perpetuating class. (In his book, *The Price of Inequality: How Today's Divided Society Endangers Our Future*, Stiglitz wrote: "The more divided a society becomes in terms of wealth, the more reluctant the wealthy are to spend money on common needs. The rich don't need to rely on government for parks or education or medical care or personal security.") "Something essentially American is lost," Stiglitz said. By which he meant the American Dream of social mobility. And then he concluded, "This is deeply disturbing."

Krugman sounded some of the same themes. He said that "the inequality we've seen since the 1980s is in large part the one-tenth of one percent pulling away" from everyone else. "This is not Gilded Age inequality," he added. "The one percent of today is overwhelmingly business executives" getting rich from earned income. "But there's a definite shift from income- to wealth-based inequality," as evidenced in the *Forbes* list of the 400 richest Americans, according to Krugman. The list's top ten includes two Waltons and two from the Koch family; its top 20 include an additional two members of the Koch family, four from the Waltons, and three members of the Mars family. The six Waltons who made the *Forbes* 400 list in 2014 had a net worth of $144.7 billion in inherited wealth—more than the GDPs of all but 54 of the world's 196 countries. Like Stiglitz, Krugman believes that politics in cahoots with extreme wealth blocks social mobility.

The next speaker, Steven Durlauf, is a professor of economics at the University of Wisconsin. He is also a co-director of the Human Capital and Economic Opportunity Working Group at the University of Chicago, an international research network linking scholars across disciplines in the study of inequality and the sources of human flourishing and destitution. Durlauf favors tougher corporate governance rules, intellectual property reform, and more financial regulation to bridge the wealth gap. He spat out terms like "marginal productivity theory," "the super-managerial class," and "quality of outcomes" as if we all knew what they meant. There weren't just economists in the audience since the event was open to the general public. And as smart as Durlauf and his policies were, I kept thinking about the typical SEIU member and how he or she probably wouldn't respond well to the impersonal and jargon-filled nature of the conversation and would want Durlauf and the others to "Get real, guys. All we want is more job security and a raise."

And so it went. When a friend asked me about the Piketty event the next day, I told him how much I admired Piketty for putting the issue of income inequality at the top of the economists' agenda. But for all the hoopla, I added, Piketty's new mathematical formula boiled down to a pretty familiar truth: the rich are getting richer. It reminded me of a joke I used to make in my speeches: "SEIU's members should win this year's Nobel Prize. You know why? We can prove that wealth doesn't trickle down, it trickles up."

I don't mean to sound cynical but there's a certain comfort level that comes when you look at the economy from on high and through data: you don't see the victims, or feel their pain. I say this as someone who had the privilege for thirty-five years of seeing SEIU's hardworking members clean floors, wipe hospitalized patients' brows, and raise other peoples' children with inspiring, unheralded dignity.

There's nothing wrong with what Stiglitz, Krugman, and Durlauf were proposing—in the short run. But the real challenge for our country has to do with the long run: Will the technology-driven economy of the future create jobs for the huge numbers of people who are going to be put out of work by technology? And, if not, how are we going to lessen income equality and sustain a middle-class economy that's robust enough to keep America from becoming the twenty-first-century version of the nineteenth century oligarchies we once abhorred?

One tongue-in-cheek commentator on Piketty's book, Tim Fernholz, of *Quartz* magazine, suggested that war can be an effective way to achieve income equality: "One of the most convincing empirical findings from Piketty's research is that World War I, the Russian Revolution, and World War II were the great levelers of the twentieth century, wiping out more than a century of capital accumulation and creating the conditions for more equitable growth in their wake."

In his review of Piketty's book, former Treasury Secretary Larry Summers suggested that Piketty should pay more attention in the future to "the devastating consequences of robots, 3D printing, artificial intelligence, and the like for those who perform routine tasks. Already there are more American men on disability insurance than doing production work in manufacturing. And the trends are all in the wrong direction, particularly for the less skilled."

For a change, I agree with Summers: less skilled workers are particularly vulnerable in the age of Moore's Law. But so are today's college graduates. And if I'm right about the continuing dearth of jobs, we won't be able to stop income inequality by simply tinkering with existing policies. We'll need a bold, alternative solution like UBI.

Given the billions of people who suffer because of economic inequality, the Piketty event was oddly unemotional; no outrage or empathy, just facts, figures, and Piketty's famous charts and formula. Walking through the lobby, on my way out, I greeted a number of acquaintances and old friends. And then, as I passed the security guard at the front desk, I finally came face to face with the human dimension of what the economists had just been discussing. That security guard. He was maybe thirty years old. He seemed to be taking his job very seriously; it was a matter of pride for him. And I wondered: What will happen to him and his loved ones a few years from now, when he loses his job to a security camera monitored by a person 7,000 miles away in India?

Remember SEIU's "Walk a Day in My Shoes" effort to gauge the commitment of the 2008 presidential candidates? Perhaps we should require every economist (and business leader, for that matter) to walk in the shoes of one of the factory workers, maids, janitors, or elderly-care workers who constitute a mere blip on their economic growth charts. What most Americans want is simple: a secure job with decent pay, raises, and benefits, so that they can afford healthcare for their family and college for their kids, so that they can retire with dignity—the American Dream.

In his closing remarks, Krugman mentioned a famous speech that Teddy Roosevelt gave on August 31, 1910, in Osawatomie, Kansas. In it, Roosevelt articulated a number of reforms that would later become the platform for his Progressive "Bull Moose" Party campaign for the presidency in the election of 1912, an election Roosevelt lost to Democrat Woodrow Wilson.

When I got home that night, I read Roosevelt's speech in its entirety and marveled at its relevance in terms of today's debate about income and wealth inequality.

Roosevelt said: "At many stages in the advance of humanity, this conflict between the men who possess more than they have earned and the men who have earned more than they possess is the central condition of progress . . . The really big fortune, the swollen fortune, by the mere fact of its size, acquires qualities which differentiate it in kind as well as in degree from what is possessed by men of relatively small means."

Roosevelt proposed a graduated income tax on those swollen fortunes, and also an inheritance tax "increasing rapidly in amount with the size of the estate." His solution to wealth inequality in 1910 was similar to Piketty's proposal after the 2008 recession. With one big difference: Roosevelt didn't see labor as a blip on a chart or as a cost in the corporate ledger; he saw it as a means toward living a full and purposeful life.

"No man can be a good citizen unless he has a wage more than sufficient to cover the bare cost of living, and hours of labor short enough, so after his day's work is done he will have time and energy to bear his share in the management of the community, to help in carrying the general load. We keep countless men from being good citizens by the conditions of life by which we surround them."

Inequality matters. We must find new ways to raise the floor and bridge the gap. Otherwise, we'll be consigning millions of American families to a needless level of anxiety, frustration, and pain.

It is this perspective—embodied in Roosevelt's famous speech—which I would keep front of mind as my journey continued. And particularly on my next stop, when my thoughts about Strategic Inflection Points and income and wealth inequality collided with the inexorable new elephant in the room.

Chapter 3

THE ELEPHANT IN THE ROOM: TECHNOLOGY'S IMPACT ON JOBS

"In technology, whatever can be done will be done," Grove observed in *Only the Paranoid Survive*. And so, whenever I talk about the future of work these days, I feel like there's a huge elephant in the room—technology's impact on jobs. Or maybe I should say a huge "robotic elephant," since the discussion typically centers on the role that robots and artificial intelligence will play in displacing the jobs we humans do.

I'll get to those robots later. But first, I need to confess the relatively long road I had to travel before I finally understood the strategic inflection point shaped by technology.

I've never been hostile or even indifferent to technology. In fact, in the early 2000s, I embraced social media when my communications staff at SEIU dismissed it as a passing fad. I was intrigued by how Howard Dean, the former governor of Vermont, used the Internet in the 2004 presidential primaries to engage and mobilize young people. By its grassroots, networked nature, social media was democratic and interactive. So I hired one of Dean's top tech advisers to develop a plan for the union to utilize social media as an organizing tool.

My skills aren't sophisticated enough to code but I loved using the emerging technologies to communicate, learn things, and stay organized. When I left the union in 2010, I switched from a PC, which had been SEIU's standard issue, to a Mac, the computer all the students and creative people were using. I liked the way I could sync up my Mac with my iPod, iPhone, and later, iPad, helping me to lead a more efficient and connected life.

Suddenly I was self-sufficient. At SEIU I had relied on my secretary to keep my calendar, return phone calls, make travel plans, and track my projects. Now most of those tasks were automated and I could do them just as quickly and effectively using my various devices. I'm quite curious, and the new technology fed that hunger. My friends started calling me "Andy, the Answer Man" because whenever anyone had a question—say, the capital of some obscure country or the breed of a certain dog—I'd start Googling under the table until I found the answer. I felt like I truly had the world at my fingertips.

In 2012, I had an epiphany about the power and reach of technology.

For months, my twenty-two-year-old son couldn't wait for the latest release from "World of Warcraft," his favorite online role-playing game. Then, on September 25, the day "Mists of Pandaria" finally came out, he mentioned how more than ten million people around the world were playing the new game within days! It had taken the entire American labor movement decades to achieve that much member power.

Everything was changing so quickly! Only eight years earlier, in 2004, the spread of high-speed broadband had enabled consumers to load photos rapidly and view video instantaneously and connect their mobile phones to the Internet. That same year, Google went public, an event that allowed it to revolutionize the way we search for information, and Facebook was founded, changing the way we stay connected to each other. YouTube and Twitter were launched in 2006, followed by the iPhone and Kindle in 2007, Instagram in 2009, and Snapchat in 2011. Almost overnight, these brands had become world famous and worth billions of dollars. Bolstered by breakthroughs in e-commerce and Cloud technology, the fledgling tech giants Apple, Amazon, and Google had become three of the most valuable and disruptive companies on earth.

I became more and more interested in these companies and in the people who started them, ran them, invented products for them, and also invested in them. I had always been a news junkie, mostly politics, business, and sports. But now I was becoming just as addicted to the latest tech news, delivered by RSS feeds from *TechCrunch*, the *MIT Technology Review*, and the blogs, wikis, and tweets of luminaries like MIT professor Andrew McAfee and Netscape co-founder Marc Andreessen.

By far my favorite source of tech news is a website called *Singularity Hub*. It was founded by two futurists: Peter Diamandis and Ray Kurzweil. Diamandis, fifty-five, is the Greek-American engineer, physician, and entrepreneur who co-founded the International Space University in Strasbourg, France, and the $10 million X-Prize competition to create a new generation of private, passenger-carrying spaceships. Kurzweil, sixty-eight, is the principal inventor of numerous technologies, ranging from the first CCD flatbed scanner to the first print-to-speech reading machine for the blind. In 2012, he became Google's director of engineering. Kurzweil opines regularly on the future of nanotechnology, robotics, and biotechnology. Much of what he says sounds like science fiction to me. But it isn't. No less a high-tech luminary than Bill Gates has said: "Ray Kurzweil is the best person I know at predicting the future of artificial intelligence."

Sooner or later most of the hundreds of predictions Kurzweil has made have come to pass. For example, in 1990, Kurzweil predicted that a computer would defeat a world chess champion by 1998. A year earlier than he'd predicted, IBM's Deep Blue beat Soviet Grandmaster Garry Kasparov. Kurzweil also predicted that portable computers, which were heavy and bulky in the early 1990s, would be available twenty-five years later "in a wide range of sizes and shapes, and commonly embedded in clothing and jewelry." (As I'm writing this sentence, Apple is releasing its first Apple Watch, signaling a major advance in wearable technology.)

In 1999, Kurzweil predicted that people would be able to talk and give commands to their computers within ten years (now we have Google Now and Apple's Siri) and that computer displays would be built into eyeglasses for augmented reality (Microsoft's Hololens and Google Glass).

In 2005, he correctly pinpointed the emergence of products like Google Translate that are able to do real-time language translation of words spoken in a foreign language. Soon you'll be able to put on a pair of virtual-reality glasses and the text will appear to your eyes as subtitles.

"Unbelievable!" say lay people like me. But that's part of the pleasure of being a tech-news junkie. You get to see the future unfold each and every day.

Some of the many headlines that caught my attention—and persuaded me that robots weren't just coming, they were already here—include:

- Schwab's is one of more than a dozen investment firms offering robo-advisers: automated, algorithm-based portfolio management services without the use of human financial planners. And a new firm called Robinhood is targeting millennials with its zero-fee stock trading app. Less than a year after launch, Robinhood claims that it has hundreds of thousands of users, and over $1 billion in transactions.
- Contour Crafting is using a giant, gantry-like robotic 3D printer to print concrete. The system can build a 2,500-square-foot house in 24 hours by following a computer design.
- Lowe's, the hardware chain, is testing a robot that greets customers and directs them to the correct aisle for purchases. Knightscope, a Silicon Valley startup, has introduced a five-foot-tall robotic guard that can roam a retail store or office building looking for intruders after closing time.
- A new seventy-two-room hotel at a Japanese amusement park will be staffed by ten humanoid robots and some supplemental humans. The Henn-na Hotel's blinking and "breathing" actroids (robots with a strong human likeness) will be able to make eye contact, respond to body language, and speak fluent Chinese, Japanese, Korean, and English as they check in guests, carry bags, make coffee, clean rooms, and deliver laundry. True to the company's motto—"commitment for evolution"—doors in the guest rooms will be accessed by facial-recognition technology. And, instead of air-conditioning, a radiation panel in the rooms will detect body heat and adjust the temperature.

- Momentum Machines, in San Francisco, has built a hamburger-making robot that can do the job of up to three kitchen workers: grilling a beef patty, adding lettuce, tomatoes, pickles, and onions, and dropping it all on a bun. It can reportedly produce up to 400 hamburgers per hour. "Our device isn't meant to make employees more efficient," co-founder Alexandros Vardakostas has said. "It's meant to completely obviate them."

- A robo-journalist helped the *Los Angeles Times* become the first newspaper to report the latest earthquake, thanks to the journalist/programmer who created an algorithm that automatically generates a short article whenever an earthquake occurs. Computer programs can now write journalistic accounts of sporting events and stock price movements. According to one expert's prediction in *Wired* magazine, 90 percent of all news articles will be computer-generated within a decade.

- A robot bartender will begin serving drinks on the state-of-the-art cruise ship *Quantum of the Seas*. The robot can create a near-infinite variety of customized drinks. Its dynamic, moving arms are capable of strong motions like shaking and also fine-motor skills such as slicing fruit and garnishing drinks.

- About 150 hospitals, most in the US, are using Aetheon's heavy-duty "trundlebots," summoned by a smartphone app, to move trolleys carrying pharmaceuticals, diagnostic materials, meals, or laundry.

- A company called True Companion is manufacturing "sex robots" with different pre-programmed personalities—for example, Frigid Farrah, who is reserved and shy, and Wild Wendy, who is outgoing and adventurous. True Companion wants to dominate the adult market for "sex robots." As it says on its website: "The US is still the world leader in certain areas of robotics—for instance, in unmanned military vehicles and in artificial intelligence. True Companion has pulled talent from organizations in the US focused on movie productions, military products as well as people from the leading artificial intelligence and animatronic institutions to provide a truly leading edge adult product which is unrivaled . . . All of our robots can even have an orgasm."

2015 was a banner year for robots, when, according to the International Federation of Robotics, the automotive industry installed 200,000 robots, followed by 69,400 in the electronics industry, 36,200 in metals and machines, and 16,500 robots in the rubber and plastics industries. The military was using 12,200 robots to do such things as defuse bombs and collect aerial intelligence, and there were growing numbers of robots being used in food processing (9,500) and dairy farming (6,200). Milking cows used to be hard hands-on work. But now a computer charts each cow's "milking speed," lasers scan their underbellies, and the cows set their own hours, lining up for automated milking five or six times a day, with the robots monitoring the amount and quality of the milk they produce.

But it's in the area of healthcare that some of the most consequential advances are being made. For example:

- There are more than twenty-five companies providing electro-mechanical, computer-driven surgical devices, or what has become known as Robotic Surgery. Among them: RoboDoc, Endocontrol, Cyberheart, and Dr. Robot, the brain surgeon.
- The Defense Advanced Research Projects Agency (DARPA) has announced a $78.9 million program to develop minuscule electronic devices that will interface directly with the nervous system in the hopes of curing chronic conditions like depression, PTSD, Crohn's, and arthritis.
- The SensiumVitals patch is similar to a bandage and is simply half an ounce in weight. Attached to the patient's chest, it checks the patient's heartbeat, respiration, and also temperature, and transmits the resultant data every two minutes to nurse stations and handheld devices.
- Super-thin and super-strong graphene is "one of the few materials in the world that is transparent, conductive, and flexible— all at the same time," according to a lecturer at the University of Manchester. As a result, graphene research is leading to experiments where electronics can integrate with biological systems. Soon implanted sensors made of graphene will be able to "read" your nervous system and "talk" to your cells.

- AliveCor's new heart monitor is a $200 FDA-cleared medical device that delivers an EKG on par with top-of-the-line $10,000 devices, using nothing but a smartphone. In a trial conducted by the Cleveland Clinic, it had a near-perfect record in detecting atrial fibrillation, only delivering false positives in 3 percent of the trials.
- IBM's Watson will soon be the world's foremost diagnostician of cancer-related ailments. Watson is being "trained" to sift through and stay up to date with all of the world's high-quality published medical information, matching it against patients' symptoms, medical histories, and test results to formulate both a diagnosis and a treatment plan.

Behind each headline lurks Moore's Law, the observation made in 1965 by Intel co-founder Gordon Moore, that the number of components in an integrated circuit doubles every two years, resulting in an exponential growth in computing power. Why does this occur? High-tech companies like Intel keep shrinking the size of transistors so that they can place more of them on each chip and in closer proximity to each together. As a result, the electrons have less distance to travel, improving the speed, power, and overall performance of computers. In 2014, the semiconductor industry manufactured 250 billion billion (250×10^{18}) transistors at a rate, on average, of eight trillion transistors a second. But some experts predict that the cost of continuing to shrink transistors will outstrip the value of doing so around 2021, putting a crimp in Moore's Law. Will that mean an end to the fifty-year exponential increase in computing power?

Not according to Ray Kurzweil, who, in *The Age of Spiritual Machines,* proposed "The Law of Accelerating Returns." Unlike Moore's Law, which only applies to the technology of semiconductor circuits, Kurzweil's Law encompasses all technological change, which occurs, he says, in paradigm shifts:

"An analysis of the history of technology shows that technological change is exponential, contrary to the common-sense 'intuitive linear' view. So we won't experience 100 years of progress in the twenty-first century—it will be more like 20,000 years of progress (at today's rate).

The returns, such as chip speed and cost-effectiveness, also increase exponentially. There's even exponential growth in the rate of exponential growth. Within a few decades, machine intelligence will surpass human intelligence, leading to the Singularity—technological change so rapid and profound it represents a rupture in the fabric of human history. The implications include the merger of biological and non-biological intelligence, immortal software-based humans, and ultra-high levels of intelligence that expand outward in the universe at the speed of light."

In terms of computing power, Kurzweil sees one paradigm replacing another: in the 1950s, we had vacuum-based computing, which gave way to the transistors of the 1960s and the integrated circuits that enabled the high-speed personal computers and mobile devices we use today. Soon that paradigm will shift to 3D computing. In fact, chipmakers have already begun creating chips with three-dimensional transistors—a process of stacking the circuits in layers so that there's no need to keep shrinking transistors. And so it goes, according to Kurzweil: Every new technology advances along an S-curve and flattens out as the technology reaches its limits. As one technology ends, the next paradigm takes over. What's next? Kurzweil sees new materials like graphene and carbon nanotubes replacing silicon. He also sees major advances in quantum computing, which will mimic the human mind and do computations so quickly that, in comparison, it will seem that today's digital computers would take millennia to provide the same answer.

WE ARE LIVING in a time of unprecedented change. Every morning, I wake up to news of an advancement in science, medicine, or technology that is more wondrous and promising than any of the science fiction I read when I was growing up. In 1972, when I graduated college, the price of the fastest supercomputers on earth was between $5 and $8.8 million (the equivalent of almost $30 and $43 million today). Forty years later, I could buy an iPhone 4 with equal performance for less than $400. What a thrill to be alive in the wonder-filled world of Moore's Law—or should I say Kurzweil's Law of Accelerating Returns. And yet, there is a dark side to all this change that will improve our lives: the loss of millions of middle-class jobs, perhaps forever, but definitely for the foreseeable future.

In September 2013, I read a study by two Oxford professors on the potential impact of computerization on 702 different kinds of work. The provocative headline from the study was that 47 percent of US jobs are at risk because of advances in machine learning and mobile robotics. The study received a good deal of attention in the financial press and seemed to warrant more discussion, so I invited one of its authors, Carl Benedikt Frey, to address a meeting I helped convene on behalf of the Open Society Foundations on the future of work.

Frey used a series of slides to show us his methodology, thinking, and results. He and his partner, Michael A. Osborne, had made several assumptions—for example, he said, "computers are basically good at routine work, from cognitive to manual work, like record-keeping, calculations, repetitive customer service, picking/sorting, and repetitive assembly." He told us that the line between routine and non-routine work (e.g., truck driving and medical diagnosis) is slowly shifting. "More jobs which used to be safe-havens to automation are going to be at risk in the future," he said. "The basic trend driving this is the growing availability of data—big data. One estimate shows that all the printed material in the world is 200 petabytes. [A petabyte is 1,000,000,000,000,000 bytes of digital information. One petabyte is enough to store the DNA of the entire population of the US—and then double it.] In 1999, we had a total of 12,000 petabytes of stored information. By 2015, we'll have 960,000 petabytes," Frey said. That's a huge amount of information for algorithms "to dig into" for the purposes of analyzing, mining, sharing, storing, and using information for every job and purpose imaginable, he added.

The low-risk occupations tended to be in education, healthcare, management, and computer engineering. It is highly unlikely that robots will take over the jobs, for example, of primary school teachers, therapists, and mental health counselors.

Then a well-dressed man who looked as though he may have been the smartest and best-connected person in the room said, "I agree with most of your findings. It's just that your predictions—your 47 percent—strike me as being much too conservative." The man seemed very certain about what he was saying, so at the end of the meeting, I made an appointment to see investment banker Steven Berkenfeld and find out if he really did know more than Frey had been telling us about technology and the future of work.

WE'RE SITTING IN a conference room on the thirtieth floor of the Barclays Building in midtown Manhattan. Sartorially, at least, we are an unlikely pair. I'm wearing a light-blue cashmere sweater, wrinkled blue jeans, scuffed up black boots, and a black leather jacket. (If it were warmer out, I'd be wearing a cotton sweater and my purple SEIU windbreaker.) Berkenfeld, fifty-six years old, is wearing a white shirt, gray tie, and custom-tailored blue pinstripe suit, set off by a mane of silver wavy hair. I sense that he'd have the same businesslike attire and demeanor had we met at a coffee shop in the suburbs on a Saturday morning, and that, either place, this trim, tan man would be at his cell phone's beck and call. He tells me that he and his wife have just come back from vacationing in Bhutan, better known as the "happiest nation in the world." Berkenfeld is a driven, hard-charging investment banker and it's hard for me to imagine him relaxing even in a place such as Bhutan. He shows me some photos he took of verdant rice fields and Buddhist monks—a stark contrast to the view outside the conference room of gray skyscrapers blurring in the November snow.

I am here to followup on Berkenfeld's unique perspective on the future of technology and work, especially his sharp-edged response to the presentation by Carl Frey. For nearly three decades, Berkenfeld has had a front-row seat at the rise and fall and rise again of both Silicon Valley and Wall Street. He keeps his finger on the pulse of the emerging technologies—and makes multi-million-dollar investments in the companies developing them.

"'The future ain't what it used to be,'" Berkenfeld says, quoting Yogi Berra, the New York Yankee great who is one of his heroes. "We have less people working and the ones who are working are working harder than ever before. We can't stop technology; nor should we. The real issue is how we manage our human resources." Berkenfeld doesn't believe that technology will make human labor obsolete, but he says our planning should be based on that scenario. "Assume technology will replace every single job that exists," he says. "The question is, what do we decide to do with people?"

He came to this conclusion by watching the future unfold at Lehman Brothers, the New York-based financial services firm, where he spent twenty-one years as an investment banker. For ten of those years, as chair of the transaction approval committee, Berkenfeld weighed in on every major deal. Then, on September 15, 2008, following a huge exodus of clients and a devaluation of its assets by credit-rating agencies, Lehman filed for bankruptcy, the biggest in US history, setting off tremors in political and financial centers around the world. Later that day, Berkenfeld was the Lehman executive who signed over the pride of the company—its thirty-eight-story headquarters building, where we're now sitting—to Barclays, which also purchased Lehman's North American investment banking and trading divisions and gave Berkenfeld a job.

His job, as managing director in Barclays' investment banking division, has given him a chance to look at the impact of emerging technologies on a variety of industries. In 2009, he focused mainly on industrial companies. In 2010, he broadened his portfolio to include "clean tech" companies in the areas of solar and wind energy, fuel cells, and electric cars. (A graduate of Cornell and Columbia University's Law School, Berkenfeld is on the boards of the Sierra Club and Green City Force.) Since 2011, he has been focusing on companies that create the technology for 3D printing and robotics.

At the Open Society Foundations meeting, Berkenfeld struck me as being an unusually quick study—he had facts at hand, saw holes in other people's arguments, and took conversations to the next level. He also had the most insightful questions. "How did you get that way?" I asked him.

"By seeing tons of deals," he says. "Before the downturn, I was seeing at least one new deal every single hour. In that flow, with so much money at stake, you develop an ability to recognize patterns, to connect the dots, to see where things seem out of whack, where a business does or doesn't make sense. And you learn to do it in a heartbeat."

After the 2008 recession, Berkenfeld began seeing a strikingly new pattern in his deal flow: "The large companies would lay off 50,000 employees and say that half of those layoffs were permanent. The small companies—even the ones that were making huge profits at the time—were also letting people go."

The rationale was always the same: the companies wanted to cut costs and increase productivity.

"It was the old story: A recession is a terrible thing to waste. You can cut your least productive employees and know that your other employees will work a little harder because they're afraid of losing their jobs."

And yet, there was a new protagonist in the story: technology—and the way corporations were viewing it.

"In the 1990s, corporations were buying new technology and adopting it but you saw no real impact on the labor force," he says. "Companies invested in technology, but they didn't bet the farm on it."

At the time, email made it easier to set up a meeting with ten people, but we hadn't reached the point, as we have in the last fifteen years, where documents fly around the world in minutes with each person adding their comments electronically to the file, saving days of work as well as mail and messenger fees. In fact, there was a lot of nervousness about technology in the 1990s, so companies kept people around in case the technology malfunctioned and these workers would need to come in and save the day.

"Remember Y2K?" he asks.

I did. On New Year's Eve 1999, at the stroke of midnight, planes were going to crash and the world was going to come to an end because the computers we had all come to rely on were going to fail, as their clocks were not capable of being programmed to account for a new century. Then nothing happened.

"When we got through Y2K with barely a hiccup, the whole mindset changed. Companies started trusting technology and especially the Internet more. So by the time the financial crisis came in 2008, CEOs could say, 'I don't need to have a pair of hands backing up the new technology anymore. I can get rid of all this redundancy.'" A convergence of other factors—in particular, Big Data and the Cloud—enabled companies to outsource more business functions. The result? Even more automation and layoffs!

That pattern continues six years into the recovery.

Each week, Berkenfeld evaluates fifteen or more proposals from executives who want to meet with his committee. Most want to take their companies public. "I'll say yes, no, or only if you do such and such—for example, an audit, or more due diligence on certain items. I've seen thousands of deals and thousands of companies and hundreds of different business models."

Nearly all of the companies are developing technologies that aim to enhance productivity and cut labor costs.

For example, one company manufactures a solar compactor that contains a new device for sending information about the status of individual garbage cans to a sanitation company's headquarters. It's easy to see why municipalities are interested in buying these high-tech compactors. Instead of having garbage trucks drive the same route every day to empty half-filled cans, headquarters can map out a more efficient route to empty only the cans that are overflowing with trash—a win-win for the city and its residents, who no longer need to spend so much time waiting in traffic behind slow-moving garbage trucks. Taxpayers will come to see the productivity-enhancing technology as a plus, since it will eventually lower the cost of collecting their garbage. But only some sanitation workers will be happy, since many of them will end up losing their jobs.

Berkenfeld gives another example. A company he recently took public manages the data centers for 500 other companies around the world. In his first meeting with the company's CEO, he asked, "How many people does it take to manage the data at each of those 500 companies?"

"I figured that each company that maintained its own data center would need to hire two, three, or as many as five people internally to manage their data, for a total of 1,000 to 2,500 data managers. But by outsourcing that task to the CEO's company, it took those other companies a total of only 180 people to manage all the data. The CEO's company had turned up to 2,500 jobs into 180, reducing by 82 percent the number of people required to run those 500 data centers."

And a similar dynamic is at play in a growing number of industries. "Every company is trying to figure out how to do more with less," explains Berkenfeld. "It's not about automating a job altogether. It's about how to make every job as productive as possible." He gives a couple of examples representing the extremes on the skills scale.

At one extreme is food service workers. "We won't," says Berkenfeld, "lose them any time soon, but we've all been to restaurants with iPads, or other devices that allow you to pay at your table. Someone is still serving your table, but that person can serve ten to twenty tables instead of five."

At the other extreme is medical diagnosis: "So much of that function can be outsourced now. We haven't seen a reduction in the numbers of radiologists yet, but the workflow of each radiologist is much higher. The same is true of robotic-assisted surgery. We won't get rid of surgeons any time soon but we'll need less of them."

More recently, Berkenfeld pointed to a study from the McKinsey Global Institute that took a long, hard look at automation and helped to illuminate some of his points. The McKinsey study suggests that the best way to understand and track the progress of automation in the near term is to shift the focus from the automation of jobs to the automation of activities within jobs. As Berkenfeld pointed out, that distinction is extremely important to his evolving ideas, because it more accurately reflects how a number of businesses are currently thinking about enhancing productivity.

The conclusions of the McKinsey study are as staggering as those of the Oxford study although different in their approach. Most notably, 45 percent of all activities that workers take on in the US economy can be automated using available technologies. This represents nearly $2 trillion in annual wages of American workers. If AI progresses and is able to process and understand natural language a little better, that number quickly jumps to 58 percent of work activities that are automatable.

Berkenfeld also pointed out that the study shed some light on the key myths around automation. First, it argued compellingly that automation of activities would impact activities at all levels of income, not just middle-income occupations as some suggest. Furthermore, it strongly defended the notion that perhaps the best "safe haven" from automation will be jobs that require creativity and emotional sensing. Unfortunately, it also pointed out that only 4 percent of work activities require creativity above a median human level and only 29 percent of work activities require sensing emotions above a median human level, suggesting that those activities that are safe from automation are relatively rare.

McKinsey's written conclusions focused mostly on the impacts for organizations and managers, using management consulting terminology like, "new top-management imperatives: keep an eye on the speed and direction of automation, for starters, and then determine where, when, and how much to invest in automation." And, "We found that the benefits (ranging from increased output to higher quality and improved reliability, as well as the potential to perform some tasks at superhuman levels) typically are between three and ten times the cost. The magnitude of those benefits suggests that the ability to staff, manage, and lead increasingly automated organizations will become an important competitive differentiator."

But it seemed to me and to Berkenfeld that McKinsey was somewhat reticent about coming out and saying it, so he summed it up for me in an email, "When 45 percent of the work activities of you, me, and our co-worker Sam can be automated, all three of us probably won't be employed for long and none of us will have all that much bargaining leverage."

For the most part, I think automation is good and inevitable. Witness the solar compactor and the social, ecological, and logistical benefits it provides. But, unless significantly more work or new types of jobs are created, increased automation will result in the loss of more cherished middle-income jobs causing considerable pain in too many middle- and lower-income American families.

After talking with Andy Grove and pondering whether the US economy is at a strategic inflection point, I concluded that the trendlines for productivity and GDP would continue to rise but wages and employment all pointed to being flat or declining. Without bold new thinking and policies, we were likely to see more income inequality and a further diminishment of the American Dream.

What Berkenfeld helps me see is technology's shaping role in the process from the points of view of companies, entrepreneurs, and the investment bankers who fund them. Berkenfeld tells me what his colleagues at Barclays and other investment banks are looking for: "Give me a business model that doesn't require a lot of capital—software, for instance, instead of manufacturing. And give me something that has a very large potential market that I can make a lot of money on. Again: software."

Why software?

"Because you can replicate it for free. That's the economics we're looking for. We're applying the same criteria to every investment and eight out of ten times we're wrong, maybe even more than that. But when we hit on that business model, it's worth an enormous amount of money to us."

As we talk, I'm struck by how little the subject of labor comes up, beyond the need to make workers more productive and either reduce or eliminate them. "Is labor a factor at all when you evaluate a company?"

"Not really," Berkenfeld says. "Twenty years ago, we used to ask, 'What's the story with labor at this company? Do they have any unions? When's the next collective bargaining group agreement?' If the company was unionized, we'd consider it a risk factor: they could get shut down for a couple of months by a strike and not hit their financial forecasts. Also, unions made it harder for companies to manage their costs. Today, you'll still find labor in IPO prospectuses, but only as a legacy factor. Labor isn't significant anymore."

What Berkenfeld says about unions doesn't surprise me, but it hits me hard to hear it, and it hurts. As union membership was declining, I used to say that it would be "worse to be irrelevant than extinct." Now that unions were even less relevant to the US economy, I ask Berkenfeld, "Is it true that corporate America views labor as a commodity, making it easier for them to lay people off?"

"Yes," he says. "If the economy were strong, as it was in 2004 and 2005, and a company with record profits said we're going to lay off a thousand workers, it would have been a big deal and newsworthy and generated negative reactions. During the financial crisis, everyone started cutting back. Even profitable companies, with very positive cash balances, eliminated jobs. I call those 'productivity layoffs.' It means a company with no financial stress lays workers off because it has become more productive and can do more with less. It can generate the same amount of revenue—and increase profits—with 5 percent less workers this year and 5 percent less next year and so on."

He noted an article in *USA Today* about how companies such as equipment maker Pitney Bowes, defense contractor Lockheed, and grocer Safeway were boosting stock performance by methodically cutting costs, which meant workers. Pitney Bowes, for instance, cut its workforce by 41 percent, from 35,140 to 16,100, during a five-year period, and its shares had gone up 60 percent in the past year.

"If that was being done in Northern Europe, Israel, China, or Brazil, there would be a huge public outcry," Berkenfeld says. "Imagine BMW giving pink slips to 2,000 workers during one of its recent highly profitable years. German citizens would be protesting in the streets. That type of outcry isn't happening here in the US because we have a different culture concerning our human capital." And it's changing, he says. "In the 1950s and 1960s, CEOs had five priorities, and they were in the following order: making a great product, taking care of customers, keeping their employees happy, growing the business, then getting a nice return for their shareholders. That's not true now. Shareholder return trumps everything, which means keeping your costs, including labor, as low as possible. Why sell bonds at 9 percent when you can sell them at 8 percent? To put people over profits in this country is almost un-American. If you have an efficient market, you just maximize profits and everything else will turn out fine."

And yet, there's another dynamic at play. Technology and the productivity it enables makes it easier for CEOs to get rid of their biggest headache: people.

"As Henry Ford said: 'Why do I always get the whole person when all I want is a pair of hands?' If I could just hire someone and put them in a box for thirty years and leave them there, that would be great," says Berkenfeld. "But it doesn't work that way. If I hire someone, I've got to train them, manage them, and fire them. I've got to worry about them getting sick, their parents getting sick, their kids and dog getting sick. If a woman gets pregnant and goes on maternity leave for three months, I have to figure out how to cover for her. She might feel discriminated against, or harassed. People want to know where they stand: to get a performance review at the end of the year and eventually a promotion. I have to work out health benefits, severance, and vacation schedules for them. It goes on and on and on."

He quotes Terry Gou, the founder of Foxconn Technology Group, a contract manufacturer which assembles the iPhone and iPad for Apple and does similar work for dozens of top tech companies. Gou is also chairman of Foxconn's Taiwan-based parent company, Hon Hai Precision Industry. According to the *WantChina Times*, Gou said, "Hon Hai has a workforce of over one million worldwide and as human beings are also animals, to manage one million animals gives me a headache."

"A million animals—I mean people—is a million headaches," says Berkenfeld. "If I don't have to deal with that, if I could just outsource those headaches to a company and say, you manage my cost center, my payroll department, my billing stuff, you do my manufacturing for me, you lay my people off, so that none of it is a problem for me, then great."

A few weeks after our meeting at Barclays, Berkenfeld sends me the results of a Harvard Business School survey: 46 percent of the school's alumni would rather invest in technology to fill their labor needs than hire humans. In another email, he reports on a "very interesting dialogue" he's been having with a Barclays' senior research analyst who covers big industrial companies like GE, 3M, Emerson, and Honeywell. Based on this analyst's discussions with CEOs, the strong bias against hiring full-time employees "starts with the very high 'all in' cost, including lawsuits, disability benefits, long-term health liabilities, and the multiplier effect (people need people). But the real concern—the thing that keeps them up at night—is that you 'never know what someone who works for you is doing.' People do 'dumb' things and those things hurt companies—they create liabilities, they damage brands, and they sometimes get CEOs fired. Rogue traders, foreign bribes, discrimination and harassment, violence in the workplace—the list is endless.'"

"I'm calling it the Lufthansa effect," writes Berkenfeld. A few days earlier, a mentally ill pilot had deliberately crashed one of that company's planes into the side of a mountain in the Alps, killing all of its

149 passengers. "I hope this doesn't sound callous—it's not meant to be—but autopilots don't intentionally crash planes."

Inevitably, our discussion about the dumb and dangerous things people do leads us to one of the hottest topics in the tech world—self-driving cars. In our next email exchange, Berkenfeld writes, "Volvo is already advertising that people who drive their self-driving cars of the future won't have accidents. There are a lot of people who make their living from car accidents—who sell insurance, who repair cars, who process the paperwork involved in accidents. Hundreds of thousands of people will lose their jobs. Maybe the pro of people not dying in accidents will outweigh everything else, but don't we also need to anticipate and plan for the job loss?"

"Yes," I write back. I'm thinking about all those truck drivers. And the cooks and waitresses who work at highway diners and truck stops. And the men and women who license trucks and drivers at the DMV. And the Teamsters locals that organize truck drivers and negotiate their salary increases and benefits so that they and their families can live middle-class lives.

Berkenfeld provided confirmation to what I saw for myself during my walk through the MIT Media Lab. "The engineers just invent stuff," Berkenfeld writes. "They're not thinking about the consequences of what they're inventing. It kind of reminds me of the Manhattan Project [the top-secret effort to produce an atomic bomb]. We'll go ahead and do it, then later we'll say, 'What did we do?'"

I don't know if I'd describe the situation in such graphic terms, and I'm sure companies and their CEOs would put it more diplomatically, but I see where his argument is coming from. I also see where it's headed—toward more technological advances and less decent-paying American jobs.

A number of very famous economists have argued that technological disruption inevitably results in new types of jobs after the initial job loss and displacement of labor. For example, it was tough going for buggy-whip makers when consumers started buying Henry Ford's cars. But look at all the jobs that were eventually created in steel mills, auto factories, and rubber-and-tire plants; in gas stations and repair shops; in car dealerships and used car lots; while building interstate highways and transporting goods from coast to coast. In the short run, self-driving cars and the other high-tech stepchildren of Moore's Law will cause job loss and displacement. But twenty years from now, according to the techno-optimists, our nation's entrepreneurial spirit and know-how will have created new types of jobs we can't envision yet, heralding an era of even greater prosperity.

However, "even if the optimists are right, the transition from the jobs of today to the work of tomorrow is going to be very disruptive for most people," Berkenfeld writes. "We're going to have a lot of youth unemployment, a lot of people in their forties and fifties getting laid off and going from $100,000 a year middle-class jobs to much less and no benefits. Technology is opening up more opportunities for entrepreneurs, and then there's a part of the population, which is much larger, being replaced by it. There are two narratives: the haves and have-nots. And the polarization is getting worse."

I agree with Berkenfeld that the transition from the economy of today to that of tomorrow is going to be rough and even devastating for too many Americans. I am not at all convinced that technological disruption (because it has in the past) will result in enough new types of jobs to fill the hole that Berkenfeld and Frey are predicting.

Doodling on a piece of paper, I draw a facsimile of the snake-like graph that helped me understand the strategic inflection points gestating since the mid-1970s. As GDP and productivity keep rising at the roof of the snake's mouth, wages and jobs keep stagnating at the bottom. Imagine plugging the snake's tail into a socket powered by emerging technologies: the mouth grows wider and wider.

MY CONVERSATIONS WITH Berkenfeld are helping me to see the strategic inflection points in a more granular light. Through his eyes and experiences I can see that entrepreneurs and venture capitalists are techno-dancing to the tune of more efficiency and productivity, which will mean fewer jobs. While robots and AI won't replace every worker, they'll make workers far more productive and cut down on the total number needed to do the work. At the same time, technology will make it easier for companies to hire contract workers instead of full-time employees—the topic of my next chapter.

It's the speed of change that keeps surprising me. When I first read the Oxford study, I highlighted a paragraph about the social intelligence of algorithms. Frey and Osborne noted a famous test that had been devised in 1950 by British computer scientist Alan Turing to distinguish whether computers can communicate as convincingly as humans. (Turing invented the first modern computer to run interchangeable software. He became known to American audiences as the hero of the 2014 film *The Imitation Game*, where he was portrayed by the actor Benedict Cumberbatch.) In an annual Turing test competition, a human judge simultaneously holds computer-based textual interactions with both an algorithm and a human. As of 2014, Frey wrote, "sophisticated algorithms have so far failed to convince judges about their human resemblance. This is largely because there is much 'common sense' information possessed by humans, which is difficult to articulate, that would need to be provided to algorithms if they are to function in human social settings." Frey implied that it would be a long time before robots could displace humans in jobs that require high degrees of social intelligence. But in a highly publicized $20,000 bet with Mitch Kapor, the founder of Lotus Development, Ray Kurzweil predicted that the Turing Test would begin to be passable by 2029.

As it turns out, however, he was wrong by fifteen years. On June 7, 2014, at an event marking the sixtieth anniversary of Turing's death, an algorithm pretending to be a thirteen-year-old Ukrainian boy convinced 33 percent of the contest's judges that it was human—a high-enough mark to pass the Turing Test.

That same week, at an arena in Sao Paulo, Brazil, an even more extraordinary techno-event would augur the future. Juliano Pinto, a twenty-nine-year-old paraplegic who was paralyzed from the waist down, performed the symbolic opening kick of the 2014 World Cup using a mind-controlled robotic exoskeleton. The exoskeleton had been created by 150 researchers under the direction of a Brazilian-born neuroscientist at Duke University. It uses a cap placed on the patient's head to pick up brain signals and relay them to a computer in the exoskeleton's backpack, which decodes the signals and sends them to the legs.

What was that again that Yogi Berra said about the future? It's changing faster than even the remarkable Dr. Kurzweil can predict. As a benchmark, here are some of Kurzweil's predictions for the next thirty years:

- By the late 2010s, glasses will beam images directly onto the retina. Ten terabytes of computing power (roughly the same as the human brain) will cost about $1,000.
- By the 2020s, most diseases will go away as nanobots become smarter than current medical technology. Normal human eating can be replaced by nanosystems. Self-driving cars begin to take over the roads, and people won't be allowed to drive on highways.
- By the 2030s, virtual reality will begin to feel 100 percent real. We will be able to upload our mind/consciousness by the end of that decade.
- By the 2040s, non-biological intelligence will be a billion times more capable than biological intelligence (a.k.a. us). Nanotech foglets will be able to make food out of thin air and create any object in the physical world at a whim.
- By 2045, we will multiply our intelligence a billion-fold by linking wirelessly from our neocortex to a synthetic neocortex in the Cloud.

It will be interesting to see how these predictions hold up. They still seem like science fiction to me, which isn't surprising, according to Peter Diamandis. "As humans, we are biased to think linearly. As entrepreneurs, we need to think exponentially." Diamandis often talks about "the 6D's" of exponential thinking. "*Digitized* technologies are *deceptive*. Before we know it, they are *disruptive*—just look at the massive companies that have been disrupted by technological advances in AI, virtual reality, robotics, internet technology, mobile phones, OCR, translation software, and voice control technology. Each of these technologies *dematerialized, demonetized* and *democratized* access to services and products that used to be linear and non-scalable. Now, these technologies power multibillion-dollar companies and affect billions of lives."

To Diamandis's point, I repeat an unattributed saying that's gone viral on the Internet. (I first encountered it on *TechCrunch*.)

"Uber, the world's largest taxi company, owns no vehicles.

"Facebook, the world's most popular media owner, creates no content.

"Alibaba, the most valuable retailer, has no inventory. And Airbnb, the world's largest accommodation provider, owns no real estate."

In the next chapter, I go to Troy, Michigan, to see how these tech and workplace trends are leading to what experts variously call "the freelancer, gig, and 1099 economy." But before we get there, I have a question for you—it's adapted from my Stern test to distinguish Luddites from citizens of the future.

How many Americans were working as freelancers in 2014?

a) 13,500,000

b) 22,300,000

c) 53,000,000

How many Americans will have made all or part of their income through freelance work by 2020?

a) 28,500,000

b) 44,000,000

c) 82,000,000

I think the answers may surprise you.

Chapter 4

THE NEW LANDSCAPE OF WORK

"Ready for the flight from hell?" she said as she squeezed by me into the last empty seat on the plane. I knew exactly what she meant. We would be spending the next two hours traveling from New York to Detroit on no-frills Spirit Airlines—"Home of the Bare Fare." That meant less foot room, seats that don't recline, and absolutely no complimentary beverages. We'd even need to pay for a glass of water.

And yet this slightly unnerved, tall, and brunette young woman— her name was Kristina—turned out to be the perfect traveling companion for a guy writing a book about the future of work, because all she could talk about was how she couldn't find any.

"I'm twenty-eight, with a degree in medical management and interdisciplinary health systems from Western Michigan," she said. "I thought I'd become an occupational therapist or social worker. I thought I was going to save the world after I graduated." But after a frustrating few months working in data entry for a Medicaid contractor, Kristina took a ten-dollar-an-hour job "answering phones and fetching coffee" at an advertising firm in Birmingham, Michigan. Over the next several months, she worked her way up to become an assistant producer of how-to videos. "But," she told me, "I think I set myself up for failure. Because it was just this awesome work environment and this amazing office culture, and you don't find that. And then the firm lost a major client, and I was kind of downsized."

And so Kristina moved to New York. I asked her why.

"I needed a fresh start," she said. "And I heard 'if you can make it here, you can make it anywhere'."

"I've heard that same song," I said.

"Yeah," she laughed. "Sinatra, right?"

But the fact was that Kristina hadn't had a single interview after four months of looking for a job through LinkedIn, Craigslist, and other online networking sites. "Producers with a lot more experience than me are a dime a dozen in New York. And companies in the medical field are hiring people with PhDs for the type of work I'm qualified to do with my BA."

Kristina was less than an hour from seeing her parents for the first time since she'd left Detroit, and she told me that she was feeling like "a huge failure—like I'm just letting them down." Her father had come to the United States from Italy when he was her same age—twenty-eight. "He only had $50 in his pocket, but he was a really good cabinet maker. And he worked hard. And he became a big success, with his own stores—the American Dream." His only goal, she said, was for his children to go to college. "Which I did. And see where it's gotten me!" On a no-frills flight back to Detroit to face the very real prospect of moving back to live in her parents' home.

IN THE LAST chapter I asked you to guess the size of America's freelance economy and I said that the answer might surprise you. It wasn't a trick question, but it's a difficult one to answer because the freelance economy (also known as the 1099, gig, or free-agent economy) is growing at such a rapid pace in a variety of old, new, and emerging categories of work.

Laura Forlano is the director of the Critical Futures Lab at the Illinois Institute of Technology. She has been studying emerging work forms since 2006. During an Open Society Foundations Future of Work session on the freelance economy, she ticked them off: "Obvious ones include contingent work, freelance work, temporary work, internships, part-time work, self-employment, project-based work, consultants, contract work, and independent work. Some new categories include free agent, on-call workers, flex workers, permatemps, and micropreneurs," she said.

"And let's not forget piecework, day labor, and informal labor," she added. "We might also include domestic workers, migrant workers, task rabbits, eBay sellers, online survey takers, hired guns, warm bodies, venture laborers, clinical laborers (who donate organs, sperm, eggs, etc.), hackers, makers, adjuncts, substitutes, cam-girls (who broadcast live and often provocatively on Internet web cams), gold farmers, prosumers, jobbies, volunteers, and contributors. And the unpaid labor we all do—like self-checkout at the grocery. That used to be someone's job."

I wondered what the future of work might look like to someone like Kristina, the young woman I'd met on the plane. "It looks like a lot of things," Forlano said. "She might be working at home, sur-rounded by file folders, or she might be an independent distributor, working for a company like Herbalife. She might be one of many in-dependent contractors sharing a co-working place, huddled around computers. Or she might be working in someone else's home as a domestic worker or nanny, or for a car service like Uber, or selling on Etsy, while working part-time in a restaurant."

The General Accounting Office (GAO) defines this type of work as "contingent" because "it takes place in a work arrangement that is not long-term, year-round, full-time employment with a single em-ployer." In 2006, the GAO estimated that 42 million workers in the US were contingent. And the number of these independent workers is growing. A 2015 survey commissioned by the Freelancers Union and Elance (a web-based platform for online, contingent work) found that 53 million workers had engaged in supplemental, temporary, or project- or contract-based work in the past 12 months. In other words, 34 percent of the total US workforce is freelance. These 53 million are equal to the aggregate number of full-time workers in 35 states.

Here is how those numbers break down, according to the survey:

- 21.1 million workers are independent contractors; they don't have an employer and work on a project-to-project basis;
- 14.3 million workers are moonlighters who have a traditional job but also freelance after work or on weekends;
- 9.3 million are diversified workers; they have multiple sources of income from a mix of traditional employers and freelance work;

- 5.5 million are temporary workers, defined as individuals with a single employer, client, job, or contract project where their employment status is temporary;
- 2.8 million business owners consider themselves freelance; they generally have between one and five employees each.

This explosion in contingent work isn't simply an American phenomenon. According to a 2015 report by the International Labour Organization (ILO), only one-quarter of the world's workers have permanent jobs. The rest—fully 75 percent of the world's workforce—is employed in temporary jobs, on short-term contract, or in informal jobs without a contract.

Last century's industrialized economy created thousands of large- and mid-sized companies that employed large numbers of people in full-time jobs to produce goods and deliver services. Thanks to my colleagues in the labor movement, millions of these jobs came with health insurance, vacations, overtime pay, and retirement pensions, and you could aspire to work for the same company for your entire career.

Sara Horowitz, the founder of the Freelancers Union, says that the current shift from employer-based employment to free agency is "on par with the economic shift" a century ago from an agricultural economy to an industrialized one. "Gone are the days of the traditional 9–5," she says. "We're entering a new era of work—project-based, independent, exciting, potentially risky, and rich with opportunities."

To better understand this new landscape of work, after reaching Detroit and wishing Kristina success in her job search, I traveled on to Troy, Michigan, to meet the head of the Fortune 500 company that first saw the business potential in temporary employment after World War II—Kelly Services, home of what, in the 1950s, were known as "Kelly Girls."

IT IS MY kind of day at Kelly—a casual Friday. Everyone in the building is wearing blue jeans. They pay $5 each for this privilege, with the money going to their local March of Dimes.

Carl Camden, the sixty-year-old CEO, is wearing stylishly faded blue jeans and a white shirt that's only partially tucked in. His smile is framed by a brown mustache. He introduces me around the office as "the voice of labor." "Here at Kelly," he says as an aside, "I like to say that we're the voice of disorganized labor."

Like many of the CEOs I've been meeting, Camden comes from humble means. His father, a military man, had a third-grade education; his mother made it through the eighth grade. For reasons he doesn't specify, Camden left home early in high school then went to college—at Southwest Baptist University, in the Ozarks of Missouri—because a minister he'd met on a beach saw some evangelical potential in him. Camden never intended to preach but he turned out to be a star debater in college, one of the best in the country. He used that skill to get a job as debate coach at Ohio State University, where he earned a PhD in psycholinguistics by the age of twenty-five. Then, while teaching and chairing the communications department at Cleveland State University, he started his own market-research firm, with the goal of using psycholinguistics to create a more persuasive form of advertising.

At age thirty-four, Camden became president of Wyse Advertising in Cleveland and started creating image campaigns for companies like TRW, BF Goodrich, and BP America. ("I was good at turning large corporations into friendly American citizens," he says.) A major bank hired him for its top marketing job. Then, a few weeks later, he got a call from Kelly. "My wife had always said we can move anywhere you want except Buffalo or Detroit," he laughs. They ended up in Troy, on the outskirts of Detroit, where he took the helm of corporate marketing at the firm that had given birth to the temp industry.

Growing up in the 1950s, I was all too familiar with the iconic image of the bright-eyed, white-gloved Kelly Girl. In the company's ubiquitous ads she was smiling and eager to please, the perfect employee. And yet by definition she was a temp—a fill in. She didn't have regular hours, job security, or benefits, the prerequisites for dignified work.

It was as if the Kelly Girl had always been there—as emblematically American as apple pie. But, as Camden tells it, the true story of the Kelly Girls presages the challenges and opportunities facing millions of Americans as they enter the free-agent economy increasingly defining the future of work.

During World War II, William Russell Kelly, a University of Pennsylvania grad with bad feet, was forced by his infirmity to join the Army's Quartermaster Corps, which was responsible for the 900,000 civilians employed by contractors to produce supplies, equipment, ammunition, and vehicles for the nation's war effort. There, he was exposed to modern management techniques and also the new generation of labor-saving equipment.

When the war ended, Kelly moved to Detroit, where the auto industry was once again in high gear. He bought twenty calculating machines and several typewriters, and began offering inventory, typing, and copying services to businesses in the booming city. "Back then, companies had ledgers that needed to be balanced every night," explains Camden. "Russ had a truck that would go through the city and pick up the ledgers at the companies and drop them off at his building in downtown Detroit." All night long, Kelly and his employees would balance the books, and in the morning, the truck would deliver the ledgers back to each customer. Kelly also transcribed recorded memos, letters, and reports for its customers, and typed them out on each company's letterhead.

In 1996, Camden interviewed Russell Kelly for the company's fiftieth anniversary. "Russ told me that the idea for Kelly Girls came when one of his biggest customers called one morning complaining that his secretary was out for the day. Russ, being a customer-oriented dude, said 'I have a light day. Why don't you borrow my secretary,' which his client happily did. A couple of weeks later Russ's secretary wasn't at her desk when he got to work. Without asking his permission, the client who'd previously borrowed his secretary had done it again, telling her that Russ wouldn't mind. Instead of getting mad, Russ saw a business opportunity and started sending clerical help on short- or long-term assignment to companies throughout Detroit."

Camden showed me an early ad featuring several typists who were Kelly Girls. It said: "These temporary employees are available to help you during business peaks, sick leaves, or vacations, as typists, stenographers, filing clerks, switchboard operators, receptionists, and general office help." There was no apparent downside to hiring a Kelly Girl: "They work right in your office on our payroll. You are invoiced for only productive hours. Each is bonded, tested, and guaranteed."

If Kelly had simply remained a booking agent, the individual Kelly Girls would have been the temporary responsibility of each company that hired them for the hour, day, or week. But Kelly decided to "own" its talent and certify certain skills, giving Kelly more power to cultivate and leverage the talent. A Kelly Girl who could type 100 words a minute, as certified by Kelly, could command higher hourly fees.

Kelly had access to an immense labor pool. By 1945 more than 2.2 million women were working in the war industries; they were building ships, aircraft, vehicles, and weaponry, in jobs that previously had been the domain of men. When the men came back from the war, employers throughout America assumed that women, as a whole, would want to stop working, so they let them go. Kelly became an outlet for the many women who wanted to continue working. As Camden explains: "Our first marketing materials were addressed to husbands, fathers, and brothers saying how it didn't reflect badly on them that the women in their lives wanted to work. We advertised how much better their wives and girlfriends would feel if they could earn their own money to pay for birthday and Christmas gifts. Imagine an American employer using that rationale to recruit women today!"

By the time Camden joined the company, in 1995, Kelly had sold its legacy business and begun dabbling in professional and technical staffing. Camden saw this new focus as Kelly's future. In the process, Kelly Girls morphed into Kelly Services—"a leading global workforce solutions company" with annual revenues of nearly $6 billion. In 2014, Kelly provided employment to over 555,000 temps in 80 countries. It still supplies warehouse workers, but it also assigns employees in the fields of engineering, information technology, finance and accounting, law, science, healthcare, and education. Kelly is also the nation's largest provider of substitute teachers, who are paid their school districts' going rate, and the world's leading supplier of scientists, who are employed on a temporary basis. These scientists can make as much as $200,000 a year.

"In effect, we function as the HR department for the contingent workforces of over 90 percent of the companies in the Fortune 500," says Camden. "Today, most of the top corporations use more talent that's not their own than their own employees to do the work. We say, 'Give us your plans, let us arrange your talent for you and, at a minimum, all of your free-agent talent. We will procure it, put it together for you, and make certain you are in legal compliance on the free-agent side. We'll do everything, even outplacement for the employees you lay off.' And because we deploy all this freelance talent, we're allowed to keep databases on it, giving us access to the best talent in the world."

Kelly's biggest client to date has been BP America, which pays Kelly to manage over "a billion dollars a year" of non-employee personnel costs (including consultants and subcontractors) and to serve as the company's global supply-chain manager. "Say they want to put up an oil rig in Norway, Angola, or anywhere else in the world. We decide what types of firms they need to work with—and who specifically. In some countries we supply the talent directly; in others, we subcontract the recruitment function to the best of their local firms."

While Camden is talking about Kelly's growing business abroad, I'm still trying to get my head around the fact that his company fills more than 2.2 million US classrooms a year with substitute teachers—a business, he says, that's been growing 50 percent a year.

"Why the boom?" I ask.

"Because principals hate doing it," he says. "They hate making all those calls and arrangements themselves, especially when our software does it so much better."

To explain how Kelly's software and system works, he tells me about Jim, an eighth-grade history teacher who can barely speak this particular day because he has a sore throat and fever.

"What is poor Jim to do?" Camden asks. "Well, at 7 p.m., Jim logs on to his computer and into our system and says he won't be at school tomorrow. The system places an automated call to the two teachers he has already specified as his two favorite subs. If those two subs don't respond—or if neither of them wants the assignment—the system goes down the list of approved substitutes in Jim's subject area and locale.

"If one of the subs on the list—Jane, for instance—wants to work the next day, she'll log into the system to see if there are any opportunities for her. It turns out that there are four schools that need a middle-school history teacher the next day. Jim's school is by far the closest, so she accepts the assignment.

"At 7 a.m., when he gets to his office, the principal of Jim's school logs into the system and learns that ten of his teachers are out—and that we, Kelly, have replaced nine of them. If Kelly hasn't filled the remaining slot within thirty minutes, the principal will get a phone call to alert him that he needs to find another way to solve the problem, which is seldom the case."

Camden claims that Kelly fills 97 percent of all vacancies, whereas the typical school only fills 60 percent on its own. "So we're much more efficient and spare principals a huge headache that allows them to focus their energies on other concerns. That's why we're seeing such a boom in this niche of our business."

DURING OUR CONVERSATIONS in New York, one insight investment banker Steven Berkenfeld shared with me is that "Software rules the world." Software makes it easy for booking agents like Kelly to separate tasks from jobs, identify workers with particular skills, and put these workers in teams that can solve problems and complete projects 24/7 and on demand, saving their client companies the cost (and, yes, headaches) of having full-time employees. A growing number of companies have built online platforms with software that connects freelancers and independent contractors with people who are looking to hire someone to complete a task, project, or temporary job. (In the next chapter, I'll be using one of those companies to help me transcribe my interview with Camden.)

Camden shares Berkenfeld's high opinion of software. "The ability to put together work in a virtual format has changed everything," he says. "We run one of the top-rated call centers for a major industrial company noted for its customer service, though there is no physical call center. We've got a piece of technology equipment that allows the call center to exist virtually; our managers monitor the call center virtually, and our talent can pick and choose virtually when they want to work.

"For example, a guy gets home and thinks: 'I've got four hours with nothing else to do. Why don't I make some extra money.' So he logs in and we'll say: 'Yup, we've got a call center assignment available,' or we'll say, 'Sorry, we're full.' If we need him, he gets paid one rate for being available, even if he's just sitting around his house with his headphones on, and another whenever a call comes in. Indeed, if a call comes in, we pay him much higher for that call center work than he'd get if he were sitting in a physical call center, where we'd have to try to figure out how to average his productive and nonproductive time." It's a win-win for everyone.

Well, almost everyone.

"If you want to ask why there are so many less warehouse jobs, it's not just the robots, which are basically smart forklifts; it's the just-in-time delivery systems and supply-chain effectiveness you get from the software," Camden says. "Companies like Amazon only keep in storage what they need to. If I'm only storing two days' worth of product as opposed to two weeks or a month of it, I've just reduced my warehouse demand by sixth-sevenths. We tend to be focused on robotics when the more important factor in workforce reduction is the smarter management system enabled by smarter technology and better analytics."

I like Camden's warehouse example, because it so vividly makes clear why there will be fewer jobs as analytics and management systems improve. I'd never argue against greater efficiency. Nor would I stand in the way of progress, particularly when it involves jobs that are so plagued with repetition and ennui. But what does it truly mean to become a society of freelancers and entrepreneurs?

After spending several hours with him, I realize that Camden is a man of three or four pet phrases. One of them is "meme"—a word I previously didn't know. According to the Oxford English Dictionary, a meme is "an idea, behavior, or style that spreads from person to person within a culture." The biggest and best memes keep replicating themselves; they go viral. Camden is always on the lookout for new memes, and once he finds one he tries to figure out how to articulate and exploit it to improve the positioning of Kelly's brand.

"Wage slave" is one of his favorite memes. As in: "The last thing I want to do is work for _____(fill in the blank with IBM, Mobil, or any big company) and become a wage slave like my dad."

"The idea that a 9-to-5 job is a good thing has been replaced with the concept that it's a bad thing," says Camden. "For at least fifteen years, workers in America—even white-collar ones—have been losing their jobs and pensions, and feeling screwed." With the bonds between employer and employee weakening, there's a lot less reason to aspire to a lifetime of working for one company or to expect a company will care about you.

Camden says that he visits "at least fifty to sixty" colleges, universities, and professional schools a year to recruit talent. When he speaks to students, he sounds the "wage slavery" meme to persuade them that freelancing is the path to a more balanced and fulfilling life than their parents may have had.

"I grew up being told I had to arrange my life around my work," Camden says. "Kelly is leading a revolution that is going to allow you to arrange your work around your life. So that you get to decide where the balance point is based on how much money you want. If you want to maximize cash, you can work this way; if you want to maximize your flexibility, you can do it this other way. You can make various sets of choices but it's your choice. It's no longer the owner of the company's choice or the government's choice how you're going to work and live. You choose!"

Kelly recently launched an ad campaign to recruit freelance lawyers. "Look what the Kelly Girl is doing now!" a woman's voice intones. What follows, on video, is footage of a smartly attired woman lawyer, with the phrase "Lady Justice."

Camden tells me about another new ad campaign. It will feature a scientist at a pharmaceutical company looking at a hard-working new clerical temp and saying: "When did Kelly start doing secretaries? I thought they only did scientists." His goal is to seed Kelly's historical values of quality, integrity, and service in each of its growing number of disciplines: "I want the day to come when a top graduate of one of America's most prestigious universities goes home and tells his parents how disappointed he is because he wasn't quite good enough to be a Kelly free agent," says Camden. "As a result, he'll need to settle for being a wage slave."

Camden's message about the freedom, flexibility, and entrepreneurial benefits of free agentry seems to resonate with many people he and I know in the Millennial generation, including our sons. His son Andrew, twenty-five, earns $100,000 a year as an engineer at General Motors, and yet Camden doesn't expect him to stay there long. Andrew just bought a 3D printer and, after work, he and a friend are using it to make drone parts in Andrew's garage. They've even started their own company. They call it "Detroit Drone."

"Are we talking about the next Steve Jobs?" I ask.

"I doubt it," Camden says. "Andrew believes in open source. He thinks it's old-generation thinking to get a patent. He says that whatever he patents now will be obsolete by the time the patent comes through. He's thrilled whenever a stranger who has used his open source software tells him it's cool. Personally, I'd never give my company's software out for free."

As Camden talks about his son Andrew, I think about my own son Matt, who is the same age as Kristina, the woman on the plane. Matt is a gifted graphic artist. His portfolio has been raved about by colleges and prospective employers. And yet, he's had trouble getting a regular paid job with benefits in any field, much less in graphic design. At first, Matt held a series of unpaid internships with various online communications firms; then he worked in a variety of retail and food establishments. In the last two years, Matt and his wife Kaitlyn have found jobs and cobbled together a living with the help of their family. Matt has a full-time job in retail, and is on his way to a career as a scuba diving instructor. All this is fine with him— really. His life is dominated by his time with Kaitlyn, friendships, the relationships he's made online, and activities he enjoys like reading, painting, and multiplayer online video games. Matt doesn't live to work, as I did. If happiness is the sign of a well-lived life, I'd rate his less work-obsessed life superior to my own.

Do all millennials take a non- or anti-traditional attitude toward work? Are they happy to be members of the emerging free-agent economy?

A survey of 1,055 millennials (Americans born between 1977 and 1995) by Ultimate Software and the Center for Generational Kinetics revealed some attitudes that might rub against the Baby Boomer grain:

- A quarter (25 percent) of millennials believe working somewhere for as little as seven months qualifies them as a loyal employee;

- Almost half (45 percent) of millennials would quit their job if they didn't see a career path they wanted at their company.
- Over one-third (34 percent) of millennials would immediately quit if their employer asked them to delete their Facebook page.
- And 42 percent of millennials, over twice the percentage of other generations, want employer feedback every single week.

But other polls show that millennials are far from uniform in their attitudes toward work. Although a plurality of millennials don't want to be wage slaves, having full-time employment with one company grows more attractive as they grow older and begin thinking about starting a family, especially for men. Not surprisingly, millennial women who are contemplating having children place a higher premium on job flexibility. At this stage of her life I'd bet that Kristina would finally like to have some security in her life—a job with vacations and benefits that will accumulate and opportunities for career growth and mentoring.

And this is one of the main problems with the free-agent economy. All that flexibility works better for some people than for others—for example, the young and unattached, and people whose skills and education command good money, and twenty-somethings like my son Matt or Carl's son Andrew and perhaps even Kristina who can always fall back and be rescued by the personal safety net of better-off parents. The meme for low-skilled workers—especially those who'd like to raise families and save for their retirement—might be "contingent work sucks." Unfortunately, contingent work will become their only option as technology continues to reduce the need for full-time low-skilled labor. For that reason, I think that low-skilled workers will embrace the idea I propose later in this book of a universal basic income, which will give them the wherewithal to raise families and save for retirement.

For most people, it's more difficult than it was to plan a career. "A job's life cycle is shorter now because of the technology," says Camden. "That makes it harder for a company to commit to a lifetime of employment. What do you do with somebody who was an awesome data entry clerk when there's no longer a need for data entry or for so many database administrators," once the next rung up on that particular career ladder. "We used to do a big business providing people to fill in for ailing or vacationing telephone operators. Well, when I use the word 'telephone operator' now, my children go, 'What are you talking about?' It's as though that job category never existed."

In this fluid marketplace of jobs, Camden and his key executives are continually looking to create new niches and businesses for freelancers. For example, Kelly has been deploying what he calls "intact teams that function as a work unit" to companies that need a particular task done: "For example, if you need a team to analyze data in the geological or natural resource area, I have a team for that."

Another growth area is older workers. "There used to be tons of jobs in this country where you were physically worn out by the time you hit retirement. Now retirement happens in stages," Camden says. "So when someone is set to retire from one of our client companies, he gets a letter like this from us: 'Hey, Jimmy, you'll be retiring soon, which is great. There are probably a lot of tasks that you didn't like to do, and some you really loved—like writing reports and memos. Tell us the stuff you really loved and we'll find you part-time work that you might still like to do—for example, writing speeches for executives.'"

Kelly has disaggregated Jimmy's job into different work streams and tasks. Once Jimmy identifies the task he wants to keep doing, Kelly may be able to sell him back to the company in a more efficient and limited way. In which case it's an overall sweet deal for both parties: the retiring employee gets extra income and enjoyable part-time work; the company gets a necessary project or type of work done. Or it can be seen more ominously: as part of the company's larger strategy to maximize profits by cutting the costs associated with full-time jobs.

In an earlier chapter, I described what MIT's Andrew McAfee has called the "Great Decoupling" of wages and jobs from growth over the last forty years. But there's been a second Great Decoupling—of workers from full-time employment, and of employees from the employers who provided them with W-2s. In a sense, this is the central challenge of the emerging 1099 economy. How do we provide health insurance, job security, and retirement benefits to workers who are, in fact, independent contractors, on their own, either because they want to be or they've been forced to be?

This has been a major challenge for Camden as he's built Kelly's empire of contingent workers. "There is no easy way in this country to provide the social network of benefits for temporary employees. If you have a job and you're employed, your compensation doesn't fall to zero when you take time off—you might get the same, less, or a disability level of compensation. But on my side of the house, you get zero. And if you have to buy certain benefits on the open market, you're screwed."

Over the years, Camden has approached several labor leaders with the idea of creating an associate union membership for Kelly's temporary workers. For their dues, the temps would get access to healthcare and retirement benefits through the union, including child care and paid leave for sickness or having a baby. But no union has taken him up on the idea.

I think I understand why. Critics of the temp industry, including many in the labor movement, claim that Camden and his colleagues try to convince US companies that permanent employees, with their benefits, vacation days, and job security, are a drag on the bottom line. In this sense, they say, the temp industry has been a major force in devaluing work and workers—undermining wages, job protections, and workers' bargaining power. But I think that most employers need little persuasion, given the self-evident cost reductions that come from deploying "just in time" workers.

By 2020, Camden estimates that over 50 percent of the total US workforce—approximately 82 million Americans—will be contingent workers. Sara Horowitz of the Freelancers Union agrees: "If I had to predict, I would say the majority of workers in the US will be doing some type of gig work on a regular basis by 2020. If you look at our study and look at moonlighters, you will see the segment that I think will really grow to majority quickly. This group may have a 'traditional' job, but they are also hosting, crafting, driving, etc. to make money."

Both Camden and Horowitz share my concern about the fundamental challenge this presents to our country and to the American

Dream. As Camden puts it: "We built a whole social structure based on the concept of a job, and that concept doesn't work anymore."

The job market, in general, is society's mechanism for organizing and distributing the work that needs to get done in that society. Personally, I find it useful to remember that our current concept of "job" is of recent vintage. As historian Bethany Moreton of Dartmouth College explained at one of our OSF forums: For most of history, in the US and elsewhere, jobs were very narrowly defined as a "piece" of work and not as work itself. The oldest meaning we can find of "job"—in the Oxford English Dictionary—was a "cartload." That is, however much a single horse could haul. It was a quantity of stuff "that you could dole out and pay on an individual rate," as in "I'll give you two bucks for hauling that cartload of shoes to the next town for me."

Paying for piecework wasn't the only or even primary way to create a "workforce" before the Industrial Revolution. According to Moreton: "You could capture one, enslave one, marry one, adopt one, or give birth to one."

The word "job" also meant "a public office or position of trust, which is turned to personal gain or advantage," Moreton says. "Another older meaning would be 'buying and selling shady investments in a hurry, creating bubbles and crashes,' if you can imagine such a thing." That meaning came about during the seventeenth century's financial revolution, when a "jobber" dealt in wholesale securities on the nascent London Stock Exchange and served as "the classic middleman, implicitly unscrupulous and parasitic, connecting brokers beyond the view of the public." According to all these meanings, "jobs" refer to breaking work down into small pieces, and distributing the work. The assumption was that doing this would degrade the outcome, says Moreton. "You don't do it as a first choice, you do it because it's efficient."

The job market as we know it—the one that evolved in the early twentieth century—depended on two factors: a strong nation-state that could enforce economic policies, and strong unions that could organize entire companies and industries and negotiate for higher wages and benefits. Before that, the relationship between employers and employees was one-sided and feudal, with the owner having all the rights and workers doing piecework jobs to cobble together a meager and uncertain living. Indeed, the majority of Americans worked in crafts and trades and had multiple sources of income.

Like most Americans, I grew up using the words "job" and "work" interchangeably. But that's not true. A job is a political construct—what we count to determine employment levels and the health of the economy. Work is an activity construct—what we do to make a living and contribute to the health of society. Since the 1930s, there's been a social construct built around the expectation of an enduring job where companies would persist and take care of you. Thanks in part to labor's decades-long campaign to bring more American workers into the middle class, paychecks from employers have become the main vehicle for delivering healthcare, pensions, and other benefits to American families. The Internal Revenue Service, the Social Security Administration, Medicare, and other government institutions have been built around this eighty-year-old expectation of an employer-based job.

It is important to note that it no longer makes sense to use the words "job" and "work" interchangeably. Increasingly, technology is making it easier for employers to disaggregate full-time jobs in the modern sense into jobs as they originally were defined—as a piece of work. Technology has helped our economy become more efficient and productive. It has also given millions of Americans more freedom, flexibility, and choice in the way they lead their lives. But in the process, it has led to the decoupling of employers and employees—the foundational relationship of middle-class opportunity and the American Dream.

The breakdown of this relationship has consequences, which I discovered when I talked to a man who helped an army of contingent workers navigate the future of work in what had become the largest and most unruly construction site in the world—the city of New Orleans after Hurricane Katrina.

Chapter 5

THE DARK SIDE
OF THE GIG ECONOMY

Before going any further in my exploration of the impact of technology on jobs, I had a task to be done. On my trip to Detroit I had recorded a ten-minute interview with Kristina, the woman on the plane, and another four hours with Carl Camden, Kelly's CEO. Now I needed to transcribe those interviews, a task I dreaded doing as much as school principals hate to find substitute teachers.

One of Kelly's original businesses, in the late 1940s, had been to help companies transcribe their daily trove of recorded letters, memos, and reports—as I described in the previous chapter. What, I wondered, would be today's equivalent of Kelly's transcription service—and how could I avail myself of that service in my current hour of need?

On my own, it would have taken the better part of two days to transcribe the four-plus hours of interviews I had recorded, even more if I factored in naps and my compulsive attempts to decode the many inaudible sections of the tape.

If it had been 2005, when I wrote my first book, I would have assigned this particular task to my secretary at SEIU. If it were 2010, after I retired from the union, I would have gone to a local college and advertised on the jobs board for an undergraduate to hire, typically for $15 or $20 an hour. Those hours—and fees—could add up.

And there was always the risk that the student would need to put his schoolwork ahead of my project, leading to a frustrating delay.

Thus, in researching my options, I was delighted to discover Upwork, one of many online platforms that connect people who need a job done with freelancers.

It takes me maybe fifteen minutes to register on upwork.com and begin the process of posting my job. There are categories for web developers, mobile developers, writers, designers/creatives, customer service agents, sales and marketing consultants, accountants, and administrative support. The last category seems most relevant, and when I click on it, a box drops down with five subcategories including web researchers, personal assistants, and transcriptionists. I've struck gold.

First I type in a description of the job: "Transcribe 10-minute interview." Then I answer several questions—for example, how long the job should take, how I'd like to pay, and the levels of experience and language fluency I'm seeking.

Each candidate has a feedback score, based on the cumulative ratings of all the people who've hired that candidate for his or her previous Upwork jobs. Also, I can ask the candidates to write a cover letter introducing themselves, which I choose not to do given the relatively straightforward job I'll be hiring them to do. Then I post the job.

Within minutes—make that seconds—Upwork sends me a list of its "top 10 recommended" freelancers according to my criteria. They are from all over the English-speaking world—three from the Philippines, two from India, one each from Canada, Kenya, and Sri Lanka, and two from the United States. There's a gulf between what the three North Americans want (from $12.50 to $25 per hour) and what the candidates from the rest of the world want ($3 to $7.50 per hour). By negotiating down, perhaps it would be possible to get one of the Americans to transcribe the tape for as low as $10 an hour. But the adventure of testing the global workforce—not to mention how low their bids are—beckons me to take the candidates from India, Kenya, and the Philippines seriously. I imagine I'm experiencing a pull similar to the one that some CEOs must feel when they consider shipping jobs overseas because of cheaper labor.

The woman from Kenya has a very high rating—4.93. Her rate is only $5.56 per hour. She's done 170 jobs through Upwork and worked a thousand hours. She claims to have done transcription work for *Morning Joe*, the MSNBC talk show, which surprises me given that show's general criticism of outsourcing abroad. But I sense that this supernaturally busy woman from Nairobi may have figured out that there's more money to be earned in subcontracting the work than in doing it herself. So I end up going with Marie J., who has twelve years of experience working as a court stenographer for the Supreme Court of the Philippines and whose overall rating is a nearly perfect 4.96.

Marie's desired fee is $7.50 an hour, but I know (from looking at the feedback and her earnings from other clients) that she has often worked for a lower rate, and my natural negotiating instinct and her prior work history says I could hire her and certainly many others for substantially less. But, morally, I don't feel comfortable going any lower, especially since Marie's court experience qualifies her to be both thorough and fast.

Several days later, her husband emails me a file with the transcription and an invoice for $4.67—*Marie's bill for the entire job!* I can hardly believe it. I've gotten the entire airplane conversation with Kristina transcribed for the cost of a couple of coffees plus change at Starbucks, where I happen to be sitting when I get the email from Marie's husband with the file. What amazes me even more is the note that accompanies it:

Hello Sir,

I am the husband of Marie. Attached herewith is the transcript which she finished two days ago but was not able to submit. She apologizes for this.

Marie was called up the other day to assist her Judge [in the Court she's working] on an emergency ocular inspection for a [Rape with Homicide Case] in a mountainous area where internet or mobile signal is remote.

She will refund the payment for this transcript considering the lateness of submission.

Best regards,

Earl J.

Remarkably, Marie and her husband want to refund her entire fee. I'm touched by how seriously they take their commitments. But Marie has done excellent work, sparing me a big headache. I tell her husband how grateful I am—and insist that she keep the payment plus the bonus I'm giving her for a job well done.

Reflecting on my first experience with Upwork, I am struck by how quickly I was connected to hundreds of independent contractors around the world. Upwork's software makes a whole world of freelance workers available to someone like me within seconds, and I can access it 24/7, on demand.

As the employer, I benefit enormously from this arrangement. I can get the work I need done without contributing to overhead, healthcare, social security, and other employee costs. And think about it: If you're an entrepreneur starting a new business, why would you pay an accountant in the US $150 an hour when you can find someone for $5 or $10 or $20 an hour in India? Similarly, if you're CEO of an established company, why wouldn't you virtually off-shore your accounting, legal research, and web design services to the best freelancers you can get in the world at the lowest price?

Technology has enabled the creation of a huge global marketplace for free-agent labor. On balance, this is very good for corporations and entrepreneurs who are seeking "a pair of hands and not the whole person" to do certain pieces of work. It's also a net-positive for free agents in lower-wage countries like the Philippines who get a source of income they wouldn't otherwise have.

But as I'm sitting here at my local Starbucks, surrounded by at least a dozen people like me who are using it this morning as their office, I wonder about the impact of the global free-agent marketplace on laptop-toting freelancers across the United States. Competing against college-educated workers around the world for a limited number of jobs, they are in a race to the bottom they can't win. Consequently, how are they going to cobble together enough of a living to feed their families, pay for health insurance, and send their children to college? How are they going to save enough of their iffy, inadequate earnings for old age?

I also worry about Marie J. in the Philippines. Now she can supplement her income by outbidding the rest of the world. But what will happen to her day job as a court stenographer and her freelance transcription business in five years as voice-recognition software gets more and more sophisticated, and cheap enough to replace her?

WHEN I INTERVIEWED him at his company's headquarters in Troy, Michigan, Carl Camden, the Kelly Services CEO, was certainly an ardent advocate for the benefits and virtues of free agentry, particularly for highly qualified professionals in fields that pay well and people who desire more freedom, flexibility, and fun in their lives. But there is a less happy side to the gig economy. I get a glimpse of it when I hire Marie to transcribe my interviews with Kristina and Camden and become part of a virtual hiring process that drives wages so low that most American freelancers can't compete.

My guide to an even darker side of the free-agent economy is Saket Soni, the thirty-seven-year-old founder and executive director of the National Guestworker Alliance (NGA), headquartered in New Orleans. NGA is the voice of the hundreds of thousands of workers who enter the United States every year on temporary visas through the US guest worker program. Mostly they work in the landscaping and construction industries. But NGA also represents women who work in the factories that process seafood that will be sold in Wal-Mart stores. And also, certain professions that weren't previously considered contingent and low-wage—for example, adjunct professors. Too often, according to Soni, the people NGA represents work in deeply exploitative conditions that rise to the level of forced labor or indentured servitude.

"There are free agents, and there are un-free agents," he explains. "As the economy spirals down, fewer people are able to make choices that we've always aspired to. The women in the seafood factory will work at a low wage because their employer's incentives from Wal-Mart force him to cut costs. A group of Brazilian welders will wait in a shack for three months before they are provided as on-call workers to a shipyard in Texas, and they won't be paid during that time. At many institutions of higher education, faculty serving on a contingent basis teach the majority of classes. These well-educated people have PhDs. But their pay is shockingly low, and they work without health coverage, union representation, or the hope of getting tenure."

Ironic, sweet, but also tough as nails, Soni is one of the most articulate young labor organizers I've encountered in recent years. Perhaps because of his background and upbringing, he has a unique take on the future of work and sees underlying patterns and connections that I find particularly insightful.

Soni grew up in Delhi, the son of a "rather low-level" clerk in India's Foreign Service. "My parents were part of a post-colonial generation in India that believed you can educate yourself out of subjugation and into freedom," he tells me. They encouraged their son to learn and care about global issues. While he was still in grade school, Saket organized a letter-writing campaign to help free anti-apartheid leader Nelson Mandela from prison. When Mandela visited India on his first trip there as South Africa's president, in 1990, Soni was one of seven student leaders to meet with him. As a result, he says, "you sort of felt like you were able to touch the levers of history"—a feeling he says he tries to stir in NGA's members as they fight for better wages and working conditions.

Soni had no intention of becoming a labor activist. He came to the United States in 1996 on a scholarship to study theater and English literature at the University of Chicago. His goal was to become a theater director. However, in 2001, he became the victim of a bureaucratic error that upended his life. The paperwork to extend his student visa wasn't sent to the Immigration and Naturalization Service—"so I fell out of status and became an undocumented immigrant."

The nation was reeling from 9/11 at the time, and Soni, like other undocumented immigrants, felt the resulting sting. "I spent two years hiding from the authorities," he tells me. "Like so many others, I became a hunted commodity and couldn't admit my identity or undocumented status to anybody. There was this feeling that you had committed a crime."

At the time, Soni shared a tiny apartment on Chicago's Northeast Side with seven other undocumented immigrants. "We each had three or four jobs in the informal economy, and we rotated sleep times because there weren't enough beds for all of us." Soni cleaned basements during the day and bused tables at an Indian restaurant at night. He also worked part-time as a taxi dispatcher. "I started hiding in the basements I was cleaning because there were rumors that the

FBI was coming—and that informants in the community were making lists of the undocumented and handing them over to the INS. I didn't want to be in the position of deporting anyone—including myself—back to India. Instead, I decided to wait the hysteria out."

Because of 9/11, Saket Soni knew what it felt like to be a vulnerable, undocumented immigrant with limited legal rights. Because of a second catastrophe that shook the nation—Hurricane Katrina—he found himself traveling to New Orleans in August 2005 to help the thousands of immigrants who had been granted temporary visas to work there in the storm's aftermath. At the time Katrina struck, Soni was working as a community organizer in a low-income housing project in Chicago. "Katrina made everything I was doing in Chicago seem irrelevant," he recalls. "It seemed very strange to get up the next day and spend it maneuvering a local alderman to fix the locks on a few doors in a Chicago housing project while there were thousands of people homeless and disenfranchised in the Superdome and no social movement gathering momentum in response to it."

Overnight, New Orleans had become the world's biggest and most chaotic construction site. President Bush responded by issuing an executive order to suspend the 1931 Davis-Bacon Act, the federal law that required mechanics and laborers to be paid the local prevailing wages on public works projects. As a result, Bush opened the floodgates for low-wage contingent workers to come to New Orleans from all over the world.

"Each morning, they bused hundreds of immigrants to the construction sites. Some were locked in for weeks, until the construction was done. You'd see workers pulling dead bodies out of homes without safety gear. You'd see one violent image after another. No one who came here to volunteer or work in those terrible first few months went back the same."

Including Soni.

"I wound up landing among a group of young lawyers and veterans of the civil rights movement who were trying to figure out what to do for the day laborers who were cleaning the casinos and rebuilding the French Quarter. Thousands and thousands of workers had come to rebuild the city, but there was no housing to speak of for them; so they had to improvise their own. There's this huge bridge spanning the

Mississippi River that cuts through New Orleans. All of the cars that had been destroyed in the storm were hauled under it. The insides of those cars were black from mud and mold. But there were day laborers living in them. Others took refuge in City Park, which had become a giant encampment of basically unpaid workers living in tents."

One of those workers, a forty-six-year-old African-American woman, had traveled hundreds of miles to New Orleans after FEMA repossessed the trailer she'd been living in since an earlier storm had destroyed her house in Arkansas. "After Katrina hit, somebody from FEMA visited her in Arkansas and said, 'We need this trailer in New Orleans.' They literally displaced the woman and drove the trailer to New Orleans for others to use. The woman followed the trailer by bus and was living in City Park when I met her, waiting for the trailer to free up again. Meanwhile, she told me she was trying to 'improve herself,' by which she meant better her circumstances financially, by getting work."

"How did people like her go about finding work?"

"That's a good question," Soni answers. "And it's where we can begin our conversation about how the situation in New Orleans sheds light on the free-agent economy and the future of work."

I ask what he means.

"In the aftermath of Katrina, New Orleans turned into a city of day laborers, with a kind of a Byzantine maze of contractors. Workers weren't employed by anybody in particular. They were brought in by labor brokers or contracted to other brokers who would place them out at construction sites. There was no clear employment relationship—just thousands of people working for people who were working for contractors who were working for labor brokers."

He tells me about a group of Native American workers from Georgia who had been approached by a broker who said a contractor there had promised him good-paying construction jobs for them in New Orleans. But once the workers got to New Orleans, the broker abandoned them—"probably because his contract didn't come through." The Native American workers were contracted by another broker to another third-party contractor. When it came time to pay the workers, this third-party contractor said he didn't have any money because his own contractor hadn't paid him yet.

"There was no clear employment relationship between the workers and the employers," says Soni. "At the same time, there was no regularity or predictability from day-to-day or week-to-week or even hour-by-hour. You were in a city of completely contingent employment without anything tying workers to anybody else for more than the few hours at a time when they were being directly supervised."

"With so much available work," I ask, "why wouldn't a contractor want to have a predictable and stable workforce?"

"First of all, the definition of contractor was made meaningless after Katrina," Soni says. "If you had a truck, you were a contractor, and most of the people claiming to be contractors had zero experience managing a workforce. Every construction site was a free-labor market, as was every street corner where day laborers gathered to find work. The primary work of a contractor was basically to bid for a contract, not to get work done. It was a law-free zone. As a result, most of the contractors were fly-by-night and here-today-gone-tomorrow."

"Was that also true for the big casinos and hotels?" I ask. From my experience at SEIU, I'd have expected the corporations that owned the casinos and hotels to hire the large industrial-cleaning companies and not small contractors to do the work.

"Yes, they hired the big national companies. But even those companies got into the practice of turning the cleanup project into the smallest number of tasks. They'd run separate workforces through each wave of those tasks. That way, nobody could accumulate seniority or history."

Like everyone else, the cleaning companies had found a way to minimize taxes, benefits, and the other expenses attached to full-time employment.

"We would constantly be responding to the next forty-five workers who had been told, 'Your work is done. Your allowance is over. You're on the street,'" says Soni. "The whole city was suffering from an extraordinary level of post-traumatic stress. And in the midst of this colossal grid failure, there was this unbelievable level of opportunism, with no rules or regulations, and the promise of billions of dollars of money."

"As in Operation Blue Roof?" I ask.

"Exactly," he laughs.

Operation Blue Roof was the name of the government-funded effort to put blue tarps on all the houses in New Orleans that required new roofs. In normal circumstances, companies would charge no more than $300 to tarp a 2000-square-foot roof. But, in New Orleans, the government was paying contractors $2,980 to $3,500 to install a tarp of that size, plus additional administrative fees.

"The guy seven layers above the person who was actually laying the tarp on your roof was earning all of this money that never found its way down to the actual construction worker who climbed up the ladder—and everybody knew it," Soni says.

As he describes this appalling behavior, I start thinking about the African-American woman from Arkansas who had followed the FEMA trailer to New Orleans. How did she make out in the end? Did she get her trailer back?

"I don't know," Soni says. "But I do know that she should have been furious about the situation, and yet she was so humble and grateful. I don't think she even had a tent when I first met her. She was sleeping under the open air on a mattress. She'd made friends with a few other women, and they'd get up at five, not knowing if their contractor was coming that day, or if there'd be any transportation to the construction site. They'd end up walking miles to get to the site, and they'd stay there all day if they had to."

He says, "I can't tell you how much this community of strangers moved me. They were living in tents, and yet they were so concerned about their personal hygiene and looking professional and maintaining a sense of dignity, and they turned those blacked-out cars under the bridge into homes, with photos of their kids and an altar to the Virgin of Guadalupe. It was like that wherever you went. Workers trying to make sense of a completely irrational employment structure. Making no or little money for their work. Getting poorer by the day, to the point they didn't have any money left to get back home."

The people of New Orleans who had been displaced from their homes fared even worse as they sought work.

"One of the furthest reaching glimpses into the future of work was when we realized that employers, who could have hired locals to do the work, chose instead to shop around for undocumented guest workers because they represented a cheaper source of labor.

The unemployment rate in New Orleans after Hurricane Katrina was 80 percent. And yet employers were saying to the Department of Labor that there was a labor shortage—that they couldn't find people to do construction, hotel, and housekeeping work. And so they went to places like Bolivia, Peru, the Dominican Republic, Vietnam, Mexico, and India to bring workers here on visas that were designated to fill labor shortages at peak season—when they, in fact, had an oversupply of local people who'd just lost their homes and couldn't find work.

"I remember one hotel that was getting paid federal money through the state of Louisiana to house people on FEMA vouchers until they found their homes again. These were unemployed adults, all looking for work, and yet that same hotel brought in guest workers from Bolivia, the Dominican Republic, and Peru who could be paid $6 an hour instead of hiring the displaced locals at the hotel for $14 an hour. And money wasn't the only reason: the guest workers were captive workers; they couldn't go on strike, they couldn't work for anyone else, and legally you could deport them."

As Soni tells me this story, I begin to wonder about the extent of what happened in New Orleans. Clearly, Katrina ushered in a hyper-accelerated shift to contingent employment, plus a diffuse and disaggregated way of organizing work. But was that shift mainly evident in the construction industry, where the need was so immediate and great, or did it spread to other industries as well?

"It spread like wildfire," Soni says. "Almost at the same moment, Filipino teachers on guest worker visas started replacing locals who had been protected by the decertified teacher's union. There was a wholesale elimination of permanent jobs from the hotels and the shipyards. And free agentry began dominating the way work was done and organized throughout the city. And, I must say, the repercussions were felt in Chicago and Northern New Jersey, which suddenly sprouted entire 'temp towns' that catered to undocumented construction workers, and in Central Pennsylvania, where 400 student guest workers went on strike at Hershey's chocolate packaging plant."

I had followed that strike pretty closely, and knew what had precipitated it after the 2008 recession: Hershey's, the largest chocolate manufacturer in North America, decided that certain types of work weren't core to their business. They were in the business of making chocolate, not packaging it—so why take responsibility for the hundreds of people who were packaging the chocolate?

Hershey's adopted a new business model to clarify that point. In 2010, it fired its direct employees in the packaging plant and subcontracted the operations of the plant to a US subsidiary of Exel, the German-owned supply chain and logistics giant. In turn, Exel subcontracted the staffing of the plant to SHS Onsite Solutions, a temp agency based in Lemoyne, PA, that subcontracted worker procurement to the Council for Educational Travel, USA (CETUSA), which coordinates cultural exchange programs for students from foreign countries.

The students came to the United States on a visa called the J-1, which enables foreign university students to work for up to four months in mainly unskilled jobs so that they can fund their travel around the country. The 400 Hershey's students came from a dozen countries, including China, Mongolia, Thailand, Moldova, Poland, Costa Rica, and the Ukraine. Each of them typically paid $4,000 to their recruiter—"for the chance to improve your English, meet Americans, and experience American culture," as the recruitment literature promised. But instead, the students found themselves packing chocolates under what a National Guestworkers Alliance (NGA) report later characterized as "brutal" conditions.

According to the report: "After above-market-rate deductions for rent and other expenses, [the student guest workers] netted as little as $1 an hour. They routinely experienced severe pain in their backs, numbness in their hands, bruising on their arms and legs, and chronic exhaustion from their daily work. When they complained about conditions, supervisors and recruiters threatened them with deportation."

"Like the guest workers six years earlier in New Orleans, they had no one to bargain with," Soni says. "Hershey's said the workers were Exel's responsibility. Exel claimed that SHS was the boss. SHS said the guest workers should talk to CETUSA. And CETUSA said the promises were made by country recruiters abroad. All of them agreed that the students legally weren't even workers; they were participants in a cultural exchange program, which exonerated all of their organizations."

In August 2011, a month before the Occupy Wall Street protests began in downtown Manhattan, the 400 student guest workers waged a sit-down strike on the floor of the Palmyra packing factory. The strike was front-page news in the *New York Times* and other major newspapers, casting a harsh light on Hershey's abuse of the J-1 student guest workers program. A decade before, the job of packaging Hershey's chocolate had paid a living wage and come with the benefits of a union contract. Those 400 packaging jobs had sustained 400 middle-class families. But now they'd been disaggregated and outsourced—not to low-paid workers in other countries, but to low-paid foreign students who had come to America to travel and learn.

In February 2012, the Occupational Safety and Health Administration fined Exel $283,000 for failing to report forty-two serious injuries in the period from 2008 to 2011.

Hershey's took no responsibility for the abuses. But, as a result of the strike, the 400 students won major reforms to the J-1 student guest worker program. Most notably, the main abusers of the program—the construction, manufacturing, warehousing, and food processing industries—are no longer allowed to utilize the program.

I was happy to hear that. Only a few hundred miles from where John L. Lewis had founded the Congress of Industrial Organizations in 1935, and I had rallied the SEIU to write a new chapter in labor's history in 2000, the American labor movement had taken a principled and effective stand against the exploitation of temporary guest workers by US corporations to deprive middle-class families of jobs.

There was something quintessentially un-American about the Hershey's story. In June 2015, an even more iconic US corporation was in the news for using temporary visas to strip away full-time middle-class jobs. The *New York Times* reported that the Walt Disney Company had laid off 250 full-time employees, replacing them with immigrants who were employees of outsourcing companies that used H-1B temporary visas to place foreigners in US tech jobs. To add insult to injury, the laid-off workers were expected to train their foreign replacements.

According to *Times* reporter Julia Preston, there are only 85,000 H-1B visas available each year, and American companies are supposed to use them to fill openings for specialized skills. However, "most top recipients of the visas have been outsourcing or consulting firms based in India, or their American subsidiaries, which import workers for large contracts to take over entire in-house technology units—and to cut costs." It is, to say the least, a worrisome trend.

ALTHOUGH I'D NEVER encountered the degree of chaos and despair Soni described in New Orleans, I'd had a long-enough career in labor to know how the process of subcontracting work can enrich everyone involved in a project except the people doing the work. As I explored the pros and cons of the gig economy, what surprised me more was Carl Camden's revelation that the free-agent, on-demand, and 24/7 economies could provide praiseworthy freedoms to higher-wage workers such as Kelly's scientists and engineers. I was also surprised how much the on-demand and 24/7 economies added to my own life as a consumer.

Because people are connected 24/7 via smartphones and computers, it has become considerably more efficient and less costly to match workers to tasks. When I needed my interviews with Kristina and Carl Camden transcribed, it was wonderful to have a world of labor at my fingertips. And you can use the online platforms to help you live all aspects of your life more efficiently. Want your house cleaned? You can book it through Handy. Need help moving, doing yard work, researching a book, or lifting something heavy? Try Task-Rabbit. Hungry for a gourmet meal? SpoonRocket promises to deliver it to your door within fifteen minutes.

I wanted to ship my bicycle from Washington, D.C., where I live, to Florida, where the son of a family friend could use it. I had no idea how to take the bicycle apart without ruining either the bike or my back, so I decided to use TaskRabbit, where I found a guy who was a champion long-distance bike rider. J.D. had lots of experience taking apart his own bike and shipping it across country to his next race. He knew exactly what to do, and then did it—for $80 plus the cost of shipping my bike to Florida.

Now I am thinking about hiring someone to hang several pieces of artwork I inherited from my stepmother. Some of the pictures are really big and cumbersome, and I've found someone on TaskRabbit who hangs paintings and photographs for exhibitions at art galleries. He'll use the right kind of hooks for each picture, and level them so they hang properly, something I could never easily do. I'd be worried about dropping the pictures or pulling the whole wall down or falling off the stepladder. It will be well worth the $20 an hour I'll be paying him for maybe two or three hours of work.

Both of these guys—the bike shipper and the picture hanger—are using TaskRabbit to make a few extra bucks at work they like doing. They don't depend on TaskRabbit to make a living. However, the free agents who rely on these online "on-demand" platforms to help pay their rent, feed their families, and educate their children are extremely vulnerable in the new economy. And a surprising number of them, I'm discovering, have master's degrees and PhDs.

The presence of free agents with advanced degrees is no more apparent than in the world of crowdsourcing. According to Wikipedia, "crowdsourcing is the process of obtaining needed services, ideas, or content by soliciting contributions from a large group of people, and especially from an online community, rather than from traditional employees or suppliers."

Internet-based crowdsourcing services are sometimes hailed as offering revolutionary new opportunities for online workers worldwide. Here, a distinction needs to be made between crowdsourcing, which is volunteer-based, and the growing crowd work industry, which uses commercial vendors to provide access to workers who complete tasks for pay. Crowd work services typically constitute an unregulated global labor market where millions of people work for as little as $1 an hour or less, without labor protections or benefits.

Wikipedia itself is probably the most famous example of crowdsourcing. In 2001, its co-founders Jimmy Wales and Larry Sanger issued an open call to anyone on the Web, including academic experts and subject enthusiasts, to create a free encyclopedia built with wiki software.

At the moment I'm writing this sentence, Wikipedia claims to feature 35,000,000 articles in 288 languages. The continuously updated English-language Wikipedia includes 4,892,042 articles and averages 750 new articles per day. Wikipedia says there are 75,000 active

contributors around the world who write and edit the prose, refer-
ences, images, and other media (including links) for the site. The vast
majority of these volunteer contributors do so without credit or pay.

From my own perspective, Wikipedia does not exploit these
volunteer contributors. The volunteers understand and believe in
Wikipedia's mission, and the Wikipedia Foundation, the 501c3 organization that supports the site, doesn't profit from their labor. That's
not the case with Amazon, Google, and the many entrepreneurial
companies that use crowd workers for data collection, to conduct
user studies, to create speech and language databases, and to complete other tasks whose purpose ultimately is to make money for
shareholders.

Sometimes, there's a thin line between crowdsourcing and crowd
work—for example, let's look at the online platform called Topcoder.

Whenever I'm around a group of parents fretting about their kids'
future, one of them will say, "I told my kid to learn how to write computer code. If you know how to code, you'll always have a job. And,
who knows, maybe you'll become the next Steve Jobs."

"Really?" I'm tempted to say as Topcoder comes to mind.

Topcoder organizes technical competitions that enable its 450,000
members (mainly freelance coders) to demonstrate and improve
their skills while helping "real world organizations"—e.g., Google,
Starbucks, NASA, and Virgin America—solve real-world problems.
The coders compete to develop lines of code in return for prizes and
recognition, resulting in great efficiencies of time and cost for the
sponsoring companies. The best of these coders may get full-time
jobs with one of these companies. The vast majority, however, end up
with little more than their expended effort.

The human data workers who help Google and Amazon develop
new technologies also fare poorly, according to experts on the emerging crowd work industry. At one of OSF's Future of Work meet-
ings, Mary Gray, a senior researcher at Microsoft Research, told us
about "The Last Mile." "Whenever a new technology is introduced,
there's always an invisible labor force put in place to complete what
the machines can't accomplish on their own," she said. These are the
workers who look through thousands of photographs and tag them
as "dog," "Mission-style chair," or "Cadillac;" who transcribe audio

clips, and who filter out racy material from news feeds—tasks that might appear simple or repetitive, and yet they are best done (at least until computers are able to do it themselves) using human intuition, emotional intelligence, and pattern recognition—at rates of pennies per task.

In addition to her day job for Microsoft Research, Gray is an associate professor in the Media School at Indiana University and a fellow at Harvard University's Berkman Center for Internet and Society. She writes frequently about digital labor and the economics of online platforms. For the most part, she writes, the employee-employer relationship is nonexistent. "The boss here is not a mid-level manager, but an application programming interface (API) deployed on a platform. The platform—owned and operated by companies like Amazon, Upwork, and LeadGenius—works in concert with an API to generate and verify workers' accounts, handle the workflow of millions of online job postings, and route payments to workers once they complete their tasks and submit them for approval." The process couldn't be more impersonal.

Lilly Irani, one of the contributors to the Open Society Foundations inquiry on the future of work, is an assistant professor at the University of California, San Diego. From 2003 to 2008, she designed user experiences for Google. She describes Google's "abundantly productive, nonhierarchical, and playful workplace" as seeming to rely "on hidden layers of human data work: subcontractors who were off the books, out of sight, and safely away from both central campus and technological entrepreneurship's gleaming promise of job creation."

Irani, too, notes the Last Mile of crowd workers that precedes the rollout of a new technology: "Google's self-driving car doesn't simply go anywhere its passengers please. For this car to drive 'itself,' a human worker has to drive around, scan, and map the car's world— including everything from curb heights to intersection angles. Machine-learning algorithms that partially automate data processing still need to be trained for every new kind of topic the algorithm might deal with."

Irani calls the people who do this sort of work "digital micro workers," and says that Google and other high-tech companies use them to train and fine-tune their algorithms and to "refine their search algorithms in the war for higher rankings with search optimizers and spammers."

One of the most potent tools in this war for higher rankings is an online platform called Amazon Mechanical Turk (AMT), which defines itself as "a crowdsourcing Internet marketplace that enables individuals and businesses to coordinate the use of human intelligence to perform tasks that computers are currently unable to do." Turkers, as the workers like to call themselves, can choose among a variety of tasks—for example, transcription, content moderation, and image classification. Because they get paid per piece of data, they are, in effect, doing cognitive piecework on demand.

The Mechanical Turk gets its enigmatic name from one of the most famous hoaxes in history: a chess-playing automaton that toured Europe and the United States from 1770 until 1854, routinely beating human chess players, including Napoleon Bonaparte and Benjamin Franklin. The automaton, a moving mechanical device made in imitation of a human being, was dressed in Turkish robes and a turban. Hidden inside, through an optical illusion, there was a human chess master operating the machine.

There's an impersonal, almost clinical way that Amazon Mechanical Turk talks about itself. A Requester creates tasks for Workers to work on. A Worker is a person who completes assignments. Master Workers are Workers who have demonstrated the ability to provide successful results for specific types of tasks across multiple Requesters. A Human Intelligence Task (HIT) is a single, self-contained task a Requester creates on Mechanical Turk. Examples of the wide variety of tasks listed on the AMT website include:

- Translate a paragraph from English to French
- Categorize the tone of this article
- Choose the appropriate category for products
- Analyze whether a website is suitable for a general audience
- Rate the search results for specific keywords

Mary Gray says that Mechanical Turk is premised on a labor model that's "essentially a bourse, where you have the buying and selling of labor in a basically unregulated fashion, with the buyers being much more powerful than the sellers of that labor." Most of the tasks are relatively simple, but at $0.08 to at most $2.50 per task, you have to do a great deal of them to earn even a semblance of a living. As independent contractors, Turkers don't get the benefits or protections of minimum-wage laws, and if a Requester doesn't think the Worker has done a good-enough job, the Worker won't get paid.

There are an estimated 500,000 people in 190 countries working for Mechanical Turk. "This is a whole class of workers that are necessary to make these artificial intelligence technologies work," says Irani. "A lot of the workers that I see on Amazon Mechanical Turk are highly educated. They're maybe doing this as a second or third job. They may be working at home, because they don't have money for childcare. Or they need extra cash because their expenses are going up. Or they're unemployed."

And to the world, even to their Requesters, they are invisible. Say the Requester is Google. "The Turkers aren't on Google's books, and they aren't in Google's equal opportunity employment statistics. Nor do they get credit or bylines for their work. Their byline is Amazon Mechanical Turk."

A thirty-six-year-old Canadian named Kristy Milland has emerged as the voice of the beleaguered Turker. Milland, who manages the TurkerNation.com website, launched a letter-writing campaign to make Amazon founder and CEO Jeff Bezos more aware of his company's obligations to Turkers. As she wrote in her inaugural letter to Bezos:

> I am a human being, not an algorithm, and yet Requesters seem to think I am there just to serve their bidding. They do not respect myself and my fellow Turkers with a fair wage, and in fact say that we should be thankful we get anything near to minimum wage for the "easy" work we do. Searching for work all day isn't easy. Having to find and install scripts to become more efficient isn't easy. Dealing with unfair rejections isn't easy. Being a Turker isn't easy. I ask that you look towards not selling us as cheap labour, but instead as highly skilled laborers who offer an efficient way to get work done. Please

stop selling us as nothing more than an algorithm and instead introduce those who use your service to the fact we are living, breathing beings who are using this money not to buy beer, but to feed, clothe and shelter our families.

Today an estimated 50 percent of the world's Turkers are American. However, you can't apply labor laws to Amazon Mechanical Turk—any more than you can to Upwork, which also operates in a global marketplace. Over the next few years, it's likely to see the outsourcing of all this American cognitive labor to lower-wage countries like India, which already is home to an estimated 40 percent of Mechanical Turk's workforce.

At the OSF meeting she attended, Gray asked for us to imagine dozens of construction or dock workers standing on a street corner or at the factory gate for piece work—a common image in the industrialized economy of the last century. For me, the 1954 movie, *On the Waterfront*, directed by Elia Kazan, came to mind. In particular, the famous scene when fighter Terry Malloy, played by Marlon Brando, goes with dozens of other men to the docks for the day's recruitment of work, only to get shut out by the corrupt boss Johnny Friendly, played by Lee J. Cobb, who has all the power.

"The notion of invisible, precarious labor is an old one," Gray said. "And now that's done through crowdsourcing." Saket Soni, who was also there, made the astute point that "the historical day labor corner had migrated to today's virtual platforms."

Gray has interviewed hundreds of crowd workers. They describe themselves as self-employed, or as small business owners. They view crowd work as a means to an end—for example, to improve their media skills, with the hope of moving into more interesting and lucrative work with those skills. Or as a second job of five to six hours per day to supplement their income. College kids may meta-tag for beer money, stay-at-home mothers to keep themselves from vegging out on TV.

"In general, the people who do crowd work don't think of the work they do as their primary identity—the way, for example, eldercare workers identify themselves by the work they do," says Gray. "This increases the impression that they constitute an anonymous, invisible workforce." And it makes them extremely hard to organize.

"For previous generations," says Soni, "work has been more than just a source of household income. It has been the arena in which workers bargain collectively and access a social safety net that allows for stability in times of crisis." The new economy turns their jobs into piecework, making it harder for workers to even consider bargaining collectively for higher pay. "Our task is to aggregate these workers in a new way and to make someone—an employer association, the state, an allied union—responsible for them," he says. He gives the example of Amazon Mechanical Turk. "There has got to be a way for Turk workers, who are obviously relevant to Amazon's equation, to leverage their own relevance a bit better."

Writes Gray: "Crowd workers today bear an unfair share of the hidden costs of this new economic engine. [They are] an on-demand workforce willing and able to contribute any time, day or night, to the growth of this economy." How can we increase their share of the new economy's success? Gray would like us to imagine "a global safety net that provides workers with a basic income and health benefits detached from the institutional digs and hours they work." She also believes that employers should be penalized for delaying or failing to pay crowd workers—one of the biggest challenges facing freelancers in general.

IN THE NEW landscape of work, there's an even bigger challenge for freelancers, according to Soni: "I think that there's this sort of cultural notion that nobody is quite a worker anymore. Everyone is an entrepreneur." America's "religion of entrepreneurship" has a powerful pull, he says. "People think that they can begin their own business and succeed. And I can certainly understand that, because we all want to feel free. But, by embracing this fantasy of being an entrepreneur, too many workers are surrendering their potential power to the big corporations." He thinks that too many big companies are exploiting the entrepreneurial dream. "It's an appealing bait and switch for a company to go to a worker and say, 'Culturally, you're not a worker anymore. Congratulations! You're now an entrepreneur.' When the fact is that you're doing exactly what you were doing yesterday and your set of choices is just as constrained."

Soni gives as one example, a nurse he'd met while he was recuperating from a surgical procedure in a hospital in New Orleans. The nurse had been working as a free agent, going from city to city and hospital to hospital, for more than five years. "Compared with other nurses, he was paid very little and couldn't afford to keep doing the work. But, he kept telling me how free he felt," Soni says. "People think there's an inherent trade-off: either you have a higher income and more benefits, or you have more freedom; it's either-or and you can't have both. But, in the process, they lose their confidence to demand something else or something more in the economy."

I've seen a version of this at the Columbia Business School, where I'm a research fellow. A lot of the school's recent graduates can't find jobs as easily as Columbia MBAs once did. To help them out in this transition period, Columbia has a Business Lab and Startup Lab, two workspaces where aspiring entrepreneurs can share an office and access to school resources. In addition, the Business School offers information on fifteen other shared space and entrepreneurial programs that graduates can potentially utilize. Often these new shared spaces can be a place for students who can't get a job to go to "work" everyday, giving them a handy answer to the inevitable question from parents and friends: "What are you doing these days?" Instead of saying that they're struggling to find a job, they can say, "I'm working on a new app," or "I'm working with some people on a new startup."

I SET OUT to discover the future of work. But, along the way, my journey has taken some alternately exciting and disturbing turns. It's been awe-inspiring to see how technology, propelled by Moore's Law, is getting smarter and cheaper, making businesses more efficient and productive to the benefit of society and our economy. At the same time, it's been sobering to see the several strategic inflection points that point to fundamental changes in our economy: wages and jobs no longer rise in tandem with productivity and wealth; the employer-employee relationship has been severed, probably forever; the 9-to-5 job is a thing of the past. For many Americans, the new landscape of work offers freedom, flexibility, and the ability to achieve their entrepreneurial dreams. For many more, however, it represents a harsh, uncertain place with lower wages and less bargaining power.

I have had two guides to the free-agent economy. Carl Camden, the CEO of Kelly Services, showed me how software-enabled free agentry works equally well to build oil rigs in Indonesia and fill classrooms in Iowa with substitute teachers. He also made a persuasive case for the free-agent lifestyle, particularly for young people who don't want to become wage-slaves like their parents were, and who'd rather achieve a more harmonious blend of work, relationships, and non-work activities in their lives.

Labor activist Saket Soni helped me see the darker side of the gig economy: how it breaks down the work of full-time employees into pieces of work, creating a law-free zone for the hiring of an anonymous and disaggregated workforce. I was struck by how this dynamic applies as much to adjunct professors and Turkers as it does to construction, warehouse, and food-processing workers in New Orleans.

What worries me most is the disconnect between this new landscape of work and America's traditional social contract. As Soni puts it: "The historical fact that benefits came with a union contract was never adjusted when unions fell away." Or when the employer-employee relationship disintegrated. There is no longer a predictable path to the middle class for most Americans. Or a social safety net to help them if they lose their job, can't work, or need a steady source of income in their old age.

The transformation of work as full-time job to job-as-piecework has grave consequences for our nation, particularly since income and benefits are still tied to the obsolete disbursement of a weekly paycheck.

"We need a strategy," Soni says. "Hope is not a strategy. Neither is nostalgia. We need a strategy for the new world of work. Otherwise, the notion of a good job will vanish, as will income, dignity, and creativity."

I wholeheartedly agree. We need a strategy for the new world of work, which is why I'll become so drawn later in this book to the idea of a universal basic income.

BEFORE I LEAVE the dark side of the gig economy, I hunger for at least a glimmer of light. I find it in the work of one of Soni's generational colleagues, Ai-jen Poo, forty-one, who has just won a $625,000 MacArthur "Genius" Award for her work organizing low-income domestic workers. Like Soni's guest workers, domestic workers are a particularly difficult group of laborers to aggregate and organize. The title of Poo's best-selling book is *The Age of Dignity: Preparing for the Elder Boom in a Changing America.* Dignity is a loaded word for her. It expresses the growing need for the type of compassionate, skilled, and professional care that will help America's booming elderly population age gracefully; it also is a call to action—to give the people who provide that care the respect and support they deserve and better working conditions.

Three facts underscore the urgency of Poo's efforts:

1. By 2050, the total number of people needing long-term care and personal assistance is projected to double to 27 million.
2. The country's 3 million professional home caregivers often work long hours for low pay and few benefits, at the expense of caring for their own families.
3. More than 80 percent of home care is provided by family caregivers without formal training, and many are squeezed between caring for their own children and aging parents.

Historically, the leaders of the labor movement were men. (In 1996, when I promoted Anna Burger and Mary Kay Henry to leadership roles in SEIU, their appointments were considered a breakthrough.) Ai-Jen Poo is part of a generation of young women activists who are charting the new territory that will define the future of work. Others include Saru Jayaraman, who is the co-founder and co-director of the Restaurant Opportunities Centers United (ROC-United) and Director of the Food Labor Research Center at the University of California, Berkeley; Michelle Miller and Jessica Kutch, the co-founders of Coworker.org, a nonprofit platform that advocates for freelancers, independent contractors, and others in today's gig-based workforce; and Natalie Foster, the co-founder of Peers.org, who you will meet in the next chapter. It's particularly important to get Poo's perspective on technology and the future of work—not only because she's one of the women shaping that future, but because domestic workers and elder care workers are two of the handful of areas with projected long-term job growth.

Poo's Taiwanese-born parents immigrated to the United States in the 1970s as graduate students because, she says, "the caliber of academic institutions and the experience here, the options, were just a whole other level." Also, her father had been a student activist in the pro-democracy movement in Taiwan, which was under martial law until 1987, and like many of Taiwan's young dissidents, he left for the US to carry out his political advocacy work. Poo's mother eventually became an oncologist at MD Anderson Cancer Center at the University of Texas. And her father, a neurobiologist, became a professor at the University of California, Berkeley.

Poo attended Phillips Academy and Columbia University, where she was one of more than 100 students who occupied the rotunda in Low Library—an action that led to the creation of Columbia's Center for the Study of Ethnicity and Race. In that sense, she was her father's daughter. But she was equally her mother's daughter. "My mother became a physician because she is a really compassionate person, and she wanted to take care of patients instead of doing the research end of medicine. She would bring home stories of the people that she would help, including Vietnamese and Cambodian refugees, and the kinds of problems she would see. The stories that she would tell!" Poo spent summers in Taiwan with her grandparents. "My grandmother helped to raise us and that's why I think the intergenerational relationship and connection is so, so important. I can't imagine where I would be without the influence of my grandparents."

In high school, she volunteered at a woman's shelter, where she saw "how only a few kinds of jobs were available to immigrant women—mainly restaurant and domestic work, and some in garment factories, where it was hard for them to make more than minimum wage." With the outsourcing of work to lower-wage countries, the factories began closing. While some of the women became home healthcare workers, the women who were undocumented tended to become domestic workers, or took other jobs where they could get paid off the books. "I started to wonder how we could improve these jobs and make them real pathways to economic self-sufficiency and opportunity," Poo says.

After college, Poo and a group of volunteers started organizing Asian immigrant women in New York City; then, in 2000, she started Domestic Workers United (DWU), whose membership primarily consisted of Caribbean, Asian, and Hispanic immigrants who were working as nannies, house cleaners, and caregivers. In 2007, DWU and eleven other organizations launched the National Domestic Workers Alliance (NDWA), which describes itself as "the leading organization working to build power, respect, and fair labor standards for the 2.5 million nannies, housekeepers, and elder caregivers in the US." As executive director, Poo led a campaign in 2010 that resulted in the passage of the nation's first Domestic Workers' Bill of Rights: domestic workers in New York are now entitled to overtime pay and other benefits, including three days of paid leave per year. NDWA has helped to pave the way for similar laws in California, Hawaii, and Massachusetts, and it has lobbied the US Department of Labor to include caregivers for older adults and disabled people in federal minimum wage and overtime protections.

Great leaders see—and seize—new opportunities. Poo noticed that more and more domestic workers who had been hired as nannies and housekeepers were now being asked to provide home care for their employers' aging relatives. In 2011, she co-led the launch of a new campaign, Caring Across Generations, which seeks affordable care for the elderly and also greater access to quality jobs for the caregiving workforce. In 2012, she was named one of the 100 most influential people in the world by *Time* magazine, and one of the world's 50 greatest leaders by *Fortune* magazine.

When I talked with this soft-spoken activist, I had just returned from the MIT Media Lab, where (as I recounted in the Introduction to this book) Palash Nandy and his colleagues were developing robots whose eyes and eyebrows using sophisticated sensors can convey the full range of human emotions in response to the emotional states of children and the elderly. Did Poo think that it was conceivable for these human-friendly robots to disrupt the caregiving industry? Most experts believe that there will be more jobs for human caregivers as the Baby Boom generation ages. Will technology make some of those jobs obsolete?

"I am an optimist," Poo says. "In moments of transformative change, there are always opportunities and openings to contend for what the future will actually look like. If we're not optimistic, we don't even see where those openings are."

She notes how technology is transforming the way she organizes domestic workers, which used to be considered an impossible task "because there's not a list anywhere of domestic workers, and no trace of them, so how do you find or organize them or bring them to scale?" Online platforms are making "it easier to aggregate workers and employment relationships in a way that we've never been able to before."

A group of caregivers in Illinois told her that Facebook helps them get through the night on their overnight shifts. "When you're alone in the middle of the night taking care of people with dementia or Alzheimer's, it's an intense, lonely job," says Poo. Similarly, "a lot of the immigrant workforce communicates with their families via WhatsApp and Skype and Facebook. Technology provides them with a lifeline to their families and their communities."

And finally, technology is helping to improve employee-employer relations, she says, particularly for housekeepers, who are often falsely accused of theft and have difficulty defending themselves because they speak a different language than the people they're working for. To improve employee-employer communication, NDWA developed an app that allows employers to articulate what they want done in their homes. "There's an agreement in English and Spanish. That way, everyone is on the same page."

As for elder care, Poo thinks that technology holds an enormous promise to make those jobs better while elevating the quality of care elders are receiving.

But how about those human-friendly robots? Aren't they potentially an existential threat to human caregivers?

"I've heard a lot about robot caregivers, and I know they're in development all over the place, from MIT to Japan, and to the extent that some of those robots can help minimize injuries, particularly in lifting and transporting the elderly, I see them as an important supplement to what caretakers do," Poo says. "But I don't see them as a replacement for people. Too often, technology ends up being about convenience rather than quality of life. And we overmedicalize elder care when what's really needed is human touch and a more humane set of solutions and choices."

Chapter 6

WITHER THE AMERICAN DREAM?

I HAD GLEANED THE perspective of several men and women who are shaping the new economy, among them: Steven Berkenfeld, who is investing in it; Carl Camden, who is creating an army of free agents for it; and Saket Soni and Ai-Jen Poo, who are trying to organize the workers in it so that they can have more leverage and job security. However, I still wanted to see the future through the eyes of someone at the helm of a big multinational company that manufactured something tangible and mechanical, like automobiles or airplanes.

Several years earlier, I had served on the Simpson-Bowles Commission with someone who fit that bill—David M. Cote, the CEO of Honeywell International, a *Fortune* 100 company that manufactures cockpits, jet engines, turbochargers, and environmental control systems. I called to make an appointment to see him. I told Cote my intentions over the phone: I wanted to hear what he thought about the future of work and the workplace. Little did I know that we'd broach a topic of even greater importance—whether America's schools could educate America's children for a potentially jobless future. Or that our conversation would lead me to the streets of Harlem, where I'd gain some startling insights into why we as a country need a universal basic income and a new American Dream.

HONEYWELL'S HEADQUARTERS IN Morristown, New Jersey, is only fifteen miles from where I was born and raised. So why do I feel like such a stranger in a strange land as I walk through the lobby of its corporate offices? I get a clue when I sign in at the front desk. As she's taking my photo for my security badge, the guard tells me, "You're the first visitor from the USA I've seen all week. We've had visitors from England, China, India, Indonesia, Qatar, and Israel. And you're the first American, maybe in two weeks."

Which is odd, since David Cote is one of the most quintessentially American men I know and epitomizes the rags-to-riches possibilities of the 1950s American Dream. Nothing in his background suggested that he would end up in the C-suite of a multinational corporation, or become one of the highest-paid CEOs in the world. He grew up in a small New Hampshire mill town. His father, who owned a service station, had a ninth-grade education; his mother, who raised five children, attended only two months of high school. "There weren't a lot of success stories coming out of my community," Cote says. "There were few role models. But my parents were determined that I would go to college, even if I ended up digging ditches for a living."

Dave wasn't so sure about the college part. By the time he enrolled at the University of New Hampshire, he had tried on being a mechanic, carpenter's apprentice, and fisherman, and found that none of those vocations fit. He was an indifferent college student— until his junior year, when his wife got pregnant and it put the fear of fatherhood into him. He upped his GPA from 1.8 to 4.0, which gave him the academic stripes he needed to get a job at General Electric as an internal auditor. He made the most of that opportunity. From 1976 to 1996, he rose through the ranks to become senior vice president of GE's $6 billion major appliances group, and by his mid-forties he was on the shortlist to succeed the legendary Jack Welch as GE's CEO. When that didn't happen, Cote joined TRW, a Cleveland-based industrial manufacturer, as chief operating officer for a year, then as CEO.

In 2002, Cote was tapped to head Honeywell. The $22 billion company had lost money two years in a row. Over the next several years, he diversified Honeywell's businesses and turned it into a highly profitable technology and manufacturing leader, with $40 billion in annual sales and more than 130,000 employees. In 2013, he was named Chief Executive of the Year by *Chief Executive* magazine, and his total compensation of $55.8 million was second among the nation's CEOs. He had come a long way. In addition to his day job at the helm of Honeywell, Cote, sixty-three, is a member of the Business Roundtable, a group of CEOs that promotes pro-business public policy. He is a director of the Federal Reserve Bank of New York City and co-chairs the US-India CEO Forum. He serves on the boards of JP Morgan Chase, the multinational banking and financial services company, and KKR & Co., a multinational private equity firm.

I'm here at Honeywell's corporate offices to get a reality check from him. I've been talking with economists, academics, union leaders, and free agents, who, with few exceptions, have painted a gloomy picture of the future of jobs and work. Cote, on the other hand, glows and occasionally booms with can-do confidence. He greets me at the door to his office with a big hug and an even bigger grin, wearing (is this the new CEO uniform?) blue jeans and a pressed blue dress shirt.

We have known each other since President Obama appointed us in 2010 to the National Commission on Fiscal Responsibility and Reform, better known as Simpson-Bowles. We were considered the Commission's odd couple—not because of our party differences (Cote is a Republican, and I'm a Democrat), but because we have such different perspectives on unions (I champion them, while Cote believes that unionization generally sounds a death knell for America's companies). SEIU's PR people tried to discourage me from getting together with Cote before the first Commission meeting, as I had proposed. They said: "CEO meets with union boss isn't usually a recipe for success." And Honeywell's PR people were just as skeptical when I called Cote to arrange the meeting. But Cote said, "If he's got the balls to call me, I should have the balls to meet with him." And we did, setting the stage for a productive relationship. Cote was a deficit hawk—he seemed willing to put almost anything on the table in terms of budget cuts, while I drew the line at Social Security and Medicare. But we discovered that we could trust and even learn from each other. And when we made the rounds together on Capitol Hill, our unexpected coupling sent a message to lawmakers: "If Andy Stern and Dave Cote can get along, surely Republicans and Democrats can make something happen" on a matter of such crucial importance to the country.

Now we're sitting in his monumentally cluttered office. Cote has traveled to more than 100 countries and brought back souvenirs from most of them, including tribal masks from Nigeria and skipping stones from New Zealand. They're scattered about, along with his collections of not-so-rare fishing caps and jerseys from all of Boston's sports teams. He reaches into his desk and pulls out a big orange piece of paper. "I have a gift for you," he says. It's a currency note for One Hundred Trillion Zimbabwean Dollars.

"Is it real?" I ask.

"You bet," he laughs. "When Zimbabwe finally abandoned this currency a few years ago to dollarize their economy, it was worth about 86 cents. I'm not saying this is what will happen to us. But it's an indication of what can happen when fiscal issues are not addressed forthrightly."

As interesting—and challenging—it would be to continue discussing the debt issue with Cote, that's not the reason I'm here. I want to get his take on the impending crisis central to this book. As Honeywell's CEO, he makes strategic business decisions with billion-dollar consequences. Net-net, does Cote think that technology will create jobs or destroy them? And how are the new technologies impacting Honeywell now?

He pauses thoughtfully, and then says, "We're putting more intelligence on the machine. That's the first thing that comes to mind." He gives an example of what that means. A year ago, his human resources managers were asked to deconstruct the job of HR specialist into its component tasks. They determined that 65 percent of those tasks could be computerized. Before, Cote tells me, "If we had 1,000 employees in HR, 300 of them were great, 400 of them were okay, and the rest didn't have a clue in terms of getting people in the company the information they needed. But now our managers and executives throughout the company can always get the right information—straight from the computer." There's no longer a middleman in conveying that information, which means fewer HR employees, but the department serves the company better. "And we're doing the same thing in other parts of the business, including financial and IT, putting more intelligence on the machine." What Cote is saying confirms what Camden and Berkenfeld told me: Technology is reducing the number of full-time employees required to do certain white-collar and middle-income jobs.

I had noticed that Honeywell had been making acquisitions in the areas of energy efficiency and climate control. I ask Cote why.

"It's conscious positioning," Cote says. He says that Honeywell has made 80 acquisitions for a total of $12 billion in sales and 50 divestures for a total of $7 billion in savings since he took over the company. He adds that he has put those savings into research and development. "I don't want to be in any business where rapid technological change puts us—or our customers—out of business." He estimates that more than half of the company's 20,000 scientists and engineers are developing software. "I even view a thermostat as a piece of plastic with a computer chip." Again, it's a matter of conscious positioning: "These days, if you want to make products that move the world forward, they need to be able to think." He describes Honeywell's new environment-control system, which he recently had installed in his home. "It's called Alto," he says. "When I want to change the temperature, I open up an app on my iPhone and say, 'Hello, Thermostat. I'm feeling cold.' Then Alto takes the temperature up two degrees. If I wake up shivering at night, I don't even need to get out of bed to warm up the room by five degrees, or to make the room lighter or darker. Alto works like a charm."

Cote is validating a story I've heard from others on my journey: software is king. He says that, thirty years from now, industrial companies that don't have "software capabilities" won't be able to compete globally with those that do.

Cote is clearly pumped by his company's success, especially its huge increase in foreign sales—a good opening for a different sort of question: "Do you still consider Honeywell an American company?" I tell him about my experience an hour earlier, when the security guard told me how infrequently American visitors come to Honeywell's corporate offices. "I know you're headquartered in the US and make investments here. But it seems that more and more of your energy and focus is overseas. What makes Honeywell International an American company?"

"Me," he says. Honeywell is American because this New Hampshire native, with his can-do attitude, boundless curiosity, and no-nonsense budget priorities, is setting the company's direction and tone.

"And how about if your successor as CEO is British or French—will Honeywell still be an American company? Could Honeywell have a CEO from China in twenty years?"

"Yes, it's entirely possible," he says. "I talk about evolution a lot. Darwin's point was not survival of the fittest; it was survival of the most flexible. And that's what we need to be—both at Honeywell and in the American economy as a whole. We need to be flexible so that we can recognize what's happening in the world and adapt more quickly than everyone else." As an example, Cote explains his business strategy in China, where Honeywell currently employs 11,000 people and does $3 billion annually in sales. "We mainly participate in the Chinese economy at a local level," he says. "I tell my guys: 'Your next big competitor is more likely to come out of China than any other place in the world. So if you can't beat the local competitors in China—by being better than them at local sourcing, manufacturing, training, and finance—you're going to be facing them in Europe and the United States.' Does that make me and Honeywell un-American? Of course not. By learning to beat the Chinese in China, we're setting the stage for beating them throughout the world."

Ten days after our meeting, Cote will be traveling to India with President Obama for the US-India CEO Forum. Cote co-chairs the forum with Cyrus Mistry, the chairman of India's Tata Group. They'll be discussing renewable energy, healthcare, smart cities, visas, film piracy, and bilateral trade policy. Cote tells me that he's bullish about India's business-friendly prime minister, Narendra Modi. "This is the first time in my twenty years of going there that I've seen this level of excitement in India's business community. It's all because of Modi. If he can get rid of some of the bureaucracy and make the government more accountable, India is poised to move."

If that happens, he says, India's brain drain will stop. More than 190,000 Indian students go abroad each year to study—mainly in the US, UK, and Canada—and most of those students prefer staying in their host countries after they graduate, because of better work opportunities and pay. On average, Indian-Americans earn close to $90,000 a year each—far above the US average income of around $50,000, according to a survey by the Washington D.C.-based Pew

Research Center. And first- and second-generation Indian-Americans thrive as professors, doctors, journalists, accountants, and engineers here.

Cote expects more of those students to return to India if Modi succeeds in improving the business climate there. But where, I wonder, will American-born graduates go to make their fortunes—or even just a decent living—in this age of technology? To India and other emerging countries?

Cote seems less worried than I am by trends pointing to more income inequality and the hollowing out of the middle class in the US. "We're 150 years into the Industrial Revolution," he says. "At first the shift from agriculture to industry was extremely painful, especially for the many people who weren't paying attention to what was happening. But, at the end of the day, it caused a whole lot of productivity and, as a result, our standard of living is significantly better."

"But where will the new jobs come from?" I keep pressing him.

"That's an interesting question," he says. "You have to think that there are going to be certain jobs that are never going to be mechanized—for example, there's still going to be a need for carpenters, plumbers, and electricians."

I tell him what I've seen with my own eyes—prefabricated housing that has the plumbing and electricity built into it. Architects and engineers who are using 3D printers to build modular skyscrapers. "Aren't you using 3D printing to make your simulated jet engines?" I ask.

"Yeah," he admits, but in the end he spits out the same conventional wisdom I've heard from so many other economists and business leaders. "I don't know exactly where the jobs will show up. But I know, in thousands of years of economic progress, they always have . . . they always do . . . they're going to come."

"Are you sure?" I keep pressing. I know that Cote has just purchased 700 acres of farmland in upstate New York. "Would you bet your entire 700 acres on our having the same number of jobs twenty-five years from now as there are today?"

"There will be even more jobs," he says without persuading me. "I just think a lot of the stuff is going to develop in ways we can't even think about, or even consider, today."

IN 2013, WHEN Cote won the American Technology Corporate Leadership Award, he said: "In these times of uncertainty, when many worry about what the future holds for their kids—for their grandkids—I take great solace in my fundamental belief that, in technology, lies hope. For technology, at its core, rejects the status quo of today in the name of hope for tomorrow."

Cote also believes in hard work. As he said in his 2013 commencement address at the University of New Hampshire: "In the Western world, we often forget the reason we live so well is because our parents and grandparents worked harder than the rest of the world to get here."

Having read those speeches, I tell him that I'm not sure that hard work and technological progress necessarily add up to a brighter future for America's children. "With automation displacing more and more workers, can we still assure our college graduates that their hard work will pay off?"

"Yes," he says sharply. It's as though I've challenged one of his core beliefs. "But working hard is only part of the equation," he says. "You have to work hard at the right stuff."

Cote is a big supporter of STEM education. Through Honeywell Hometown Solutions, a philanthropic program, he and his company support the teaching of science and math in communities around the world, starting with preschool.

"We need more engineers, not more lawyers," he says. He points to how the US only graduated 450,000 US citizens as scientists and engineers in 2007, whereas China graduated about 950,000—"and that's with only about one-third as many college-age eligible kids going on to college on a percentage basis. That means when it equalizes, China will graduate about 3 million scientists and engineers a year to our 500,000. We need that Sputnik moment that mobilizes our kids to want to be engineers and scientists."

According to Cote, America's students will have a brighter future if they major in STEM subjects. "Think about all the kids who graduate in political science, history, psychology, and sociology. They worked hard and got an education, but if they had focused on math, science, and software capability, wouldn't they be employed in a different way? That's not to say that history majors will be irrelevant in the future," he says. "But I think the average math major is going to do a lot better than the average history major. Don't you agree?"

It is hard to disagree that the average math major will probably earn more money than the average history major in their lifetime. But I don't agree with Cote that the next generation of Americans will get better jobs—or end up better off than their parents' generation—simply by studying more science and math and by learning how to code. Especially in the emerging gig economy, where well-educated Americans compete for piecework against scientists, mathematicians, and coders around the world, and where they need to cobble together a living without job security, pensions, and the other benefits that used to come with full-time employment.

A new study challenges Cote's belief that a STEM education is the best route to a middle-class life. According to *New Yorker* writer John Cassidy: "Beginning in about 2000, for reasons that are still not fully understood, the pace of job creation in high-paying, highly skilled fields slowed significantly." To demonstrate this, economists Paul Beaudry, David A. Green, and Benjamin M. Sand divided the US workforce into a hundred occupations, ranked by their average wages, and looked at how employment has changed in each category. Since 2000, they showed, the demand for highly educated workers declined, while job growth in low-paying occupations increased strongly. "High-skilled workers have moved down the occupational ladder and have begun to perform jobs traditionally performed by lower-skilled workers," they concluded, thus "pushing low-skilled workers even further down the occupational ladder." In his new book, *Will College Pay Off?*, Peter Cappelli, a professor of management at Wharton, reports that only about a fifth of recent graduates with STEM degrees got jobs that made use of that training. "The evidence for recent grads," in Cappelli's analysis, "suggests clearly that there is no overall shortage of STEM grads."

As Michael S. Teitelbaum wrote in *The Atlantic*, "A compelling body of research is now available, from many leading academic researchers and from respected research organizations such as the National Bureau of Economic Research, the RAND Corporation, and the Urban Institute. No one has been able to find any evidence indicating current widespread labor market shortages or hiring difficulties in science and engineering occupations that require bachelor's degrees or higher, although some are forecasting high growth in occupations that require post-high-school training but not a bachelor's degree. All have concluded that US higher education produces far more science and engineering graduates annually than there are S&E job openings—the only disagreement is whether it is 100 percent or 200 percent more."

And despite Cote's bullishness on Modi, the outlook for STEM graduates of India's engineering colleges isn't any better. The number of engineering colleges in India has gone up from 1,511 in 2006–07 to 3,345 in 2014–15, giving the impression of a booming job market in that country for engineers. In truth, an estimated 20 to 30 percent of India's 1.5 million engineering graduates this year may not find a job at all.

As Glenn Hubbard, the dean at Columbia's Business School, says: "The elevator's broken. Young people are trapped on the same floor their parents were when they boarded it." My sense is that most middle- and upper-income parents in the US know this and they're starting to worry. If that's the case, how does the American Dream look to parents and young people who are trapped on the elevator's lower floors?

WALK INTO THE spacious lobby of the Harlem Children's Zone, on 125th Street in New York City, and you see evidence of its intent all around: drawings and paintings by young people, posters advertising parenting classes, a video showing kids in grades K–12 engaged in active learning, with parents and teachers deeply involved in their lives.

The Harlem Children's Zone (HCZ) began in the early 1990s as a one-block pilot effort "to address all of the issues children and families were facing within a finite geographic area: crumbling apartments, rampant drug use, failing schools, violent crime, and chronic health problems." In an area where 60 percent of the families live below the poverty line—and 75 percent of the children scored below grade level on statewide reading and math tests—the goal was to create a pipeline of coordinated, best-practice programs that would give these children and their families seamless support from birth through college. It worked so well that the pilot grew from one block to 20 blocks to 60 blocks, and now, to 97 blocks of Harlem, serving 13,700 youth and 13,200 adults a year.

President Obama modeled his national Promise Zone Initiative in part on the HCZ. In his 2013 State of the Union Address, he announced his plan to designate a number of high-poverty urban, rural, and tribal communities as Promise Zones, with the federal government partnering with and investing in those communities to create jobs, leverage private investment, increase economic activity, expand educational opportunities, and reduce violent crime. "Anybody in this country who works hard should have a fair shot at success, period," the president said. "It doesn't matter where they come from, what region of the country, what they look like, what their last name is—they should be able to succeed." In 2014, he announced that the first five Promise Zones would be funded in San Antonio, Philadelphia, Los Angeles, Southeastern Kentucky, and the Choctaw Nation of Oklahoma.

Geoffrey Canada, the sixty-three-year-old founder of the Harlem Children's Zone, was born in the South Bronx and is an example of what the American Dream is all about. His mother was a substance-abuse counselor. After his parents divorced, when Geoff was four, his father played no real role in his life. In his memoir, *Fist Stick Knife Gun: A Personal History of Violence*, Canada wrote about growing up in a culture of fatherless poverty and 24/7 street violence. He was able to overcome his surroundings and earn a BA in psychology and sociology from Bowdoin, a master's degree in education from Harvard, and honorary doctorates from Columbia, Princeton, Tufts, Dartmouth, and numerous other colleges and universities. Canada was the star of *Waiting for Superman*, a 2010 documentary about America's troubled public schools, which showcased the cradle-to-college programs he had initiated so successfully for schoolchildren and their families in Harlem. That same year, Mayor Michael Bloomberg offered Canada the job of running the public school system in New York City, the largest in the country, which he declined in order to continue focusing on his Harlem Children's Zone.

I've known Canada for almost ten years. We both serve on the US advisory board of the Open Society Foundations. We were both profiled on the May 11, 2006, edition of CBS's *60 Minutes*, in segments separated by a report on the Dixie Chicks, the controversial country music group that criticized President Bush's War on Iraq. Although our inclusion in the same edition was serendipitous, it's clear looking back on the show that Canada's efforts in trying to reform public education paralleled mine in the labor movement. We shared the similar goal of continuing to make the American Dream a possibility for all Americans by bringing both the labor movement and public education into the twenty-first century.

In his segment, Canada expressed his goal of giving Harlem's impoverished kids the same advantages middle-class and upper-middle-class kids get in the suburbs. "They get safety. They get structure. They get academic enrichment. They get cultural activity. They get adults who love them and are prepared to do anything for them."

His promise to parents who live in the Harlem Children's Zone was: "If your child comes to this school, we will guarantee that we will get your child into college. We will be with your child from the moment they enter our school till the moment they graduate from college." To Canada, college is the promised land—and the key to the American Dream—because young people who graduate college are more likely to get a good job and see the connection between education and a good life, thus breaking the generational cycle of poverty.

With all that I've learned about college's diminishing return on investment for middle-class families, I wonder if Canada still sees college as the best path out of poverty for the kids at HCZ.

We're sitting in his conference room, which overlooks the hustle and bustle of the newly revitalized 125th Street, the commercial center of Harlem. In his dark suit, Canada looks like the chief executive of a big company making a presentation to his board. He gets up from his seat at the table and walks over to a map of New York City's five boroughs. "It shows the incarceration rates of all the different areas of the city," he tells me. When he talks—and listens—Canada makes loose-limbed gestures with every part of his body: his eyes, mouth, arms, and hands, even his legs. And now he's using those various body parts to point to perhaps the darkest area of the map, a section of Harlem and the Bronx about a half-mile from the Harlem Children's Zone. "The darker the area," he explains, "the higher the percentage of people in jail. But there are dark spots all over the city.

When I show this map to rich folks, they look at the dark areas near where they live and wonder: how did all this crime get so close to where my wife shops, where my kids go to school, where I go to work each day—'ah, it must be those housing projects nearby.' And then I point to the 97 blocks of the Harlem Children's Zone and tell them, 'Not one of my kids is in jail. We have 881 kids in college and not a single kid in jail.'"

Canada considers college to be the best antidote to a life of crime. "My kids are very ambitious," he says. "I mean, you want to see capitalism in action, just take a walk in the 'hood. They all want to be rich. They all want Rolexes—the real ones—and the latest-thing newest car. The idea I'm trying to sell them is that there's another way besides criminal activity to get these things and education is the key."

But isn't a booming economy the other antidote to crime?

"Yes it is," he says. He mentions a report he read at the end of the Clinton Administration in 2000, when the unemployment rate was 4.0 percent, the lowest it had been since 1968. "The economy was so strong, the report said, that companies were hiring black men with felonies. In the end that's what a booming economy does: you need employees, whether they have a college degree or not, whether they've graduated or not, whether they've committed felonies or not, you need bodies. We haven't seen anything like that for a long time."

Canada doesn't think there's an appetite politically in the United States for a public-sector jobs program. "And I see no way that the private sector will create enough new jobs for people in the communities like mine that are struggling. Or in any community, for that matter." He's noticed the unemployment rate going down. "But that's a lie," he says. "There are a huge number of folks who have given up looking for work. It may sound like everything is rosy again but it's not."

Like David Cote and me and everyone else I've interviewed for this book, Canada believes in the virtue of hard work. "A lot of great things happen when you work. And something else happens when you don't work, and when a whole generation doesn't work. What's the first thing that happens when entire communities don't work? Alcoholism, drug abuse, early teenage pregnancy, crime. In the 1970s and 1980s, that was just a black movie. But now it's playing everywhere—in rural America, for instance, with its terrible meth problem.

"If you want to see where we're going as a nation," Canada continues, "go to inner-city Chicago, Detroit, Pontiac, Flint, and Cleveland. The critics say, 'Look at these people: they have lousy values, they took to drugs.' But this had nothing to do with anything but work leaving. When work disappears, people don't have money to buy stuff. The economy erodes. The infrastructure gets neglected. And then there's the social piece: people lose their way."

Despite all the government assistance programs, nearly 16 million Americans fall below 50 percent of the poverty line, according to the US Census Bureau. That's the equivalent of a family of four living on $34.40 per day, or $8.60 per person. As *New York Times* columnist Eduardo Porter writes: "No other advanced nation tolerates this depth of deprivation. It amounts to one in twenty Americans—a share that has refused to shrink despite five decades of economic growth." Porter attributes this ignominy to the overhaul of the welfare system in 1996, which increased benefits for poor people who worked, are married, and have children, and decreased benefits to the lowest-income Americans who didn't fulfill those criteria. As Porter poignantly writes: "By believing the poor are not exerting enough effort, we allow ourselves not to care." This permits politicians—and voters—to go normally about their business while 16 million Americans, including most of the children who attend school at the Harlem Children's Zone, live on $8.60 or less a day.

Thus far on my journey, I had mainly seen the American Dream through the eyes of people who have been the beneficiaries of their parents' and grandparents' hard work and full employment. With the exception of Saket Soni's guest workers, this is the first time I've reported on a community that's inherited a generational legacy of poverty, crime, and joblessness. The kids who've been lucky enough to get into the Promise Academies of the Harlem Children's Zone are getting a better shot at success than their parents and grandparents did. Will it matter?

In 2015, 100 former Promise Academy students graduated from college: 70 with four-year degrees and 30 with two-year degrees. Only about half of them had jobs six months later. "The kids thought it would be easy to get jobs once they had the degrees. It's not," Canada says. "It's really hard for my kids to get internships, or to connect with the labor market and find a career path."

I tell Canada what David Cote said: that it's increasingly important to study the right subjects—STEM subjects—if you want to succeed in today's economy.

"I get that," Canada says. "Right now, everyone's saying: 'You should go into STEM and become an engineer.' I get the same pressure from my board. They say that we should teach more coding to our kids—and plumbing, too. My kids don't look down on plumbers, they'll do anything to earn a buck. And if there's really a shortage out there, and we could get a thousand kids to be plumbers, I'm all for it. But I've given up trying to predict which jobs will be around ten years from now because, in every single industry, I know entrepreneurs who are trying to figure out how to do those jobs without people."

That's what Steven Berkenfeld told me based on his evaluation of hundreds of proposals each year from entrepreneurs: most of whom are developing software that will enable companies to do more with less people. And it's also what I saw at Honeywell, where David Cote is putting more intelligence on the machine, lessening his need for human resources specialists.

"Apparently, the hardest thing to teach a robot is how to change a baby," says Canada. He stands up and goes through a mimic's routine of changing a baby's diaper. Then he gestures incredulously at me, as if to signal the fact that changing a baby's diaper is no big deal. "There are all these kids at Stanford trying to make a billion dollars, trying to find the next big thing, and you're telling me that they're not going to figure out how to teach that robot how to change a diaper! People keep saying that there are certain jobs computers will never be able to do. Really? This cat is out of the bag and it's not going back in again. Technology is going to deprive a lot of people of work."

I ask Canada if he ever thinks about giving his students a more realistic sense of their prospects for success in an economy with less jobs and more income inequality.

"No," he says defiantly. "You will defeat young people if you let them know it's a crapshoot out there—that, if we don't get it together as a nation, you're screwed."

He tells me about the day he took Geoff, Jr., then twelve, to visit the Promise Academy. There were 500 kids in the hallways saying, "We will go to college," as they do each morning when they recite the school's creed. Geoff, Jr., criticized his father for brainwashing these kids. "I told him he's right, but I'd never apologize for it. One way or another, these kids are going to be brainwashed and end up believing that they're a certain kind of person. Part of the issue in going to college isn't about getting the degree; it's how you end up thinking about yourself. Do you think you're smart? If you don't think you're smart, this is a tough place to grow up. If you do think you're smart, you accept the responsibility for messing up—for not doing your homework, for not going to class. I think the idea of the American Dream—that you work hard, go to school, get a good job—is worth selling. Pulling yourself up by the bootstraps—it's worth selling."

But how much more would it be worth selling if America found a way to deliver on that promise? And if we offered our children a dream that all of our citizens could achieve?

As I LEAVE the Harlem Children's Zone, with its goal of breaking the cycle of poverty and making a middle-class life possible for marginalized African-American young people, I feel as sad as I've felt to date on my journey. Because my friend Geoffrey Canada is using the hope of the discredited American Dream to motivate young people to take responsibility for their own lives. The risk, of course, is the big let-down ahead for those young people—for all of America's young people—if we don't offer them a more achievable dream, one that delivers on its promises. I don't blame Canada for choosing to perpetuate the myth—at least he's honest enough to acknowledge it for what it is. Nor do I blame people like Carl Camden and David Cote for perpetuating it, because the myth was a reality for them and it's hard to imagine a more motivating narrative to pass on. I feel less charitable, however, towards the politicians running for Congress and the presidency who'd have us believe that tinkering with a few policies will be enough to restore the American Dream to its 1950s luster. We need a more radical solution—for instance, the universal basic income I put forth later in this book.

My need, at this point in my journey, is to get a bigger-picture view of what I've been learning. By bigger picture, I don't mean a macroeconomic view, which always seems so impersonal to me, but to get a sense of what's been happening over a span of generations to real families as they grapple with economic change.

To do that, I seek out Dorian Warren, a young historian who has a talent for putting the ebb and flow of labor policy in terms that personalize it for me.

I meet Warren at Rockefeller Center, where he is a regular contributor at the MSNBC cable news channel. When I get there, MSNBC is having a terrible day. Its early afternoon news show, which is just ending as I walk in, is drawing only 11,000 viewers in the prized 25–54 demographic—an abysmal ratings number. Warren, who appears on *Morning Joe* and other programs, has just been given his own online news and opinion show, which he calls *Nerding Out*. It's part of the network's strategy to gain the younger viewers who get the little news they consume not on cable or broadcast television but on their cell phone and other mobile devices. I could talk to Warren all day about the struggling news industry. Or about his other daytime job—as an associate professor at Columbia University, which puts him at the nexus of another industry being disrupted by technology. But, after talking with Cote and Canada, I'm here to get this gifted young thinker's perspective on the historical relationship between jobs, work, and the American Dream.

"For the majority of our history," Warren says, "we've had an economic system of capitalism, yet operated under the medieval rules of feudalism. Until the 1930s, there was no real freedom in the workplace. I think my personal family narrative was how I made sense of this history." And then he takes me through the generations:

"My great-great-great-grandparents were slaves," he says. "They were the property of their masters—on plantations in Georgia, Mississippi, and Oklahoma.

"My great-great-grandparents were the first generation born into freedom, after the Civil War. But they still had the same jobs as their parents did in slavery—agriculture and domestic work—and their status was still tied to plantation owners."

That status began to change at the beginning of the new century.

"My great-grandparents were sharecroppers and domestic workers. They were part of the first migration north of blacks from the Jim Crow South. One of my great-grandfathers served in World War I, which brought him to Chicago. The others followed. They were pulled North by industrialization and the promise of freedom— freedom from racial violence, and freedom to work and make a decent living in their own communities."

In the Jim Crow South, the employer-employee relationship took the form of master and slave, and then plantation owner and indentured servant. In both cases, the owner had all the power. Did that change after the Great Migration north?

"My grandparents were born in Chicago between 1910 and 1920," Warren says. "All four of them were janitors. It was the first time in my family's history that anyone held a non-agricultural or non-domestic job, or didn't work as someone's slave or indentured servant. It was the first time anyone in my family had mobility and the freedom to find other work.

"My paternal grandmother was a janitor for her entire career," he says. "My maternal grandmother was a 'janitress,' as she called herself, in the Chicago public school system. She'd do little things on the side, like make lampshades, to make extra money. When she was in her fifties she went to community college and became a truant officer for the last five years of her working career. Her husband, my maternal grandfather, also worked in the Chicago public schools as a janitor; then he worked his way up to become the super of his school, making sure it was heated in the winter and that everything was fixed and functioning."

In many ways, Warren's grandparents were first-generation immigrants to a new country. I find myself reflecting on my own family's narrative. My paternal grandfather came to the United States from Russia in the early part of the twentieth century to escape persecution and find opportunity; he became a butcher in Newark, New Jersey, eventually with his own stand. He died when my father was just fifteen. My father worked his way through college and became a lawyer with a small law firm; he built it up until it became the second largest law firm in the state. He used to say, "It was easy for me to become more successful than my father, Andy, all I had to do was go to college. It will be very hard for you, given what I have been fortunate enough to accomplish, to become more successful than me." Had he lived long enough, I am sure he would have been very proud to say he was wrong—the American Dream.

Warren's father dropped out of high school when he was fifteen; he lied about his age and enlisted in the Air Force. "He was in every American conflict from Korea to Afghanistan," Warren says. His mother grew up in the Ida B. Wells housing project on Chicago's South Side. In 1955, her parents moved to a middle-class neighborhood called Chatham, where almost everyone was a police officer, teacher, or firefighter. When they moved in, they were the third black family on a mainly Irish-American block; by 1962, the whites on the block had fled to the suburbs, and the neighborhood was all black. Still, there was a sense of having made it. By owning their own home, these middle-class blacks had achieved a big part of the American Dream. And with the help of the US government and military, they were able to pass along that dream to their children—for example, to Warren's mother.

As a young woman growing up in the 1960s, his mother had two options—nursing school or teachers college. She chose the latter. She worked as a teacher in the Chicago public school system for forty-five years. Her union membership gave her health and vacation benefits and a pension when she retired. "In Chicago—where you have meat packing, autos and steel—the industrial unions were absolutely critical in creating the black middle class," Warren says. "But I would argue that public-sector unions, like the teacher's union, played an even larger role."

Warren's parents divorced when he was one. He and his mother moved in with his grandmother. Then, when Warren was ten, his mother bought the house next store. "I grew up on a middle-class block with other black kids whose parents worked in the public sector."

Growing up, Dorian Warren's house was filled with books. His grandmother bought an expensive set of encyclopedias, which Warren and his brother "devoured." Like David Cote's mother—and my own—Warren's insisted that he get as much education as he could. "That was the mantra in my family. Because no one can take it away from you. My mother also said: 'Do better than me.' Which meant:

'Don't become a teacher. It doesn't pay enough.' And here I am," he laughs.

He didn't set out to be an academic. He majored in political science at the University of Illinois, and planned on applying to law school. But his mentor, a woman professor, refused to give him a recommendation to law school. "She said we have too many black lawyers and not enough black PhDs." Warren got offered full scholarships to four graduate schools, including Yale, where he got a master's degree and PhD in political science. After his third year of grad school, he moved back to Chicago and worked as an organizer for UNITE-HERE Local One, a union representing workers in the hospitality industry. He wrote about Local One's history in his dissertation.

At the age of thirty-six, Warren, the descendant of slaves, is an accomplished scholar, pundit, and activist. He has taught at both Columbia University and the University of Chicago, and he has received research fellowships and grants from the Ford Foundation, CUNY's Murphy Institute, and the Russell Sage Foundation. Warren specializes in the study of inequality and American politics. He has written three books, including one about labor policies at Wal-Mart. He serves on the boards of the Applied Research Center, the Center for Community Change, and the *Nation* magazine.

Frustrated with department politics, Warren was about to leave Columbia when I met with him. He wants to use social media and other online technologies to engage young people in political dialogue and activism. In that sense, Warren is an optimist. And yet, he sees the future through the lessons he's learned from the past.

For example, Warren sees African-Americans as "the canary in the coal mine" for the American economy. In the nineteenth century, miners used canaries as an early warning signal for toxic fumes in their coal mines. If the canary, with its fragile respiratory system, gasped for breath, the miners knew to exit the mine. When cotton-picking was mechanized and the North became industrialized, African-Americans knew that it was time to exit the rural South. Between 1910 and 1970, more than six million of them headed north to cities like Detroit and Chicago for jobs and to build middle-class lives.

In the late 1950s and early 1960s, the jobs in those cities started leaving and as a result, blacks became unemployed at twice the rates of whites. After the 1963 March on Washington for Jobs and Freedom, civil rights leader Bayard Rustin warned of the dangers of automation and income inequality: "Automation deprives more Negroes of jobs than any other single factor, including prejudice," he wrote. "Under automation, we are faced with a new civil war situation all over again. Once again, the union cannot endure only half free. It cannot survive if it is divided into those who receive high incomes and those who are unemployed and subsist on the dole."

Geoffrey Canada painted a picture of what happens when jobs disappear from the inner cities of places like Chicago, Detroit, Cleveland, and New York City. Once-proud neighborhoods become battlegrounds of despair. Does the same fate await the rest of America when technology makes millions of jobs—and workers—obsolete? Or, taking a cue from the dead canary, can we leave the old American Dream behind and begin fashioning a new American Dream our children will be able to achieve?

WHEN AUTOMATION TRANSFORMED the rural South, Dorian Warren's family became part of the great migration of African-Americans to the industrialized North. Natalie Foster's family, which worked as tenant farmers in Oklahoma, went West. They were driven from their home by drought, economic hardship, and bank foreclosures in the 1930s. And like the Joad family in the novel *The Grapes of Wrath*, they set out with thousands of other "Okies" to California in search of jobs, land, and dignity.

They didn't find what they were looking for, and ended up back in Oklahoma. But soon the nation was at war, and Foster's mother's brothers went off to join the fight. When they got back, they were able to go to college on the GI Bill and get unionized work that enabled them to join the middle class. Foster's mother went to college, became a teacher, then fell in love and married an evangelical minister who took a job with a congregation in Stafford, Kansas, just outside Wichita, where, in 1979, Natalie was born.

In terms of this book, thirty-six-year-old Natalie Foster was born at the beginning of the "great decoupling," the phenomenon of increasing productivity and stagnating wages. Politically, she grew up during the Reagan Administration, with its socially Darwinistic policies of lower taxes, smaller government, and demonizing the poor. She was also part of the first generation of high-school students to use the Internet to learn. She grew up believing that "information should be available and free and that it can be accessed anywhere at any time and right now at our fingertips." In the middle of conservative Kansas, she could look up the poets of the Beat Generation and connect in chat rooms with people from all over the world who shared her interest in what Allen Ginsberg, William S. Burroughs, and Jack Kerouac had to say to young people in 1950s America.

Both her family and their congregation valued service—"in part, so that we could save souls for the next life." But when she went to college in Malibu—at Pepperdine University, which was affiliated with the Churches of Christ—she started volunteering on weekends in Los Angeles on Skid Row. Working mainly with homeless people, she found her orientation shifting—from saving souls for the afterlife to helping people better their lives in the here and now.

The year she graduated college two planes tore into the World Trade Centers in New York City, and the world became a scarier place. By then, Foster had moved to Atlanta and begun her life as an organizer—first for Green Corps, which trained environmental activists, then for the Sierra Club, where she led campaigns to stop coal mining in Appalachia and protect the Great Smoky Mountains National Park. She joined MoveOn.org as deputy organizing director and used the power of the Internet to build opposition to the war in Iraq. Then it was back to the Sierra Club, where she built and ran an online organizing department that fused traditional field organizing, social media, and grassroots fundraising "to protect and explore the planet." A great gig. But then the White House called and, in April 2009, Foster became the digital director of Organizing for America, with the job of running President Obama's digital strategy in the successful fight to pass comprehensive health reform.

That's how I got to know Foster—as a colleague and leader in the fight for better healthcare. After that triumph, she ran the president's digital team out of the Democratic National Committee to help counter the Tea Party's "revolt" to overturn Obamacare during the midterm Congressional elections. (At the end of that grueling fight, Obamacare was battered, bruised, and yet still standing.) By then,

Foster and the man she would marry, Matt Ewing, an equally accomplished organizer who describes himself as a "do-gooder in startup land," decided to move to California, as her "Okie" grandparents had done during the Great Depression. In terms of this book, Foster and Ewing wanted to see what they could do through technology to bring a sense of calm and community to the United States of Anxiety. And that's why I wanted to speak with her—because her new focus had been on revitalizing the American Dream for the citizens of the new economy.

In May 2011, Foster joined with environmental and civil rights activist Van Jones to start an organization called "Rebuild the Dream." Its mission, using digital technology, was to "advance highly inventive solutions that are designed to protect and expand the middle class, while creating pathways to prosperity for those who are locked out of it." According to Foster, "Other than labor unions, there really wasn't a whole lot of organizing around the American middle class, and the middle class was slipping away. We wanted to organize an open source, leaderless American Dream movement, but that's not what people wanted. People were too pissed off at the inequality in the country. Six months later, on Wall Street, the Occupy movement inserted inequality into the mainstream conversation, and the anger spread."

Meanwhile, Foster was beginning to get wind of another trend: "People all over the globe were turning to one another to build a peer economy—from babysitting cooperatives and time banks to people sharing homes, cars, skills, and time as a way to help them pay the bills, work flexible hours, and spend more time with their families." She saw this peer economy as an alternative to the economic model that has been dominant for decades: "After generations of centralized wealth, production, and control, here was a new, distributed model that creates more value for everyone involved."

In 2013, Foster co-founded Peers, a member-driven online community for the new economy. The two other co-founders were James Slezak, now the director of strategy at the *New York Times*, and Douglas Atkin, the global head of community at Airbnb. In interviews, Foster mentioned how much the Peers community reminded her of the people back home in Stafford, Kansas, where her parents still lived. Stafford's only general store had just closed. "And the community came together and collaboratively funded their own, locally-owned store to replace it," Foster said. "Not just as a place to buy stuff, but as a community and social center. All over the world people are turning to one another to build the economy they want to see—and that's what Peers is about."

Foster and her colleagues started by holding potluck-style dinners in homes, cafes, and other venues where people would share their experiences and hopes for the new economy as they broke bread and got to know each other. At an event Foster attended in Oakland, "one woman was talking about how she and her neighbors had organized a babysitting cooperative. Other people were talking about how much money they were making driving for Lyft or delivering for Shyp, which was just launching at the time." There were Dinners with Peers in ninety-two cities around the globe, and in places as varied as Nairobi, Kenya, and Tulsa, Oklahoma.

From these dinner conversations, Foster could tell that there were a variety of reasons people were joining the peer economy. For example, some people were refugees from a retail job where they had a very strict schedule that made it hard for them to plan their lives or find extra work or another job. The sharing economy let them make income on their own terms, in entirely new ways, and by putting together a series of gigs. "So it was less like a job," she says, "and more like 'how do I create my livelihood?'"

Currently, Peers claims 500,000 members. On the Peers website you get a sense of how the new economy is shaping up. Here, at a glance, are the main job categories, with some of Peers' listed companies and how freelancers working for them make their money:

Ridesharing, Carsharing, and Delivery: Uber and Lyft—by driving passengers who need a ride; Shuddle—by driving kids for busy parents; Sidecar—by sharing your ride with your community; Relay-Rides—by renting out your car for longer terms; Munchery—by delivering quality prepared meals to diners; Postmates—by delivering goods via car, bike, or scooter, or more; Spinlister—by renting out your bike, surfboard or snow sports equipment; Instacart—by delivering groceries to your neighbors; Shyp—by packaging and shipping packages for your community; Dolly—by helping people move their stuff.

Homesharing: Homestay—by hosting travelers in your home and guiding them through your city; Airbnb—by renting out your home, apartment, or spare bedroom; Vrbo—by renting out your home or vacation home.

Business: In addition to Upwork (as discussed in Chapter 4), there's Thumbtack—through creative, professional, and skilled freelance jobs, and Blogmutt—by writing blogs for companies in need of fresh content.

Errands and Cleaning: Handy—by providing household services; and Job Runners—by completing a wide range of errands, chores, and everyday jobs.

Care: Urbanbabysitter—through babysitting or nanny jobs; DogVacay—by taking care of dogs; care.com—babysitting, petsitting, senior caregiving, and housekeeping jobs.

Teaching: InstaEdu—by tutoring college students; and CoachUp—by coaching athletes in your area.

Skills and Talents: In addition to TaskRabbit (as discussed in Chapter 5), there are Gorrilly—by letting people see your favorite products in person; Feastly—by cooking meals at your home; Etsy—by selling handmade goods, vintage items, or craft supplies; Sparkplug—by renting your musical instruments and equipment to musicians; and Vayable—by leading cultural experiences for travelers.

On its website, Peers also features links and reviews of companies and organizations that can help you manage your business and your insurance, tax, legal, and financial issues.

In 2014, Foster left Peers. I asked why. "Matt and I were both running startups. And we had a little boy. That's an awesome television show for Silicon Valley," she says, "but it'd be a terrible life to live." So, after turning their startups "over to very good hands," they took a six-month sabbatical in Oaxaca, a city in the south of Mexico. When they came back, her husband joined SolarCity, a startup that was "bringing community organizing to the sales of solar panels," and Foster became a fellow at the Institute for the Future Approach in Palo Alto, a nonprofit that helps organizations make decisions about their long-term futures. One of her main concerns, she says, is "that the Uber driver looks a lot like my father now." In fact, her father left his ministry and moved to Colorado, where he's become a self-employed handyman. Natalie helped him build the website for his new business. "He's doing great, building up a strong reputation through word-of-mouth and online platforms like Yelp. But he doesn't have access to the social safety net—and neither do Uber drivers or other self-employed people in the sharing economy. So I've become very interested in helping to rethink these protections."

I BEGAN THIS chapter with the American Dream of a small boy in rural New Hampshire who grew up to be the CEO of a huge multinational corporation. I went on to tell the stories of children in Chicago, Harlem, Oklahoma, and the middle of Kansas who pursued and for the most part fulfilled their twentieth-century American Dreams. Now this chapter ends in the fall of 2015 with one mother's dream for her three-year-old son in San Francisco. His name is Huxley but his parents call him Huck. When I ask her why, Foster says, "So he could be Huxley in a suit and Huck in overalls." For me, these names have literary resonance: British writer Aldous Huxley's *Brave New World* and American writer Mark Twain's coming-of-age stories about Tom Sawyer and Huckleberry Finn along the mighty Mississippi River. And I wonder, if Twain were alive today, how would he frame three-year-old Huckleberry Ewing's coming-of-age story in this brave new world of technological disruption and change?

"When you think about Huck's future, what's your dream for your son?" I ask Foster.

"Wow," she says. "It's hard not to be dystopian about his future. There's climate change and all these students graduating college under the weight of massive debt. But, really, my dream for Huck is that he finds himself living in a society that values equal opportunity for all its children. And that he's able to find and make a living from work he truly loves."

Chapter 7

EN ROUTE TO A
NEW AMERICAN DREAM

Earlier, Andy Grove's insights on the strategic inflection point helped galvanize my thinking about the impact technology was having on jobs, work, and the middle class. But then, in April of 2014, I had an experience that brought the issue home to me in a very visceral and personal way. I was at the Full Frame Film Festival in Durham, North Carolina and saw the premiere of the documentary *The Hand That Feeds*, which had been written, directed, and produced by the socially conscious young filmmakers Rachel Lears and Robin Blotnick.

Lears and Blotnick tell the story of one man's courageous fight to organize a small group of restaurant and bakery workers at the Hot and Crusty Bagel Cafe on East 63rd Street on Manhattan's Upper East Side. Mahoma Lopez, an undocumented Mexican immigrant, makes sandwiches at the café. The film reports that the café's affluent clientele do not realize that Lopez and the other immigrants behind the counter work as many as twelve hours a day, seven days a week, for sub-minimum wages and without vacations, health insurance, or overtime pay. Lears and Blotnick also reported that employees risk getting fired if they call in sick.

The situation gets so intolerable that Lopez, the shy sandwich-maker, is compelled to speak out against these degrading conditions and persuade his co-workers to unionize. For two months, Lopez and his co-workers go without pay as they picket Hot and

Crusty—an act of defiance all the more courageous in light of threats to turn them into the Immigration and Naturalization Service and face the all-too-likely chance that they will be deported. Members of the fledgling Occupy Movement occupy the café in solidarity with the strikers. Hot and Crusty's owner follows through on his threat to close the café before he'll accept a union. But in the end, with the support of a talented group of lawyers and organizers and a new owner willing to recognize the union, Lopez and his twenty-two co-workers win a contract with benefits—a rare victory for organized labor in an era when so many powerful people are trying to bury it.

Along with the rest of the audience, I jumped to my feet as the film ended and applauded the workers and organizers who had worked so hard to achieve this inspiring win. However, as I left the theater, I found myself getting overwhelmed by a different emotion—a wave of doubt and despair that was deeper than any I'd experienced since I realized that Congress would not be passing the 2009 Employee Free Choice Act, which would have made it easier for unions to organize workers. At the end of fifty-two days of some of the most brave, creative, and thoughtful organizing efforts I'd seen in decades, only twenty-three workers had benefited directly from the strikers' victory. Multiply their efforts by a thousand—or even ten thousand— and you'd make only the smallest crack in the great wall of inequality that now divides the wealthiest 1 percent from the other 99 percent of America's families.

Healthcare reform, in contrast, showed that it's still possible to organize a campaign that moves the needle. In 2010, after five years of smart and persistent organizing by SEIU and other groups, a president who got elected on a platform of change signed the "Patient Protection and Affordable Care Act (ACA)." As of March 2015, the US Department of Health & Human Services reported a total of 16.4 million new Americans covered due to the ACA through the marketplace, Medicaid expansion, young adults staying on their parents' plan, and other coverage provisions.

Unions alone would never have been able to accomplish a victory of such magnitude as healthcare reform through traditional organizing and collective bargaining campaigns. It took strategic partners, including some very odd bedfellows, as well as the president's bully pulpit to make healthcare reform a reality. If we want to transform the US economy at this anxiety-inducing inflection point for our nation, it will take a similar effort. Technology's exponential growth has the potential to displace nearly half of America's workers and put the American Dream that inspired our parents and grandparents out of reach not only for our children, but also for generations to come. As with healthcare reform, it will take a broad coalition of strategic partners—and leaders who genuinely understand the urgency of this moment—to strengthen the middle class and keep the dream of a better future alive for our children and grandchildren.

Who will lead that effort? Unions are still important for achieving victories like the one Mahoma Lopez led, but their role in the new technology-driven economy is markedly more limited, especially if there are significantly fewer jobs and, thus, significantly fewer members to represent. And, as we've seen, the technology-driven economy places a premium on innovation and new ways of thinking. The people running unions, unfortunately, have not been creative enough, to date, in responding to the challenges of a changing economy, as evidenced in their slow response to Uber, Airbnb, and other disruptive ventures, and in the difficulties unions have faced while trying to organize freelancers. Most union leaders have a single-minded devotion to the collective bargaining model as the only way to represent workers.

So what is the new culture-shifting idea, the new mechanism for driving large-scale change? That's the question I started to ask myself in earnest as I left the movie theater in Durham. The generation of activists I had just applauded is as talented, strategic, and committed as any I've known. However, if I was twenty-five instead of sixty-five and wanted to make a needle-moving difference for workers in the future, I wouldn't choose to hitch my star to either a labor union or a perpetually underfunded community organization. I'd tether it to an issue that could make a difference in the lives of all Americans, not just workers, and to an organization that was capable of scaling up a truly national effort, as the government had done with Social Security, Medicare, and Obamacare.

Over a period of four years I had been discussing the future of the economy with some of the most influential economists and policy makers in the world. They included two Nobel laureates in economics, Michael Spence of NYU's Stern School of Business and Joseph Stiglitz of Columbia University. Glenn Hubbard, now the dean of the Columbia Business School and formerly chairman of the Council of Economic Advisors during the presidency of George W. Bush and economic advisor to Republican presidential candidates Mitt Romney and Jeb Bush; and Jared Bernstein, who had served as Vice President Joe Biden's chief economist, brought me the thinking of leading advisors to top people in the Republican and Democratic parties.

Policy analysts Susan Lund of the McKinsey Global Institute and Teresa Ghilarducci of the New School outlined the best- and worst-case scenarios for me in terms of job creation, unemployment, and retirement security. Sara Horowitz, the founder of the 165,000-member Freelancers Union, deepened my understanding of the challenges facing workers in the 1099 economy. I had long discussions beyond those reported earlier with CEO's David Cote of Honeywell and Carl Camden of Kelly Services, and with the billionaire movers and shakers Ronald Perelman, who underwrites the fellowship I hold at Columbia University, and George Soros, who is chairman of the Open Society Foundations, which sponsored the initiative I organized about the future of work.

I asked them: Why do you think the latest economic recovery is producing no jobs and such anemic wage growth? Also, what do you see as the main challenge we face in maintaining a growing middle-class economy in the age of technology?

I had presumed that most of these people would be concerned about technology's long-term impact on jobs. But technological unemployment hardly came up in these conversations unless I specifically raised the topic. And when it did, Honeywell's Cote was typical in saying, "Don't worry, the jobs will come, as they always have in these times of technological disruption."

It struck me as both odd and troubling that so few of the experts seemed to be as worried as I was about technology's long-term impact on jobs, especially when the trends suggested that this time the narrative of technological disruption might have a tragic ending—not "the jobs will come, as they always have" but "a lot of the good jobs are gone forever and the new ones aren't sufficient in either number or quality to sustain the American Middle Class."

I was so taken by this possibility that I titled my first slide show "A Jobless Future," and presented it at Columbia's Business School and various conferences with a prophetic certainty that left little room for argument. Occasionally, some students or policy makers in the audience would challenge me with equal force and certitude. They would cite very reputable scholars who disagreed with my more "alarmist" views and ask me to prove why this current technological revolution was different from the previous ones in agriculture and industry, which had ended up producing even more jobs. It took me awhile to realize when debating the future that no one can be proven wrong; that Andy Grove was prescient in appreciating that at a strategic inflection point the implications " . . . are often not clear until events are viewed in retrospect."

So, let me pause and offer my assumptions about jobs and the future.

First, I agree with scholars like Andrew McAfee and Erik Brynjolfsson and think we are already seeing and feeling the impact of digital and information technology in the economy. Furthermore, I believe that we are on the brink of a paradigm-shifting impact over the next fifteen to twenty-five years. My assumptions were summed up well by Derek Thompson, a senior editor at *The Atlantic*, in an article that explored "A World Without Work."

Thompson wrote, "It does not mean the imminence of total unemployment, nor is the United States remotely likely to face, say, 30 or 50 percent unemployment within the next decade. Rather, technology could exert a slow but continual downward pressure on the value and availability of work—that is, on wages and on the share of prime-age workers with full-time jobs. Eventually, by degrees, that could create a new normal, where the expectation that work will be a central feature of adult life dissipates for a significant portion of society."

Although I personally do think this time is far different from previous moments of massive technological change, it is more important to recognize that, while experts may disagree on the degree to which robots and software will reduce or create jobs, there is an emerging shared agreement among many leading scholars, academics, and technologists that big disruptive changes are on the way.

Some, like Larry Summers, are beginning to rethink old positions as the impacts of change reveal themselves. "When (I) . . . was an MIT undergraduate in the early 1970s, many economists disdained 'the stupid people [who] thought that automation was going to make all the jobs go away,'" Summers said at the National Bureau of Economic Research Summer Institute in July 2013. "Until a few years ago, I didn't think this was a very complicated subject: the Luddites were wrong, and the believers in technology and technological progress were right. I'm not so completely certain now."

Summers now argues that "if current trends continue, it could well be that a generation from now a quarter of middle-aged men will be out of work at any given moment." From his standpoint, "providing enough work" will be the major economic challenge facing the world.

But views amongst experts remain diverse and still largely split as demonstrated by a 2014 Pew Research Center study that asked 1,896 experts about the impact of emerging technologies. The web-based instrument was fielded to three audiences. The first was a list of targeted experts identified and accumulated by Pew Research and Elon University during five previous rounds of the study, as well as those identified across twelve years of studying the Internet realm during its formative years. The second wave of solicitation was targeted to prominent listservs of Internet analysts, including lists titled: Association of Internet Researchers, Internet Rights and Principles, Liberation Technology, American Political Science Association, Cybertelecom, and the Communication and Information Technologies section of the American Sociological Association. The third audience was the mailing list of the Pew Research Center Internet Project, which includes those who closely follow technology trends, data, and themselves are often builders of parts of the online world.

The Pew researchers found that "half of these experts (48 percent) envision a future in which robots and digital agents have displaced significant numbers of both blue- and white-collar workers—with many expressing concern that this will lead to vast increases in income inequality, masses of people who are effectively unemployable, and breakdowns in the social order." But another 52 percent did not.

And accurately predicting the future is hard even for the best of techno futurists. As Brynjolfsson and McAfee acknowledged in *The Second Machine Age*: "Computers are so dexterous that predicting their application ten years from now is almost impossible."

Finally, there is an ongoing debate about the nature of automation in general. Some, like the authors of the Oxford study mentioned earlier, suggest that whole occupations could be automated at scale due to advances in technology and artificial intelligence. Others, like the McKinsey Study on the four fundamentals of automation, suggest that a better way to understand the course of automation is to take a task- or activity-based approach, especially in the near term.

I'm sympathetic to the McKinsey argument, and think it is likely the best approach for trying to predict the course of automation in the near term, say, over the next ten to fifteen years. It suggests that at the core of the argument over automation is really the idea of the sweeping ability of technology to diminish the need for labor by changing or taking over certain tasks and functions. This is how things have already taken hold; the starkest example is an Amazon warehouse, but McKinsey cites many others including airport kiosks and the role of IBM's Watson in diagnosing disease. These recent changes haven't eliminated jobs completely but they've eliminated a number of activities that used to be done by humans. This type of progress has and will continue to allow firms to trim back the workforce for years to come.

I think the 'activity-based' progression of automation, suggested by McKinsey, will continue the steady elimination of tasks and the resulting reduction in jobs until one of two major game-changing events occur. The first will be the adoption of driverless cars and trucks for transport and delivery, which will erode or eliminate the largest occupation in twenty-nine states, an employment upheaval of unprecedented proportions. The second will be the arrival of the more promising and staggering advances in artificial intelligence, the type that intellectual and business leaders, such as Elon Musk, Bill Gates, and Stephen Hawking, fear could truly revolutionize society in unpredictable ways, take hold and radically reinvent the way we work and live.

Despite the seemingly split decision and at this point a hung jury amongst experts, I still found myself closely aligned with Thompson's conclusion: "But the possibility seems significant enough—and the consequences disruptive enough—that we owe it to ourselves to start thinking about what society could look like without universal work, in an effort to begin nudging it toward the better outcomes and away from the worse ones." This problem is potentially big enough that we must turn our attention now to what we could possibly do in the face of these changes.

SO OFF I went in search of solutions. My first stops were discussions with economists, experts, and policy makers. I consistently posed the question to friends, former colleagues, and leading experts, "What policies will actually help in the face of technological unemployment?"

It quickly became clear to me that "timing" would be a very important factor in thinking about the right policy solutions. The people I spoke with, and their recommendations, largely fell into three buckets.

First, those people and solutions that focused on the present. Side-stepping my questions, these folks largely refused to even acknowledge the possibility of technological unemployment, or suggested that thinking about it and planning for it largely distracted resources and brain power away from solving some of our more immediate issues (of which there certainly are many). While I often found myself frustrated in these conversations, I do want to pause and say that I admire their focus and dedication on the here and now. These are people fighting to raise the minimum wage, to work on real-time scheduling problems, to battle existing economic inequality, to build union power, and to ensure we have fair and inclusive immigration policies. This is noble, important, valuable work and I would never want to diminish the work and efforts of these people. However, the policy solutions they offered me simply ignored the problem I was trying to solve and, so, I've largely left them to do the critical work of taking care of today's problems, and continued my journey for future-oriented solutions.

The second group of experts and suggestions I've come to call the "mitigators." These were folks who weren't quite ready to admit that technological unemployment might require radical solutions but seemed convinced that this new wave of technological innovation would certainly have some impact. Their policy suggestions mimicked their beliefs. They were not radical enough to adjust to what I believe is an entirely new paradigm, but their ideas did hold some promise for mitigating the near-term effects and helping to harness some of the positive benefits of the evolution. Each of these mitigating policies, which should be carefully considered in the near future, deserves more attention, so we'll dive into them a bit more later in this chapter.

The final camp are the true believers (of which I count myself one), in the sense that they believe that technological unemployment is eventually inevitable and believe that more radical and big-thinking policy solutions will be needed in the next fifteen to twenty-five years. The leading voices amongst this group include Andrew McAfee and Erik Brynjolffson, Albert Wenger, Steven Berkenfeld, Martin Ford, and myself. To be clear, no one in this group thinks these solutions need to be applied today, but we all feel the pressing need to consider, debate, and better understand these policies for when they may be needed. If my many years in Washington, DC taught me one thing, policy change, especially drastic policy change, doesn't happen overnight and it doesn't happen without building a pathway to victory and a powerful coalition of supporters. We'll visit two of the leading suggestions for more radical policies that could help our society adapt to and thrive through technological unemployment at the end of this chapter and in the next chapter as well.

The best policy suggestions that emerged from my time spent with "the mitigators" included: focusing on education and innovation, which are indirect approaches but could help to better prepare our workforce and drive some small-scale job creation in the near term; developing a new version of the stimulus package and investing in infrastructure, which could stimulate growth and provide potential job growth in the early stages of automation; reworking and simplifying the earned income tax credit while simultaneously raising the minimum wage, which could raise the income floor and ease the transition for lower-wage workers; and finally, mandating a shorter workweek, a more historic than contemporary idea, that could spread out the available work and income in the short term.

LEVERAGE TECHNOLOGY TO IMPROVE PUBLIC EDUCATION

The specter of a jobless future brings the inevitable response of improving K–12 public education to make the US economy more competitive and adaptive to the type of technologies that are in development. There is continuing controversy about issues such as curriculum and funding, but no matter how hot the debate there is no question that people in America place high value on a well-educated populace. And polls also provide evidence that a majority believe, as I do, that access to good education is a basic human right.

Unfortunately, recent statistics related to education are frustrating. The college "wage premium"—essentially how much more a college education versus a high-school education gets you paid—has been flat since 2000. And real earnings for college graduates have declined.

As of this writing, in early 2016, there has been a three-year decrease in college enrollment as parents debate the return on investment (ROI) for a college education that can saddle their children with the burden of paying back sizeable student loans. They are making this decision in the context of a twenty-year trend of automating and outsourcing manual work that will continue as driverless cars and trucks, touch-screen checkout and ordering, and automated warehouses get fully implemented. Now that trend is also starting to affect white-collar professionals whose work involves many routine tasks. We are seeing automation take an increasing toll on the jobs available for lawyers, accountants, medical diagnosticians, insurance adjusters, stockbrokers, and software coders.

Still, the mitigators strongly believe that smart investments in education can make a small difference in the near term, and I am apt to believe there is some truth to this. McAfee and Brynjolffson, in

The Second Machine Age, offer a good roadmap for the type of investment in education that may make a difference over the next ten years. First, they write, we need to leverage emerging technology to deliver quality education to as many people as possible. MOOCs, or massive online open courses, could have an important role to play in the process, because of their unique ability to disseminate leading education products and teachers to millions of people cheaply. Second, we need to support and elevate good teachers, and ensure that we pay teachers enough to reflect the value of their work. If we are going to expect high-quality education, we need to find a sustainable way to deliver high-paying jobs to teachers.

This type of investment is not simple, but it could make a difference in creating a more dynamic education system that will help stave off technological unemployment and buy us time to develop and implement more broad sweeping reforms.

INVEST IN INNOVATION

As a short-term policy, continuing to support innovation in industry-shifting technologies is a smart policy for two reasons. First, these innovations continue to create jobs, new industries, and businesses that fuel short-term growth. Second, they help to create a better standard of living for Americans and people across the globe. We should continue to invest and encourage our best and brightest to think of new ways to harness the power of these technologies to make the world a better, fairer, and more just place. At the same time, we must keep in mind the limited scale and nature of this job creation. As McAfee noted in a presentation he made to the Open Society in 2014, the "big four" firms of the twenty-first century (Apple, Amazon, Facebook, and Google) have fewer than 200,000 full-time employees in the US combined.

CREATE A NEW VERSION OF THE STIMULUS PACKAGE

The American Recovery and Reinvestment Act of 2009, better known as "The Stimulus Package," featured a smorgasbord of policies that helped millions of people get back on their feet after the 2008 financial crash: increasing the length of time that out-of-work people could collect unemployment insurance, delivering new energy efficiency and renewable energy research and investment, temporarily increasing the Earned Income Tax Credit (EITC) payout for families with more than three children, increasing the child care, housing, and college credits and adding a new payroll credit, offering subsidies to businesses that hire welfare recipients and the long-term unemployed, and additional business tax incentives. As we transition to a world with greater automation and with fewer incentives for businesses to hire, we should attempt to institutionalize these measures and hope that the multiplicity of approaches either kickstarts or eases the transition to a new economy.

INVEST IN INFRASTRUCTURE

Many economists, including Larry Summers of Harvard, Jeffrey Sachs of Columbia, and Larry Mishel of the Economic Policy Institute, suggest that America's best strategy for creating jobs is to invest heavily in infrastructure, as we have in previous recessions. President Franklin Roosevelt's Works Progress Administration (WPA), the largest-scale infrastructure effort ever undertaken, provided enormous numbers of infrastructure jobs to help ease the pain of the Great Depression through temporary employment, and bridged the gap till spending related to WWII helped to lift America out of its more than decade-long downturn. The WPA also had lasting and positive long-term impacts including 650,000 miles of new or improved roads, 124,000 new or improved bridges, 1.1 million new or improved culverts, 39,000 schools built, improved or repaired, 85,000 public buildings built, 8,000 new or improved parks, and 18,000 new or improved playgrounds and athletic fields. And although "shovel ready" projects in the 2009 American Recovery and Reinvestment Act overpromised short-term stimulus, in the long run all of those projects and many more could provide new economic opportunities. There is certainly a need to improve the nation's run-down bridges, roads, airports, and railways—and to build a cyber-infrastructure suitable for the twenty-first century. Not all of this work can immediately be done by machines, so if we invested in them now we could, again, ease the pain of the transition and offer a source of income for many Americans in the near term.

Congress, as of this writing, has not funded these efforts because they would add to the national debt and grow the size and role of government, two things that conservatives in Congress are staunchly opposed to. We can overcome this hurdle through alternative funding that would temporarily reduce taxes on the estimated $2.1 trillion dollars of revenues that American corporations have banked offshore, and then allow these earnings to be repatriated with a share of the taxes set aside as seed capital for a permanent infrastructure bank. If all of those profits were repatriated at the corporate tax rate from 10–20 percent it would produce $210–420 billion in new revenue. The concept of a US infrastructure bank has broad-based support from organizations as varied as the US Chamber of Commerce and the AFL-CIO and from US senators on both sides of the aisle, including Sen. Rob Portman (R-OH) and Sen. Deb Fischer (R-NE) and Sen. Chuck Schumer (D-NY) and Sen. Mark Warner (D-VA). Chamber of Commerce head Thomas Donohue has said, "A national infrastructure bank is a great place to start securing the funding we need to increase our mobility, create jobs, and enhance our global competitiveness. With a modest initial investment of $10 billion, a national infrastructure bank could leverage up to $600 billion in private investments to repair, modernize, and expand our ailing infrastructure system." While Senator Warner suggested, ". . . we need to find additional ways to upgrade our nation's infrastructure, and this bank will help us strike the right balance between near-term discipline and investment in future growth."

I couldn't agree more; making these investments in the next decade will have positive short-term benefits and prepare us better for life in a more technologically advanced society, ensuring that we have less catching-up to do.

RAISE THE MINIMUM WAGE AND SIMPLIFY THE EARNED INCOME TAX CREDIT

While often discussed as separate policies, I think it is important that we not only focus on raising wages in this country, but also modernizing and simplifying the earned income tax credit.

In 2012, Carl Camden, the CEO of Kelley Services, and I proposed raising the national minimum wage, in stages, to $12.50 an hour, an amount that would allow an individual supporting a family of three to live modestly, at about 30 percent over the federal poverty line based on a forty-hour workweek. That level would offer workers a way to escape poverty, feed their families, buy basic medical insurance, and live in secure housing without significant government support. Since then, SEIU's "Fight for $15" campaign has blown past what was then seen as a "radical" idea, and the campaign has persuaded several municipal governments to raise the minimum wage in their cities, stirring even more discussion of raising the federal minimum wage. One of my mantras is that people who have demonstrated a willingness to work should not be poor, and if you work the equivalent of a full-time job you should never live in poverty.

Think about the indignity and sense of failure that a growing number of workers feel when after a long day on the clock, they come home to their family knowing that despite their hard work, they can't feed them, cover their medical insurance, or pay their rent without government support. What message does that send about the righteousness of work and the pride of taking personal responsibility for your family?

While raising the minimum wage doesn't solve the problem of technological displacement, it can play an essential part in slowing the race to the bottom created by too many workers seeking too few jobs. And it can help make work pay for those people who have low-wage jobs.

When paired with raises to the minimum wage, the EITC, a refundable tax credit that has been in use since the mid-1970s, can lift the floor for low- to moderate-income workers and their families. The EITC has avoided much of the derision and partisan bickering that other social safety net policies suffer from and provides approximately $60 billion to the 24 million working poor, largely financed by taxes on wealthier Americans. However, despite its broad-based support, the EITC is far from perfect. First, the EITC does implicitly subsidize low-wage work in our economy and serves as a boon to low-wage employers. If the EITC did not exist, theoretically people would be less willing to take low-wage jobs. This is why EITC reform and raising the minimum wage need to go hand in hand. Secondly, the EITC is paid out through the tax filing process as refundable tax credits. However, EITC recipients tend to be low-income and short on time and bandwidth to understand how the system works. The filing process is extremely difficult and made even more so if you have multiple streams of income like the forty-three million independent workers who are self-employed in the gig, on-demand, or 1099 economies. Third, as stated in a Center for Budget and Policy Priorities report, "In contrast to the EITC for families with children, the EITC for childless workers remains extremely small—too small even to fully offset federal taxes for workers at the poverty line. Under current law, a childless adult or noncustodial parent working full-time, year-round at the federal minimum wage is ineligible for the EITC."

An updated and improved version of the EITC should be both simple and flexible enough so that benefits would accrue automatically and make it easy for workers with or without children to collect benefits despite jumping from gig to gig—for example, as a worker went from his day job at the car wash, to his evening shift as an Uber driver, then finally to his late-night session on Mechanical Turk. This would eliminate the need for costly, time-consuming, and hair-pulling returns that limit the effectiveness of the current program.

MAKE THE WORKWEEK SHORTER

Historically, workweek reduction has been touted as a mechanism for increasing employment while giving individual workers more time to enjoy their lives. The Fair Labor Standards Act of 1938 established the five-day, eight-hours-a-day workweek standard we still observe today. There is nothing sacred about those numbers—during the Great Depression, President Hoover wanted to reduce the workweek to thirty hours to avoid layoffs. This policy might still make sense in the short term for certain companies and industries—for example, government, healthcare, and banking. But increasingly, it will be hard to standardize a thirty- or thirty-two- or thirty-six-hour workweek in an economy like ours that has fewer people working set hours and in full-time jobs. And it is hard to imagine a national policy where workers maintain the same income while employed in a reduced workweek.

————

THE MITIGATOR POLICIES are smart, useful, and necessary in the short run to raise the floor, create jobs, restore dignity, and ease the pain. Many great individuals and organizations are already hard at work on finding ways to deliver these solutions to Americans. But it is crucial to keep policies such as these in perspective and not project them as long-term solutions to the tsunami of technological change that will destroy millions of formerly decent-paying jobs in the next two decades. America could, for example, pour a trillion dollars into infrastructure between now and 2020, but how will that help bricklayers and plumbers make a living ten years from now, when a recently developed bricklaying machine can lay bricks more accurately and faster than the most skilled craftsperson, or when the new 3D printing technology and emerging technologies will enable builders to embed plumbing and electrical wiring in wallboard before they assemble a house or even skyscraper? The EITC is essentially a great tool for subsidizing low-paying jobs. But if there are far fewer jobs twenty years from now, our real need won't be to supplement what jobs pay, but to create enough jobs to replace the ones technology is rendering obsolete.

We can also keep raising the minimum wage higher and higher—to, say, $50 an hour—but in a world of fewer and fewer jobs, that's only going to soften the blow for an increasingly small nucleus of people as the gulf between the richest 1 percent and the rest of society continues to widen.

Shorter workweeks can be effective for a time. But if the number of people without a traditional employer continues to grow, then the policy of shorter workweeks will only impact the diminishing number of jobs that remain regulated and standardized. It's not likely that shorter workweeks will apply to white-collar salaried jobs, where hours aren't established by law, or to part-time employees in the gig economy. Also, as we've seen in Europe, shorter workweeks can create competitive disadvantages for countries with employers who can move or situate their work in multiple locations around the world.

Innovation and the hope that it will spur new economic growth also has its limits. The 2013 Oxford Study is required reading for anyone who believes that technology will not massively disrupt jobs. It concluded that 47 percent of jobs in the US are at risk of being eliminated due to software, robotics, and machines learning artificial intelligence. One of the myths that innovation believers spout is that automation will only replace repeatable tasks. While this is true in the short term, automation is creeping into more complex and white-collar tasks and will soon impact those as well. The entrepreneurs Steven Berkenfeld is funding are creating software that helps companies produce more—and more efficiently—with fewer people in work that once involved brain work like writing, researching, diagnosing, teaching, and investing.

The idea that the technologies that we are creating today could be the engine of job growth in the long term seems very unlikely. The most persuasive arguments for why this is unlikely to be the case have been made by McAfee and Brynjolfsson, who suggest that technological change is faster and more pervasive than ever before and the focus of this change is on creating cheap ways to automate jobs. In both of their recent books, they explain how computers, digital technologies, and robotics are accelerating. McAfee has also written on his blog, "The pace and scale of this encroachment into human skills is relatively recent and has profound economic implications. Perhaps the most important of these is that while digital progress grows the overall economic pie, it can do so while leaving some people, or even a lot of them, worse off."

Brynjolfsson and McAfee explain in the *New York Times*, "[T]echnologies are going to continue to become more powerful, and to acquire more advanced skills and abilities. They can already drive cars, understand and produce natural human speech, write clean prose, and beat the best human *Jeopardy!* players. Digital progress has surprised a lot of people, and we ain't seen nothing yet. Brawny computers, brainy programmers, and big data are a potent combination, and they're nowhere near finished." This does not bode well for the innovation-leading-to-job-growth line of thinking.

An important part of the argument that McAfee and Brynjolfsson lay out that hasn't been widely reported on is the role of general-purpose technologies, or GPTs. GPTs are technological innovations that interrupt the normal march of progress. Past examples include steam power, electricity, and the internal combustion engine. They are, quite simply, the most important technological innovations in history. Many feel that the computer is the most recent GPT. GPTs typically improve over time and lead to numerous complementary innovations (e.g., networking, Internet, business computer software). Therefore, having a static view of the impact of computerization makes little sense to Brynjolfsson, McAfee, and others, as they see the impact of computerization as an ongoing, accelerating impact, one that feeds off itself in delivering ever-expanding possibilities for new invention and automation.

As Brynjolfsson and McAfee argue, the technologies we are developing now really are different. Before the "digital revolution," other industrial advances gave humans more power and strength, but did not affect mental work: people were still needed to think. Even in the beginning of the digital revolution, as McAfee told Thomas Edsall of the *New York Times*, "Computers became better at math, and at some clerical abilities, but we people were still miles ahead in other areas. So employers needed to hire humans if they wanted to listen to people speak and respond to them, write a report, pattern-match across a large and diverse body of information, and do all the other things that modern knowledge workers do." Employers also needed people if they wanted lots of physical tasks done, including driving a truck or vacuuming a floor. The same with most tasks involving sensory perception, such as determining if a soccer ball has crossed a goal line." But as McAfee pointed out to Edsall, "All of the above abilities have now been demonstrated by digital technologies, and not just in the lab, but in the real world. So employers are going to switch from human labor to digital labor to execute tasks like those above. In fact, they're already doing so. I expect this process of switching to accelerate in the future, perhaps rapidly, because computers get cheaper all the time, are very accurate and reliable once they're programmed properly, and don't demand overtime, benefits, or health care." But as computers and the digital revolution mature, and technology and big data begin to encroach on and then exceed many of the skills of knowledge workers, putting our blind faith in 'innovation' in hopes that it will create jobs seems to be misplaced optimism.

Call me a true believer in the speed and extraordinary consequences created by technology if you want, but it's almost impossible for me to envision any of the mitigating policies, even if they are implemented in ideal form, producing a net increase in middle-income jobs twenty or twenty-five years from now. Combine technological unemployment with the two great de-couplings (growth from income, and work from jobs), add a dash of globalization and income inequality, and you get a highly combustible brew. Yes, timing matters. The policies listed above—a new stimulus package, infrastructure investment, upgrading the EITC, bolstering unions, raising the minimum wage, and shorter workweeks—might keep the brew from boiling over for a while. But if these mitigating policies remain our main long-term strategies for reinvigorating the economy, our leaders will be walking us toward the edge of the cliff with a blindfold over our eyes.

The one recurring fear I have about this moment is that while academics, elite policy makers, and people in positions of responsibility nearing the last third of their work lives (older people like me), and their children, are more likely to be spared from the first wave of the disruption, the people working in the 47 percent of jobs at risk of technological elimination will be on the front lines of a disaster, and they are our friends, children, neighbors, and fellow Americans. Andy Grove offered this more prodding guidance, "Success breeds complacency. Complacency breeds failure. Only the paranoid survive." And "Complacency often afflicts precisely those who have been the most successful. It is often found in companies (and I would add countries) that have honed the sort of skills that are perfect for their environment. But when their environment changes, these companies may be the slowest to respond properly. A good dose of fear of losing may help sharpen their survival instincts."

Unless we are afraid—even paranoid—about losing millions of American jobs because of technological disruption, it's unlikely that we'll keep our survival instincts sharp and prepare wisely and skillfully for a potentially jobless future. Unless we take that threat seriously now, our children and their children will pay the price of our complacency.

Andy Grove gave the following advice to companies, but it's just as applicable to our nation as a whole as we grapple with economic change and uncertainty: "An organization that has a culture that can deal with these two phases—debate (chaos reigns) and a determined march (chaos reined in)—is a powerful, adaptive organization."

Such an organization has two attributes: First, it tolerates and even encourages debates. These debates are vigorous, devoted to exploring issues, indifferent to rank and include individuals of varied backgrounds. And, second, it is capable of making and accepting clear decisions, with the entire organization then supporting the decision.

May our nation have the wisdom to freely debate our course, and then steer together in a direction to ride this tsunami of change to a new and glorious future.

————

THE MORE I tried to imagine our likely future as a technology-rich society with significantly fewer jobs, the more anxious I became. Like almost everyone I knew, I'd feel lost and certainly diminished if there wasn't work that paid me a living wage. Besides paying the bills, work provides us with opportunities to contribute, be validated, become part of a community, and feel pride. It gives purpose to our lives.

So it was only natural that my initial thought for a solution to the coming tsunami of technological unemployment would be to guarantee a job for every American who wants one. That, as noted above, was part of President Roosevelt's program to attack long-term unemployment during the Great Depression. The WPA put eight million Americans to work building bridges, parks, roads, hospitals, and airports. Could that be the solution to the joblessness ahead—a twenty-first-century jobs-for-all program? There's certainly a lot of work to be done: in addition to fixing our crumbling streets, bridges, and railroads, people could get paid to coach their neighborhood sports teams, remove graffiti, provide child care, mentor teens, drive senior citizens to doctors' appointments, and tend their community garden. As long as we could design a system to track and subsidize these efforts—which shouldn't be hard, given the software already designed for the sharing economy—we could create a sector of the government dedicated to funding and administering work that benefits the common good.

However, the more deeply I considered such a program, the more complicated it became. Not least, how could we get the American people to agree upon a set of activities that everybody would value equally enough to fund? Would these new publically funded jobs be in addition to or would they ultimately displace private-sector funded workers?

Imagine the fiery debates that would take place in Congress and throughout the nation as Americans argued about the nature and value of child care versus elder care, or whether composing music is a more culturally enriching and valuable enterprise than developing a video game, or whether we should really pay our fellow citizens to reduce their carbon footprint or distribute family-planning information to teenagers, activities that might offend a large number of Americans on religious or ideological grounds. Inevitably, a handful of people in a government agency would end up deciding the value of a particular job or category of work for the entire country at the expense of individual differences and choice.

Also, a guaranteed jobs program would require a huge government bureaucracy. And it would involve the type of intricate tracking mechanisms that inevitably raise concerns about personal freedoms and privacy. Are we really going to force adults to work at jobs they don't want? Are we going to monitor and drug-test the millions of Americans who take these jobs and treat them like criminals if they slip up? After satisfying America's genuine infrastructure needs, will a guaranteed jobs program with the best intentions devolve mainly into make-work or a way for big companies to replace their own workers?

The more I put a twenty-first-century WPA to the test, the more expensive it became. It'd be a lot easier and more efficient just to give people cash.

Giving people cash, not a job, is the central feature of a universal basic income (UBI), in which every citizen in a country or region receives a certain amount of money on a regular basis without having to do anything to be eligible for that money.

At first the notion of "money for nothing," as the Dire Straits song goes, was alien to everything I had worked for in my life. But the more I researched UBI, the more the idea intrigued me. It has a long history in the United States, beginning with Thomas Paine and other Revolutionary War period social thinkers. After a hiatus of 200 years in the US (but not in Europe), the idea returned to prominence in the 1960s and 1970s as poverty issues grabbed the headlines. The Rev. Martin Luther King, Jr., and President Richard M. Nixon both wanted to give Americans a guaranteed minimum income with no work requirements. Our nation was very close to having a basic income policy: in 1970, the US House of Representatives passed a plan that was to be funded by a negative income tax, only to have the US Senate reject it.

More recently, supporters from both the right and the left have turned to a basic income because it offers the clearest and simplest path to creating a floor that keeps people out of poverty. Conservatives see it as a means of eliminating costly and inefficient welfare programs. Libertarians view it as a way to encourage greater individualism and personal choice.

As you might suspect, my main reason for supporting UBI is its potential to deliver economic justice and security at a time when globalization and technological progress make it harder for Americans to find jobs that pay a living wage. But I'm also drawn to it because of its potential to reinvigorate and give new meaning to the American Dream.

I arrived at this conclusion while reading the small yet growing body of literature on the nature of work and leisure in a "post-scarcity" society where people are able to enjoy their lives without worrying about starving or going homeless. The perspective of writers like Philippe Van Parijs, a Belgian philosopher and economist, and Peter Frase, an editor of *Jacobin* magazine, offers an appealing alternative to the current status quo where Americans work longer, harder, and more productively than ever, with no increase in wages.

As measured by hours spent in the workplace, Americans who do have jobs work an average of 1,836 hours a year, up 9 percent from 1,687 in 1979. By contrast, Germany's work hours declined from

2,387 hours annually in 1950 to 1,408 in 2010; during that same period, France's fell from 2,241 hours to 1,552 annually. Some of the increase in the number of hours worked by Americans has to do with the nature of 24/7 work amongst professionals in the global economy; and part has to do with low-wage workers who need income for their families.

And those statistics only cover the amount of time we spend at work. Thanks to cell phones, laptops, and the ability to work remotely from home or anywhere else, the Protestant work ethic that fueled America's industrial prowess has taken a disturbing turn. We take work home with us at night and on weekends. Work invades our dinnertime, story time, commuting time, and vacation time.

Sound familiar?

"We now live in an 'always on', 'always connected' world," says Professor Jon Whittle, who heads the School of Computing and Communications at Lancaster University in the UK. "And the ubiquity of smartphones and social media has blurred the boundaries between work and life. For many of us, the first thing we do when we wake up in the morning is to grab the smartphone by our bed—which doubles as our alarm clock—and check our work email; all this before we have kissed our children good morning. Technology also means that our switches between work and life have become frequent and rapid. It's no longer the case that we switch off from work when we leave the office. Rather, we go home and are constantly switching back and forth between family and work roles, dipping into work-related social media even as we are cooking dinner for our spouse."

In other words, it doesn't matter where you are: if you're lucky enough to have a job or paid work to do, you are probably working.

Work has been at the center of Western culture and civilization since the sixth century, when St. Benedict declared "Ora et Labora! Pray and Work!" as the twin pillars of a spiritually balanced and fulfilling life. By the 1100s, the work a person did became part of his name and identity, as evidenced in the proliferation of surnames such as Shoemaker, Thatcher, Weaver, Carpenter, and Smith. In the industrializing societies of the eighteenth and nineteenth century, the soil of capitalism was fertilized by the Protestant work ethic, with its emphasis on hard work and frugality.

The German sociologist Max Weber, who coined that phrase in his 1905 book, *The Protestant Ethic and the Spirit of Capitalism*, was particularly interested in Calvinism, which extolled the spiritual merit of being productive in one's labor or occupation, i.e., one's "calling" in life. Believers were encouraged to make money, to be successful in business, and to reinvest their profits rather than spend them on frivolous pleasures. The Protestant work ethic fed the distinctively American Horatio Alger narrative—that a person born of poor parents could climb the ladder of success through hard work and perseverance in the face of hardship.

Those theologies took root in a world of limited resources—of scarcity, which persisted in the United States until the middle of the last century. The statistics underlying the reality of everyday life for many people make for shocking reading: "In 1900, 1.75 million children between the ages of ten and fifteen—almost one-fifth of all children in that age cohort—were in the work force. Children provided one-fourth to one-third of the incomes for working-class families, which spent more than 90 percent of their household earnings on food, shelter and clothing. In 1900, Americans spent nearly twice as much on funerals as on medicine, and less than 2 percent of Americans took vacations."

Fifty years later, after the United States emerged from World War II as the most productive and technologically innovative country in the world, ordinary Americans, freed from the yoke of scarcity, were able to share in America's unprecedented new affluence. In this age of abundance, middle-income factory workers could buy a home in the suburbs, with all the latest gadgets and amenities. They could afford to buy a new car every two or three years. They could send their kids to college, take an annual two-week vacation, and save for a comfortable retirement.

The literature I began to read asked why, in the age of abundance, Americans continue to work so hard. In their essay, "In Praise of Leisure," father and son authors Robert and Edward Skidelsky argue that the material conditions for living "the good life" already exist in the affluent parts of the world, including the United States, and so legislative bodies in the US and elsewhere should use policy-making to limit work hours and create a society where citizens have the leisure to lead more fulfilling and interesting lives.

Robert Skidelsky is an economic historian and author of the Wolfson award-winning three-volume biography of the British economist John Maynard Keynes; his son Edward is a philosopher. They acknowledge that their thinking is far from new. In the eighteenth century, the Scottish moral philosopher Adam Smith, often called "the father of economics," pondered the question: What happens after economic growth has ensured that we all have enough? And most famously, in an essay he wrote in 1930 called "Economic Possibilities for Our Grandchildren," Keynes predicted that, sometime around the year 2030, "man will be faced with his real, his permanent problem— how to use his freedom from pressing economic cares, how to occupy the leisure, which science and compound interest will have won for him, to live wisely and agreeably and well." Keynes believed that the real purpose of economic growth is to free people from work, not to encourage people to keep working harder and harder in pursuit of capital.

With 2030 just a bit more than a decade into the future, it seems clear to me that technology is going to keep making the US economy more productive, efficient, and competitive. We will remain a very rich country, wealthier than any nation in the history of the world. We will have high-paying jobs for fewer people, however, and the gap between the wealthiest 1 percent and the rest of us will continue to grow. So how can we assure that every American lives at or above the poverty level, and that we maintain the aspirational engine of the American Dream at a time when the old verities (work hard, go to college, and follow the rules) no longer assure a better future for our children?

Through a universal basic income.

As the Belgian philosopher and economist Philippe Van Parijs elegantly puts it: "The UBI is called 'basic' because it is something on which a person can safely count, a material foundation on which a life can firmly rest." Van Parijs helped me understand that UBI isn't simply anti-work, which would have been a turn-off for me; nor does it discourage an ambitious person from making money. As Van Parijs notes, "Any other income—whether in cash or in kind, from work or savings, from the market or the state—can lawfully be added to [a UBI]." UBI doesn't lower the ceiling on what a person can earn; it simply raises the floor.

Peter Frase opened my eyes to the fact that a UBI would enable a much larger portion of the population to exist and thrive outside of paid labor. That had been a huge worry of mine. With technology changing the nature of work, how were people going to survive financially if they didn't have jobs with benefits? Frase broadened my view by putting the emphasis on people's enhanced ability to thrive. If their basic needs were provided for, real people, not just rich people, would be empowered to make their own work and lifestyle choices. They would be less beholden to take and keep a crappy job just to make ends meet, or to work for substandard pay when their time would be better spent taking care of a sick child or dying parent. They could cut back on their hours or drop out of the labor market at will—to pursue an altogether different and more fulfilling way to make a living, or to pursue a more meaningful life that wasn't as centered around work.

Rich people have those choices, and so should everyone else.

The freedom to choose the life that you want for yourself and for your family. That's the new American Dream. And UBI can help all Americans to achieve it, as the next chapter shows.

Chapter 8

A TWENTY-FIRST-CENTURY SOLUTION TO A TWENTY-FIRST-CENTURY PROBLEM

A T FIRST BLUSH it seems almost un-American—a universal basic income (UBI) that grants an income to every US citizen without any obligation to work or perform a socially mandated task.

In a country that celebrates hard work as the path to fulfillment and riches, the idea of getting money for nothing—even if it's just enough to keep you and your family off the debt collector's call list and above the poverty line—is heresy. And yet, in some ways, UBI is as idealistic, optimistic, and American as the Declaration of Independence and its foundational principle that "We hold these truths to be self-evident, that all men are created equal, that they are endowed by their Creator with certain unalienable Rights, that among these are Life, Liberty and the pursuit of Happiness."

Even with our current economic problems, we live in a land of abundant wealth and resources. And UBI is rooted in the belief that every human being should have at least the basic means to choose the life they want for themselves and their families. At a time when the tried-and-true twentieth-century solutions are failing us, UBI has the potential to give our troubled economy a twenty-first-century shot in the arm by transforming the technological disruption that's been causing us so much anxiety into a force for self-fulfillment and the common good.

If these sentiments sound lofty and gilded, as I'm sure they do, my hope is that the conversations that take place within this chapter inspire you to see UBI as a policy that can raise the floor and reinvigorate our nation's founding principles while providing new scaffolding for the American Dream.

THE FIRST MAJOR proponent of a basic income in the United States was the political theorist Thomas Paine, one of the nation's founding fathers. Almost twenty years after he wrote *Common Sense* (1776), the pamphlet that inspired Americans to seek their independence from Britain, Paine penned *Agrarian Justice* (1795), which offered a philosophical rationale for a guaranteed minimum income:

"It is a position not to be controverted that the earth, in its natural, uncultivated state was, and ever would have continued to be, the common property of the human race." Once cultivated, however, "it is the value of the improvement, only, and not the earth itself, that is in individual property." Hence, Paine reasoned, every owner of cultivated lands "owes to the community a ground-rent for the land which he holds."

Paine proposed that the revenues from ground rent be used to fund his plan for a basic income.

In hindsight, Paine's plan was as radical and prescient as his call for liberty had been: "There shall be paid to every person, when arrived at the age of twenty-one years, the sum of fifteen pounds sterling, as a compensation in part, for the loss of his or her natural inheritance, by the introduction of the system of landed property. And also, the sum of ten pounds per annum, during life, to every person now living, of the age of fifty years, and to all others as they shall arrive at that age."

Paine wanted to provide each US citizen with a basic stake of 15 pounds sterling when they turned twenty-one, and an old-age pension of ten pounds per year when they reached the age of fifty.

His proposal was never adopted, but it has inspired other people—most recently, social entrepreneur Peter Barnes—to fashion funding schemes for a basic income based, as Paine's was, on recouping our natural inheritance through taxes on the people and corporations who own and use it.

From 1790 to 1940, the locus of new thinking about basic income shifted to Europe, where the idea gained its greatest momentum in the aftermath of the First World War.

In his 1918 book *Roads to Freedom*, the philosopher and mathematician Bertrand Russell proposed "that a certain small income, sufficient for necessaries, should be secured to all, whether they work or not." He believed that human beings have a fundamental right to a basic income.

He also proposed that a larger income "should be given to those who are willing to engage in some work which the community recognizes as useful." Today, this is commonly known as a participation income.

Although Russell wanted to give people who did socially useful work a bonus, he didn't believe that human beings should be defined by the work they did, or obligated even to do it. "When education is finished," he wrote, "no one should be compelled to work, and those who choose not to work should receive a bare livelihood and be left completely free"—an argument that finds favor with libertarians who support a basic income.

In 1918, the Quaker political leader Dennis Milner, a member of Britain's Labour Party, argued for a "state bonus," essentially a weekly UBI paid to all citizens to end the poverty that was so rampant and devastating in postwar Britain. Major C.H. Douglas, a British engineer and social philosopher, added the rationale that his country's overall "productive power" was a "joint result of current effort and of the social heritage of inventiveness and skill" of all the people; hence, "all the citizens should share in the yield of this common heritage." The economist James Meade, later a Nobel laureate, endorsed Milner's ideas and referred to basic income as a "social dividend" to be funded out of the return on publicly owned productive assets.

In 1948, as Europe dug its way out of the ashes of World War II, and its colonies in Asia and Africa began to assert their independence, the idea of a basic income was embedded in the new United Nation's Universal Declaration of Human Rights. As Article 25 states: "Everyone has the right to a standard of living adequate for the health and well-being of himself and of his family, including food, clothing, housing and medical care and necessary social services, and the right to security in the event of unemployment, sickness, disability, widowhood, old age or other lack of livelihood in circumstances beyond his control."

It was in the United States that basic income made its next big showing. In his 1962 book *Capitalism and Freedom*, the libertarian economist Milton Friedman proposed a "negative income tax"—a form of basic income delivered through the federal tax system that provides subsidies to persons or families whose income falls below a certain level. "The basic idea is to use the mechanism by which we now collect tax revenue from people with incomes above some minimum level to provide financial assistance to people with incomes below that level," Friedman wrote. One of his biggest goals was to dismantle the welfare state that President Franklin Roosevelt had put in place through his New Deal. Friedman was convinced that a negative income tax would reduce the need for the social safety net and also its expensive, inefficient bureaucracy.

Another libertarian, the Nobel Prize–winning economist F.A. Hayek, later wrote: "There is no reason why in a free society government should not assure to all, protection against severe deprivation in the form of an assured minimum income, or a floor below which nobody need descend."

Hayek made his case on the basis of common interest—he wrote that all of us might need "insurance against extreme misfortune" in our lives—but also because society has a moral duty to assist those within "the organized community . . . who cannot help themselves."

The fact was: decades after the Great Depression of the 1930s, and after the United States had emerged from World War II as the most affluent country in the world, poverty was pervasive in America. In 1964, President Lyndon Johnson unleashed his Great Society campaign of social programs to fight poverty. But by the spring of 1968, it was clear that his focus had shifted to the war in Vietnam. In response, more than 1,000 economists signed a document urging Congress "to adopt this year a system of income guarantees and supplements." As signatory John Kenneth Galbraith, the nation's best-known economist, wrote: "The answer or part of the answer (to poverty) is rather clear: everybody should be guaranteed a decent basic income."

Another signatory, James Tobin, a Yale professor who would later become a Nobel Laureate in economics, favored giving each American household a basic income credit that would vary in amount according to the size and composition of their household. These "demogrants," as he called them, could be supplemented with any other type of taxable income.

While Tobin and Galbraith were lobbying Congress to create a basic income, the Rev. Martin Luther King, Jr., was planning a march on Washington to serve as the focal point of his national Poor People's Campaign. King expressed his reasons for supporting a basic income in his 1967 book *Where Do We Go From Here: Chaos or Community*. He wrote that each of the government's poverty programs was aimed at "first solving something else"—for example, the housing problem, or hunger, or the education deficit. Instead of this indirect approach to poverty, "I am now convinced that the simplest approach will prove to be the most effective—the solution to poverty is to abolish it directly by a now widely discussed measure: the guaranteed income."

King's critique of the current welfare system was withering. "The contemporary tendency in our society is to base our distribution on scarcity, which has vanished, and to compress our abundance into the overfed mouths of the middle and upper classes until they gag with superfluity. If democracy is to have breadth of meaning," he wrote, "it is necessary to adjust this inequity. It is not only moral, but it is also intelligent. We are wasting and degrading human life by clinging to archaic thinking."

Like Paine, Russell, and so many of the earlier proponents of a basic income, King emphasized the fact that we live in a period of abundance, not scarcity, and that technology gives us the tools, resources, and moral imperative to end poverty.

"The curse of poverty has no justification in our age," King wrote. "It is socially as cruel and blind as the practice of cannibalism at the dawn of civilization, when men ate each other because they had not yet learned to take food from the soil or to consume the abundant animal life around them. The time has come for us to civilize ourselves by the total, direct and immediate abolition of poverty."

The 1968 petition of Tobin and his fellow economists gave the Nixon Administration the impetus it needed to pursue its own plans to eliminate poverty. In 1969, a presidential commission unanimously recommended the adoption of a guaranteed income with no work requirements, to be funded by a version of Friedman's negative income tax. The US House of Representatives adopted the plan, which was supported by groups as varied as the Ripon Society, a centrist Republican policy organization, and the liberal National Council of Churches. But in 1970, and also in 1972, the US Senate rejected the plan.

Democratic presidential candidate George McGovern featured a version of Tobin's demogrants in his party's 1972 platform. After McGovern's defeat and Nixon's impeachment, basic income moved from the arenas of politics and policy-making to the halls of academia in the US.

With one major exception:

During the construction of the Trans-Alaska Pipeline in the 1970s, the state of Alaska got an unexpected windfall from the money oil companies paid for leases to look for oil and secure drilling rights. To safeguard future income from oil, Alaskans amended the state constitution so that they could put 25 percent of that money into a dedicated fund, which would become known as the Alaska Permanent Fund. To gain public support for the idea, Gov. Jay Hammond, a Republican, wanted to pay an annual dividend to all of Alaska's residents in proportion to their years of residency. The US Supreme Court, citing the "equal protection clause" of the 14th Amendment, ruled that Hammond's funding scheme was discriminatory against immigrants from other states. So Hammond turned his dividend into a universal basic income given to any person who is officially a resident of the state. Each year, around 650,000 Alaskans receive a dividend from the Permanent Fund. It has grown from $386 per person to slightly over $2,000 per person over the years, going up and down at times with the stock market and price of oil. The program has proved enormously popular. Supporters credit it with making Alaska the most egalitarian of US states—and for helping residents in Alaska's impoverished rural areas deal with unemployment rates that can go as high as 60 percent.

Before I turn to my own basic income plan, I need to cite three other, very different plans that have been proposed in recent years.

In their 1999 book *The Stakeholder Society*, Yale Law School professors Bruce Ackerman and Anne Alstott proposed giving a one-time $80,000 grant to each US citizen on their eighteenth birthday. The grants would make all of America's young people significant stakeholders in the nation's wealth and future. As they begin their adulthood, stakeholders could invest the money, or save it, or use it to help finance a college education, the purchase of a house, or the start of a new business. Ackerman and Alstott proposed funding the grants through an annual tax of 2 percent on the property owned by the richest 40 percent of Americans. Even though an $80,000 grant would give young people a head start as they embark on their adult lives, it doesn't go very far in an economy where people will need a non-labor source of income for the rest of their lives just to get by.

In his 2006 book *In Our Hands: A Plan to End the Welfare State*, the libertarian political scientist Charles Murray proposes a basic income scheme, funded and implemented as follows:

"Henceforth, federal, state, and local governments shall make no law nor establish any program that provides benefits to some citizens but not to others. All programs currently providing such benefits are to be terminated. The funds formerly allocated to them are to be used instead to provide every citizen with a cash grant beginning at age twenty-one and continuing until death. The annual value of the cash grant at the program's outset is to be $10,000."

Murray believes welfare programs hurt the people they aim to help—and that they're largely responsible for the decline in marriage and the high rates of teen pregnancy in the United States. Take away government support, he says, and teen girls will think twice before getting pregnant again. Give people a basic income and they'll be more likely to take responsibility for their lives.

I don't agree with Murray's premise that welfare incentivizes teens to have babies out of wedlock; nor do I believe that taking away government support will cause teenagers, poor people, or anyone else to take more responsibility for their lives. The only reason to eliminate welfare programs is to use the money to finance a better way of helping poor people—UBI. Murray seems to want to teach poor people a lesson. But the point of UBI is to give poor and lower-income people more freedom to choose their own lives, the essence of democracy. Some people will choose to take more responsibility for their lives, and some will not, which to my mind is just fine, because that's how people behave when they are allowed to choose freely, whether they are born rich or poor.

In his 2014 book, *With Liberty and Dividends for All*, the social entrepreneur Peter Barnes introduced a basic income plan inspired by Thomas Paine's idea that all people have a right to income from wealth we either inherit or create together. He gives air, water, and the electromagnetic spectrum as examples of our common inherited assets, and intellectual property rights (i.e., patents, copyrights, and trademarks) as wealth that we create together. That's because the federal government, in granting these rights, gives the people and companies that hold them a temporary monopoly on making money from the intellectual property. Noting that most of the more than $5 trillion asset value of the nation's intellectual property rights accrues to companies in the software, entertainment, and pharmaceutical industries, Barnes believes that it's perfectly valid for US citizens to expect these companies to pay the government a fee for not letting others infringe on their intellectual property.

Barnes's big idea is to create a Sky Trust (also referred to as a "clean air trust") modeled on the Alaska Permanent Fund. Companies that profit from using (and often polluting) the air would pay user fees to the Sky Trust. In turn, the trust would pay a monthly dividend to all US citizens over eighteen years old. "If you want to use nature's gifts to all of us to dump your crap, we can regulate you," Barnes says. "But we can also make you pay us for the right to use what rightfully belongs to everybody." Barnes applies the same criteria to the corporate use of other common assets and believes the government would be able to collect enough fees from all these assets to fund a dividend of $5,000 per adult per year.

Barnes isn't interested in raising the income floor. His main goal is to reduce pollution. He doesn't want to give the government any additional money to spend; he'd rather give the fees the government collects directly to citizens to help boost their incomes. Unlike my plan, Barnes's keeps the welfare system in place. For that reason, I think his plan runs the risk of unintentionally hurting the poor—because once lawmakers become aware that the new program puts more income in the pockets of low-income people, they will be tempted to raise the income limit for people to qualify for the earned income tax credit (EITC). Or they'll cut welfare allotments in order to accomplish other policy goals—like fighting a war, or giving corporations or upper-income people yet another tax break.

The Alaska Permanent Fund is the most enduring basic income program to date. (Due to the income it can obtain from its natural resource of oil, Alaska is uniquely situated to charge fees to fund its dividend.) There has been one other intriguing US experiment, however. In 1996, the Eastern Band of Cherokee Indians in North Carolina's Great Smoky Mountains opened a casino and elected to distribute a proportion of the profits equally among its 8,000 members. According to a study by Elizabeth Jane Costello, a professor of medical psychology at Duke University, by 2001, when casino profits amounted to $6,000 per person yearly, the number of Cherokee living below the poverty line had declined by half. Among the children who moved out of poverty because of the supplements, the frequency of behavioral problems declined by 20 percent. Minor crimes declined, and on-time high school graduation rates improved. She studied three different cohorts of Cherokee children: ages nine, eleven, and thirteen. Ten years later, the children who received the income supplements earliest in their life had benefited most in young adulthood and were one-third less likely to suffer mental-health and substance-abuse problems in adulthood. It also improved parenting quality. As Moises Velasquez-Manoff wrote in an "Opinionator" column in the *New York Times*, quoting a community resident he'd interviewed: "Before the casino opened and supplements began, employment was often sporadic. Many Cherokee worked 'hard and long' during the summer, she told me, and then hunkered down when jobs disappeared in the winter. The supplements eased the strain of that feast-or-famine existence, she said. Some used the money to pay a few months' worth of bills in advance. Others bought their children clothes for school, or even Christmas presents. Mostly, though, the energy once spent fretting over such things was freed up. That helps parents be better parents," she said.

There have been several other basic income experiments, mainly in Canada, Africa, and Europe.

In the mid-1970s, the tiny Canadian town of Dauphin (the "garden capital of Manitoba") acted as guinea pig for a grand experiment in social policy called "Mincome," funded jointly by the Canadian federal government and the province of Manitoba. Their aim was to determine if a guaranteed minimum income acted as a disincentive to work. During the five-year experiment, only two groups of people were found to work fewer hours: adolescents (because they felt no pressure to support a family) and new mothers (because they wanted to spend more time at home with their infants). There were several other findings: As expected, poverty disappeared. And, unexpectedly, hospitalization rates went down, especially for admissions related to mental health and to accidents and injuries, while high-school completion rates went up, suggesting that a guaranteed annual income, implemented broadly in society, may improve health and social outcomes at the community level.

In 2008 and 2009, a basic income experiment in the impoverished Otjivero-Omitara region of Namibia produced a number of intriguing outcomes. There was an increase in entrepreneurship, evident in the fact that the average income grew 39 percent beyond the basic income and that many recipients were able to start their own small businesses—for instance, baking bread, making bricks, and sewing dresses. The guaranteed basic income had increased households' buying power, creating a local market for these goods. Among the other outcomes: the basic income reduced the dependency of women on men for their survival and gave them a greater measure of control over their own sexuality, freeing them from the pressure to engage in transactional sex. It gave HIV-positive residents more time and resources to travel to the town of Gobabis to get their medication. The number of children considered underweight fell from 42 percent to 10 percent. Dropout rates fell 40 percent, partly because parents had more money to pay school fees and for uniforms. Household debt fell, savings increased, and there was increased ownership of livestock and poultry. Finally, there wasn't the expected increase in alcoholism, partly because the community committee reached an agreement with local shebeen owners not to sell alcohol on the day the government disbursed the monthly grants.

In July of 2015, it was reported that the Namibian government was "strongly considering" a national basic income program.

The Dutch city of Utrecht is expected to begin a yearlong basic income experiment in January 2017, although not universal. Selected recipients will receive a monthly basic income of 900 euros for an adult and 1,300 euros for a couple or family, with no restrictions on how it must be spent. More than 46 percent of the Dutch working-age population is employed part-time, so the experiment is part of a greater debate on whether to raise the floor by raising the minimum wage or by utilizing forms of non-labor income. The test in Utrecht is meant to explore how the behavior economically and socially of people who receive a basic income compares with that of welfare recipients. The cities of Tilburg, Groningen, Maastricht, Gouda, Enschede, Nijmegen, and Wageningen also are considering the experiment.

Switzerland will hold a nationwide referendum on an unconditional basic income in 2016. If the referendum passes, basic income will become a constitutional right. It has been interesting to watch the referendum take shape. The petition for a referendum was started in April 2012. Within a year it had 70,000 signatures. By October 2013 more than 130,000 citizens had signed the petition, which meant that a referendum on an unconditional income had to be held. To publicize the petition, supporters emptied a truck filled with eight million coins in front of the Federal Palace in Bern. The level being proposed is 2,500 Swiss francs per month, the equivalent of $2,650 in US currency. The governing Swiss Federal Council has urged citizens to vote against the initiative on the grounds that it would force women back into housework and care work, cause low-cost jobs to move abroad, and necessitate a tax hike to fund a UBI. It will be fascinating to see how the vote turns out.

According to a recent poll, 69 percent of Finns support the idea of a basic income, with the median respondent calling for a minimum of 1,000 euros a month (about $1,083 in US currency). In 2017, Finland will begin a two-year pilot that promises to be the most rigorous test yet of a basic income in a developed country. Finland's center-right government has set aside 20 billion euros (a little under $22 billion) to fund the trial, which will look at a variety of models, including a full basic income that replaces most means-tested benefits, a partial basic income, and a negative income tax in which benefits pay out as people earn more money.

I will also be watching closely to see what happens in Canada over the next few years. In October 2015, the Liberal Party, led by Justin Trudeau, won 184 of 338 seats in Canada's House of Commons and drove the Conservatives out of government after nearly a decade in power. A plank in the Liberty Party's platform reads: "BE IT RESOLVED that the Liberal Party of Canada advocate for a federal pilot of a basic income supplement in at least one Canadian town or city, in cooperation with the appropriate provincial and municipal government(s)." It will be interesting to see if the Liberty Party can build, as it intends, on the 1970s Mincome experiment in the province of Manitoba.

And there is momentum building for UBI across the pond, in England, where the prestigious Royal Society of Arts (RSA) recently endorsed UBI as the best practical solution for the challenges facing the British economy. In a major report on basic income, Anthony Painter, RSA's director of policy and strategy, wrote: "A rapidly changing economy and labour market, growing public concern about the workings of our welfare system, the aspirations of citizens, particularly younger ones, for greater freedom, control and responsibility are all contributing to a moment of inflection." Pledging to help "shift the idea more towards the mainstream and practical reality," he added, "The time is right for an idea which has had powerful advocates for centuries to move to the centre of the debate about the kind of country, the kind of government and the kind of lives we want in the twenty-first century." Why is it significant for the RSA to put its considerable weight behind the idea of a universal basic income? Its current president is Princess Anne of the British Royal family, who succeeded her father, Prince Philip, and her mother, Queen Elizabeth II (when she was a princess) in that role. Since its founding in 1754, the RSA has counted such illustrious thought-leaders as Charles Dickens, Adam Smith, Benjamin Franklin, Karl Marx, Thomas Gainsborough, and William Hogarth among its 27,000 elected Fellows. And among its current Fellows are innovators such as the theoretical physicist Stephen Hawking and the computer scientist Tim Berners-Lee, best known as the inventor of the World Wide Web.

WHY NOW, AMERICA

THE IDEA OF a basic income has been around for hundreds of years. And for the most part, it has remained just that: an idea. So why do I think it's time to have a very serious conversation in this country about making a universal basic income a reality in twenty-first century America? Because as we move from an industrial economy to one based on digitization, our economic system is irreparably breaking down.

I'm emboldened in that statement from a conversation I had with Albert Wenger, the managing partner of Union Square Ventures, a New York-based venture capital firm best known for its early investments in Zynga, Tumblr, Twitter, and Etsy. Wenger has founded or co-founded tech companies in the areas of data analysis, investment, and management consulting. He has degrees in computer science and economics from Harvard, and a PhD in information technology from MIT. He spends a lot of his time thinking about how technology will change the workplace, and here's how he explained the fundamental loop of the industrial economy to me—and why it is breaking down: "In the industrial economy most people have a job and sell their time for a wage, then they use that money to buy products and services that are produced, for the most part, by other people who are selling their time. That fundamental loop is breaking down because we can make more and more things without people. It's not a matter of 'This will happen.' It's already happening, as we can see everywhere in the data"—and as I've noted several times earlier in this book.

Technology will keep making us more productive and efficient, but with fewer people. It's impossible to predict exact numbers and there is no timetable for the transition from the industrial economy to the one that's taking shape. "But one thing's for sure," investment banker Steven Berkenfeld says. "The transition will be a mess." As Berkenfeld points out, the poor, the marginalized, and lower- and middle-income families will bear most of the transitional pain. The rich, less so. This becomes evident when I ask Berkenfeld to imagine what would happen if his own son, who is twenty-two, was suddenly to lose his job as a management consultant, or if that job became part-time or was turned into piecework.

"Well, I would have to cover his medical insurance," Berkenfeld says. "And I would need to take into account that he won't be making any money when we go on our family vacation, since he's only getting paid for the days he works. Right now, I guarantee the $2,000-a-month lease on his apartment. If he lost his job, he'd probably have to move back home with us. Everything would change. He'd be much more dependent on us."

Of course, everything would not change for the Berkenfeld family. Berkenfeld and his wife might be inconvenienced for a while, but their son would come out fine in the end, as would my own son, Matt, if he lost his job. Young people like them have a safety net with deep pockets—their parents. And they are born with a particular type of guaranteed basic income—the parental basic income, what I call PBI.

Also, parents with financial means give these kids a foot up in the job market. "If you're rich and connected, your kid will be able to work for you or one of your friends or use one of the connections you have," Berkenfeld says. "It's children from middle-income and lower-income families who won't have similar options."

I am very concerned about the social safety net for workers. Historically, benefits came with a full-time job and membership in a union. It was the union that negotiated healthcare, workers' comp, sick leave, and other benefits on behalf of its members, and those benefits helped workers and their families lead a more secure middle-class life. But now, with unions and benefits both falling away, American workers are more vulnerable if they get sick or hurt on the job. "We need a new social contract," says Saket Soni, Executive Director of the National Guestworker Alliance and the New Orleans Workers' Center for Racial Justice, who we met earlier in Chapter 5. "And we need a new mechanism for people to update the social contract."

When I refer to a jobless future, I'm by no means suggesting that there won't be any jobs. However, I do think that we are heading toward a world with fewer overall jobs—perhaps tens of millions of them. In that world, the jobs that are left will either be extremely well paying and secure (at the top/winner take all), or contingent, part-time, and driven largely by people's own motivation, creativity, and the ability to make a job out of "nothing."

The current social contract puts this second category of worker at a disadvantage.

You have to be employed to benefit from policies like raising the earned income tax credit or the minimum wage. If you're unemployed, a higher EITC won't put any extra money in your pocket. If you're working part-time, a higher minimum wage will add to your total income for the hours you work, but you're vulnerable to getting your hours cut. When you work hourly for pennies as an Amazon Mechanical Turk, no one will be paying you for sick leave. Nor will anyone be giving you sick leave, unemployment insurance, or a pension if you've been forced to become self-employed or an entrepreneur because you've lost your full-time job, or even if you've freely and happily chosen that path.

Ours is a consumer-driven economy: How can it even function, much less thrive if so many fewer people have money to spend? Technological unemployment threatens our economy, and also our American way of life. An underclass of youth without hope and jobs is capable of becoming violent and spawning terrorists. For all these reasons, technological unemployment is a national security issue.

Steven Berkenfeld joins me in thinking that we need to take a lesson from the way the military deals with contingencies: "If this were the military, the generals would have different scenarios for what they'd do if 5 percent, 10 percent, or 40 percent of the workforce faced a jobless future." The military prepares for every possibility. Let's follow their example and bring together a group of economists, policy-makers, futurists, politicians, business leaders, labor organizers, and everyday Americans to hash out a realistic plan for UBI, even if we never execute the plan.

After years of focusing on creating more middle-class jobs and raising wages, I find myself drawn to a policy that gives every American over the age of eighteen a basic income without any work requirement. My support for UBI is born from a belief that we must attack poverty at its core—a lack of income—rather than treating its symptoms. Also, with major technological advances eliminating

more middle-class jobs, new systems of universal support are required. Lacking good jobs and satisfying work, the next generation
will desire to build a life outside of poverty and low-wage work, and
we should endeavor to give them that opportunity.

Let's begin with UBI's historically biggest selling point.

UBI IS A BETTER SOLUTION TO POVERTY

LIKE THE Rev. Martin Luther King, Jr., and so many other advocates of
a basic income, Michael Tanner, a senior fellow at the Cato Institute,
believes that UBI is potentially the best solution we have to poverty.
Tanner, a libertarian, says that the first ten years of President Johnson's War on Poverty were "relatively successful" in reducing poverty,
"and then it levels out." In 1964 the poverty rate was 19 percent. By
1966, it had fallen to 15 percent. In 2012, it was still 15 percent, according to the latest US Census figures. The federal, state, and local
governments spend $1 trillion on anti-poverty programs each year.
"But to what end?" he asks me. "We've been spending more and more
money developing more programs, without getting any additional
benefit, for over forty years. Maybe we need to re-think the whole
approach."

According to Tanner, the biggest problem with current anti-
poverty programs is that they "infantilize" the poor. "We treat poor
people like they're three years old. If you want people to be responsible adults, you need to treat them like responsible adults. If they're
poor because they lack cash, we should give them cash and let them
take charge of their lives."

Tanner also says that the welfare system "ghettoizes" the poor.
"It forces them to live in the one area of town that offers them free
public housing, grocery stores that accept food stamps, and doctors
who take Medicaid." Most of the payments are made directly to the
providers; as a result, the people being helped by welfare most likely
never see the money and "they don't learn to budget or choose among
competing priorities," like most Americans are expected to do.

I've seen firsthand how programs meant to help the poor can stig-
matize them and perpetuate the culture of poverty. In my first labor
union job, I represented thousands of the workers at Pennsylvania's

Department of Welfare who administered the state's anti-poverty programs. The state welfare bureaucracy had huge overhead costs, too much red tape, treated people as supplicants, and enabled too much waste and fraud. It created perverse incentives for people to avoid work and to remain poor, and it allowed too many people to fall through the cracks.

I've also seen how much the welfare system humiliates poor people and punishes the unemployed—the terrible indignity of standing in the unemployment line for hours, then having to prove that you've been out looking for a job at least five times that month, even though there aren't any jobs. Geoff Canada of the Harlem Children's Zone thinks that the welfare system is predicated on keeping people down. "Our capitalist economic system can only work if we make people feel bad about being unemployed," he says. And he predicts that middle-class kids who can't get a job will get the same degrading treatment as the poor do when technological unemployment gets worse.

A basic income is simple to administer, treats all people equally, rewards hard work and entrepreneurship, and trusts the poor to make their own decisions about what to do with their money. Because it only offers a floor, people are encouraged to make additional income through their own efforts: As I like to say, a UBI gives you enough to live on the first floor, but to get a better view—for example, a seventh-floor view of the park—you need to come up with more money. Welfare, on the other hand, discourages people from working because, if your income increases, you lose benefits. In contrast with welfare, there's no worry about phase-out problems, marriage penalties, people falsifying information, or having more babies to get a bigger check with UBI.

"It's clearly the simplest of all the options," Tanner says. "You pick a number—a dollar amount for the monthly disbursement—and then you mail a check. That's the one thing the government does really well. It's almost neurotically good at mailing everyone their check on time."

I laugh. The government is extremely efficient when it comes to mailing checks, and Tanner is 100 percent right about UBI's practical virtues. But let's not forget UBI's greatest appeal—its potential, as Dr. King pointed out, to eradicate poverty.

UBI GIVES WORKERS MORE FREEDOM AND CHOICES

I ASK ALBERT WENGER, the venture capitalist, if he's afraid that his colleagues on Wall Street will label him a socialist because he supports a universal basic income.

"Not in the least," he laughs. "If anything, UBI makes markets work better."

I ask him how.

"For one thing, it gives all the participants in the market real options. Right now, too many people in the labor market don't have options. As a result, we need crutches like the minimum wage and unemployment insurance, and we end up regulating the market in a way that discourages activity." He is on the same page here with labor organizer Saket Soni who believes that UBI "would free people, presumably, to make decisions, rather than force them into deeper competition to hang onto jobs."

UBI would also increase workers' bargaining power. The ability to say, "Pay me a lot more than that, if not I'll stay home" gives workers tremendous leverage in the face of abusive employers, bad workplace conditions, and inadequate wages. That increased leverage should have a positive impact on the wages of people who are unskilled and semi-skilled since they will face less competition from workers forced by financial necessity to seek jobs they don't want.

UBI is a game-changer for labor. As basic income advocate Timothy Roscoe Carter points out: "In any negotiation, a person who can walk away from a deal can always exploit a person who cannot. Capitalists can always walk away from labor, because they can just live off of the capital they would otherwise invest. It will never be fair until labor can just walk away. A basic income is the ultimate permanent strike fund."

And UBI provides options by enabling workers to move their families to a place where there are better jobs, giving poor and middle-class Americans more of the same kind of choices available to those with higher incomes. Economic handcuffs and fear of poverty limit Americans' choice of employer, and their ability to leave crappy jobs, start a new career, work fewer hours, take time with their family, get healthy, start a business, go back to school, or search for a new line of work. That choice, that freedom, exists today, but only for the extremely wealthy and their families.

As Wenger says, "UBI will enable people to do a lot of things financially that are impossible right now." He gives the example of a young person who is barely getting by in New York. During the past three years, the city of Detroit has been selling houses in some of its more run-down areas for $500 if the buyer is willing to rehab the house and help revitalize the neighborhood. It's a fabulous opportunity for resourceful and adventurous young people, and for couples who don't otherwise have the means to buy a house and start a family. But that young person in New York can't take advantage of this amazing offer. Why? Because he doesn't have the money to get to Detroit. And, once he gets there, he won't have a job to pay for his food and other basic expenses. "We have these weird cycles where people get trapped in places that are too expensive for them," Wenger says. "A universal basic income will help change that. It will let people move to places they can afford, where they can live a better life."

In addition to giving people more freedom and choices, UBI will enable them to become more financially independent, making it less likely for people to get manipulated by someone else who controls their finances. People in abusive relationships will be able to escape them more easily. And women, now less financially dependent on their husband's income, will be freer to pursue their own financial goals.

Like Wenger, Carl Camden, the CEO of Kelly Services, sees UBI as unleashing a flow of new economic activity. "When a highly compensated guy like me generates another million dollars of income, most of that money will go to savings," he says. "But if you give that million dollars to people who make relatively little or nothing at all, almost all of the money will be spent. It reenters the system immediately, with velocity, which is what you want in a government program."

Economists also point to the "multiplier effect." Every extra dollar going into the pockets of low-wage workers adds about $1.21 to the national economy. Every extra dollar going into the pockets of a high-income American, by contrast, only adds about 39 cents to the GDP. That's because the richer person can fulfill more of their more important needs and wants with the rest of their money than the poorer person can. By transferring money from high earners to low and middle earners, where the effects of spending are amplified, UBI will have a major ripple effect on the entire economy.

UBI will help the economy in a second way: it might seem counter intuitive, but a UBI applied in a "fewer jobs future" would enable a broader range of people to take bigger career risks, and to put their energies into activities that drive new types of "work," new sources for income, and new inventions. In an article in *Quartz* magazine titled "Entrepreneurs don't have a special gene for risk—they come from families with money," business journalist Aimee Groth summarizes new research analyzing the shared traits of entrepreneurs. She notes, "the most common shared trait among entrepreneurs is access to financial capital—family money, an inheritance, or a pedigree and connections that allow for access to financial stability. While it seems that entrepreneurs tend to have an admirable penchant for risk, it's usually that access to money, which allows them to take risks. And this is a key advantage: When basic needs are met, it's easier to be creative; when you know you have a safety net, you are more willing to take risks."

By the same token, UBI would also make it easier for entrepreneurial activists to create worker's organizations, particularly experimental ones like Ai-Jen Poo's National Domestic Workers Alliance or Saket Soni's National Guestworkers Alliance. And more people will be willing to take the risk of joining these organizations, because even if the organizations fail, their members, bolstered by a basic income, wouldn't need to be as afraid of being fired by their employer and left without any source of income.

PEOPLE ARE STARTING TO COALESCE AROUND UBI

WHY NOW, AMERICA? Because there is a coalition developing among conservatives, liberals, progressives, and libertarians in support of a basic income. Within the last year, UBI has been debated by mainstream commentators in the pages of publications such as the *Washington Post*, *Slate* magazine, *The Atlantic*, and the *New York Times*. Thought leaders who a few years ago whispered their support of UBI are beginning to voice it louder.

Amitai Etzioni, a world-renowned sociologist who is also a professor of international relations at George Washington University, came to basic income as a policy solution after the 2014 congressional elections. While interviewing middle-class Americans, he discovered that "many are even more concerned with losing what they have than with gaining more of the same. True, they are bitter that their real income has not increased for years on end, and they sense that they will be unable to provide a better life for their children than they had. However, they are even more concerned about the fact that they are no longer sure that the job they have will be there tomorrow; that Social Security will be there when they retire; and that their pension fund will not be retroactively diluted and is properly funded . . . They read about millions who have been kicked out of their homes in recent years. In short, they feel insecure, and for good reason . . . Finally, many people seem to not believe that the policies Democrats tout—such as increasing the minimum wage and investing in education and infrastructure—will return the economy to a high-growth pathway and lift most people's wages in the foreseeable future, and neither do I." One of the remedies he proposes is a twenty-first-century version of the negative income tax, "which in effect provides a floor underneath which the income of many millions of Americans may not fall. It should be expanded and reissued as a basic income security plan."

Five-time US presidential candidate Ralph Nader, a long-time champion of the idea, has become increasingly vocal lately in his support of a basic income. On his radio show, Nader compared basic income to the work he did as a consumer advocate to get smoking banned on airplanes in the 1970s. "Once we shifted people's perceptions—so that they saw the ban as a health issue, and not as a personal freedom one, the ban became status quo. I hope the same thing happens with basic income."

Vinod Khosla, founder of Sun Microsystems and renowned venture capitalist, recently said, "Looking forty years out, I find it hard to imagine why we won't need to support half the population to not work but pursue other interests that are interesting to them."

And if some of the tech elite of Silicon Valley have their way, UBI will become national policy far sooner than forty years from now. In an article he wrote for *Vice* magazine, called "Why the Tech Elite is Getting Behind Universal Basic Income," reporter Nathan Schneider described a scene at a conference he attended:

"After one speaker enumerated the security problems of a promising successor to Bitcoin, the economics blogger Steve Randy Waldman got up to speak about 'engineering economic security.' Somewhere in his prefatory remarks he noted that he is an advocate of universal basic income—the idea that everyone should get a regular and substantial paycheck, no matter what. The currency hackers arrayed before him glanced up from their laptops at the thought of it, and afterward they didn't look back down. Though Waldman's talk was on an entirely different subject, basic income kept coming up during a Q&A period."

Netscape creator Marc Andreessen told *New York* magazine that he considers UBI "a very interesting idea." Sam Altman of Y Combinator, the boutique incubator, has called its implementation "an obvious conclusion." You've met many of the tech elite intrigued by UBI in this book—including Wenger, Berkenfeld, and the Singularity Hub's Peter Diamandis. Others include the young Italian entrepreneur Federico Pistono, author of the book *Robots Will Steal Your Job, but That's Okay*, and Marshall Brain, the founder of HowStuffWorks .com, who has written a novella called *Manna* about a basic-income utopia.

Former US Labor Secretary Robert Reich came out strong for UBI in the fall of 2015. In the final chapter of his book *Saving Capitalism: For the Many, Not the Few*, Reich expressed his deep fears about the future of capitalism: "Absent some means for sharing the increasingly large rewards that go to a few people and their heirs . . . the middle class will disappear," he wrote, "and capitalism as we know it will not survive." As a solution, Reich suggested providing "all Americans, beginning the month they turn eighteen and continuing each month thereafter, a basic minimum income that enables them to be economically independent and self-sufficient."

Reich noted how a basic income could transform American society and culture by enabling young people to follow their passions and callings rather than "their narrow need" to acquire things, and by freeing "budding poets or artists or scientific theorists" to pursue their dreams. UBI, as Reich describes it, is tailor-made to help young people build the emerging gig, artisan, and sharing economies.

Later in this chapter, you'll get a closer look at some of the ideologically strange bedfellows who are beginning to coalesce around UBI. "It's such a fascinating and unlikely alliance," says historian Dorian Warren. He compares it to the late 1960s, when basic income drew the support of liberals like the Rev. Martin Luther King, Jr., and conservatives like President Richard M. Nixon. "The stars are starting to realign," Warren says. "Both sides are slowly being pushed to the same position on UBI, and eventually they'll have to get there, they'll need to make it policy, because the only alternative is social and political instability, and insurrection." Which is exactly what Wenger told me when I asked him if he viewed UBI as a necessity or as part of an ideology. He said, "I think it's absolutely essential! If we don't do it, we're going to wind up with more and more inequality and everything will explode."

ARE WE AT A TIPPING POINT?

I HEAR MORE and more parents getting deeply and genuinely angry about the high cost of a college education and how their children are accumulating a crushing level of debt, even as they graduate college and can't find a job that pays a living wage. That will be the tipping point for UBI, when the death of the American Dream becomes a painful fact in an increasing number of middle-class homes; and, yes, we're almost there.

Steven Berkenfeld predicts that the nation's colleges will provide the tipping point, but for a different reason and according to a different scenario:

"It will start when a big-state governor like New York's Andrew Cuomo, who is under pressure to keep costs down, recognizes that it's really inefficient with today's technology to have someone teaching Macroeconomics 101 at every one of the campuses of his state's university system. So I can see him saying, 'Let's hire the most famous and most charismatic economics professor around—maybe someone from Harvard or MIT—and have him teach Macroeconomics 101 on a single webcast that goes to all the campuses. We'll hire graduate students to run break-out sessions and administer tests at the various campuses, and pay them pennies.' That's the tipping point."

I ask Berkenfeld why.

"Because economics professors will be losing their jobs," he says. "The guys in their fifties and sixties, who already have tenure, are set. But what are these twenty-six-year-old grad students and adjunct professors going to do? Write a blog? Share their cars? Take a job at Home Depot for the medical benefits? You can't make a living that way. So they'll be forced to confront the problem just as American families are experiencing it. And I bet we're going to see a lot more dissertations and op-eds, as a result, on topics like technological unemployment, UBI, and the future of work."

Geoffrey Canada and I find ourselves talking about Europe—how all over that continent there are new extremist political parties that are anti-immigrant or based on racism being formed because the voters are fed up with the existing parties and sense that, whoever gets elected, it won't make any difference in their lives. "Will the same thing happen here?" I ask Canada. That's what George Soros, the most progressive of billionaires, says he's afraid will happen if income inequality grows. Economic insecurity does not breed progressivism. As its most natural consequence, it breeds politicians like Jean-Marie Le Pen, the anti-immigrant xenophobe who founded France's far-right National Front Party.

"George isn't alone," Canada says. He tells me about a fund-raiser he had attended the week before. "I was the only non-billionaire at the table," he says. "When someone brought up the subject of income inequality, the richest of the billionaires looked around and said 'the guillotine's right around the corner.'"

"What did the other billionaires do?"

"Well, they didn't laugh. They nodded knowingly."

That doesn't surprise me. Some of the wealthiest people I know are afraid for their lives and their children. They remember the 1960s, when people had a choice between a young black power leader, Stokely Carmichael, and his call for "Burn Baby Burn" and an older generation led by Martin Luther King saying "Give Peace a Chance," and there were plenty of activists who chose "Burn Baby Burn." They know about the kidnappings of the wealthy taking place in third-world countries, how families like theirs never go anywhere without bodyguards and in an armored car.

I tell Canada about a meeting I attended at the Democracy Alliance, a collection of philanthropic and political donors who support progressive organizations and their leaders. We were divided into groups and asked to offer solutions to a number of worst-case scenarios. Ours was: It's 2017. Republican Rand Paul is president. His first action is to eliminate all government programs. In response, there are riots in the streets and rich people fear for their lives. What would you do if you were one of the rich people? "The rich people in my group already knew what they were going to do," I tell Canada. In fact, they were already doing it."

"Let me guess," Canada says. "They were buying real estate in New Zealand."

"Or in some other safer country. How did you know?" I ask Canada.

"Because income inequality is going to get worse and worse, and there's a tipping point," he says. Then he throws his long arms into the air. "I want to say this to Republicans and Democrats alike: How are we going to make sure that this next generation can fully participate in the American Dream. There's no other place I wish I was born, or where I could have had a better life. But I really do think that we're going to destroy this country if we don't start to take this structural problem seriously."

UBI GIVES US A CHANCE TO CREATE THE SOCIETY WE WANT

IF ANYONE HAS faced her fair share of structural problems, it's Diana Farrell, the president and CEO of the JPMorgan Chase Institute, a global think tank dedicated to delivering data-rich analyses and expert insights for the public good. From 2009 to 2011, Farrell served as Deputy Director of the United States National Economic Council (NEC) and Deputy Assistant on Economic Policy to President Obama. She played a major role in restructuring the nation's auto industry.

During one of our many conversations, I ask Farrell if there was anything she learned when she was working around the clock to save

America from economic collapse that might be relevant to my interest in UBI.

"We don't live for money—or for the economy," she says. "We live for a society in which the economy is a part. That's the biggest lesson I learned. We tend to treat economic issues as all-important when, in fact, they are just levers to create the society we want."

Seven years after the recession, Farrell finds herself worried about the historically high percentage of Americans who count themselves among the long-term unemployed. She says, "It's a real problem when so many people who would like more work can't get it."

I raise the prospect of even more unemployment twenty years from now, when technology has displaced as many as 47 percent of today's jobs.

"A world in which there's less work for people, and where no one has any vested interest in the work, is very frightening," she says. "The challenge of the post-work world will be [in] helping people participate constructively in the economy. Not just the best and the brightest, but those who may not be as skilled, hardworking, or visionary."

Intriguingly, Klaus Schwab, the founder and executive chairman of the World Economic Forum in Davos, pointed to this same challenge in a January 2016 interview with the Swiss newspaper *Blick*, when he said that "human development/fulfillment doesn't necessarily have to be of an economical nature. It can also occur culturally and socially." His conclusion: "We need solutions that guarantee everybody a minimum income."

Carl Camden says that UBI is potentially an answer to the challenge Farrell voices—but in a way that transforms UBI from an unconditional basic income into a participatory income that requires people to volunteer or work at activities that are "truly beneficial to society."

"For example?" I ask.

"Raising the banks of the Mississippi River by six feet from Minnesota down to Louisiana," he says. "We should do that, as citizens, in response to the melting of the Arctic ice cap."

Camden isn't an advocate yet but he believes that a basic income can be a catalyst for "redefining American citizenship," and for demanding much more from our citizens. According to Camden, we should expect every US citizen to vote 95 percent of the time. And help our neighborhoods "work better" by keeping up their lawns and clearing their sidewalks of snow. "Now we tell people to enjoy being a citizen without any expectation that they fulfill the obligations that come with citizenship," he says. "But, to protect the nation's health, I think that people should get vaccinated and vaccinate their children. Every citizen should help to keep the nation's infrastructure in shape, because it serves us all. And you should commit a certain amount of time to volunteering each year, in addition to a year or two of military service or some other way of serving the country. With the obligation of citizenship come the rewards of citizenship. And we can make part of the rewards financial."

I tell him what I like about his idea: "You're redefining citizenship at a time when most Americans don't think much about what it means. You're inviting individuals to make an investment in America, with UBI sealing the deal." Also, his ideas are seductive. I find myself adding to his list: citizens should reduce their carbon footprint, save energy, reduce water usage. I begin seeing UBI as a mechanism for engaging younger people in the environmental activism they value, and older people in leaving a sustainable planet as their legacy for future generations. And I see the same technology that powers the sharing economy—and Camden's Kelly Services—as being a vehicle for helping people find service opportunities and tracking their volunteering hours online.

But then I find myself remembering why I think that UBI should be simple and pure and not tied to any requirements at all. By turning UBI into a platform for a more committed and engaged citizenry, aren't we making it too layered and complicated to succeed? Aren't we opening it up to endless debates on what we, as Americans, should value and do, instead of leaving those issues up to the more efficient, free-choice mechanism of people simply spending their money?

UBI may be just one more lever to create the society we want, as Farrell suggests, but we should be careful about letting that lever rust while we endlessly debate the nature of the society we want to create.

WON'T UBI MAKE PEOPLE LAZY?

THAT'S TYPICALLY THE first question I'm asked about UBI. Many Americans think that if you give people cash, they'll never want to work again, which is a very bad result because, as everyone knows, "An idle mind is the devil's playground."

Conceptually, the biggest hurdle for many people is the fact that UBI doesn't have a work requirement. "I think if you ask the average business person, everyone is terrified that, given an option not to work, people will walk away from their jobs and it will undermine capitalism in this country," says Geoff Canada. "The poor people I know feel the same way; they equate not working with all the welfare queens and deadbeats out there. Encouraging people not to go to work will drive the country crazy," Canada warns me.

Of course, UBI doesn't discourage people from working; it enables them to not take jobs that pay too little relative to the fulfillment they offer. Most people will want to keep working, because they aspire to a more comfortable lifestyle, or they want to send their children to camp or a private college, or they need the income to travel and pursue their interests, or they want to contribute to their community, their nation, and the world.

Still, Canada has a good point when he says that advocates for UBI must make every effort to keep UBI from having "the feel and stigma of welfare," and to keep the monthly disbursement number sufficiently low that "you won't get rich on what we give you, but you'll be able to put together a way to get around through public transportation or a bike; you won't starve, you'll find a place to live, it won't be glamorous, but it will be okay." Albert Wenger agrees with Canada on the disbursement number: "It should be enough for people to feel like they can take care of the most important things in their lives but not think, 'I'm all set,'" which would discourage incentive.

A CHANCE TO REEVALUATE OUR PRIORITIES

SUPPORTERS OF UBI believe that, instead of discouraging work, it will encourage people to reevaluate their values and set new priorities for themselves and their families.

"Americans get confused about needs and wants," says Wenger. "UBI helps to clarify the difference. Not everybody needs a Mercedes, for instance. That's a want."

In forcing people to make such distinctions, a UBI can help individuals determine how much they truly want a certain object or lifestyle, and how to go about getting it. For example, a person who wants a Mercedes may choose to work harder in his commission-based sales job so that he can afford that particular car. My brother-in-law Keith, on the other hand, values trail biking above other activities. In his case, a basic income would offer him the freedom and flexibility to spend more of his time in the park, either on his bike or volunteering to beautify the trail.

Says Wenger: "We've deluded ourselves into believing that work is the only legitimate way of creating purpose in someone's life—and that a job is so central that we have to organize everything else around it." He points out the anxiety-inducing nature of our obsession with work: "We terrorize our kids to be afraid that if they're not doing their homework, they won't get into the right school and get the right job. It's very hard psychologically for people to get away from that."

When I talked with Steven Berkenfeld, he and his wife had just returned from a week's vacation to Bhutan, which has been called "the happiest country in the world." I ask him if he'd ever consider living there. "I'm an American," he says, "in my own way as patriotic as they come. But instead of moving there, I'd like to figure out how to make America a bit more like Bhutan. We have to move away from being a society that values the dollar more than anything else."

Dorian Warren sees UBI as an opportunity to redefine the purpose of work and leisure. "I don't think we can go into any discussion of basic income with the notions we currently have about the sacred nature of hard work," he says. "The fact that robots are coming is a great thing. It means more time for leisure. To take a walk in the park without feeling guilty or constantly looking at the messages on your phone. We need to redefine what work is—and reclaim leisure as being an equally important value.

"I know lots of workers who take deep pride in their craft," he adds. "Could those welders and agricultural workers who are proud of what they do enjoy doing it fewer hours and on their own terms?

Would they enjoy spending more time with their kids and grand-kids? I'm sure they would."

THE FRAMEWORK FOR A NEW AMERICAN DREAM

I WONDER WHAT the American Dream would look like if it weren't so anchored in the Protestant Work Ethic. How would we frame this new American Dream? What would we aspire to as individuals and as a nation?

Warren says he would want "an America where everyone has the opportunity to thrive." That's the theme of the Center for Commu-nity Change, a Washington, DC–based nonprofit whose mission is to help low-income people change their communities for the better. "By enough to thrive, we mean clean air, a healthy community, and good public schools," says Warren, who serves on the organization's board. "But I think there should also be an element where everyone has enough income to live your life as you see fit without harming other people. And where you can find meaning in your life without it being so attached to work."

When Michael Tanner gives his formula for a successful democ-racy, he talks about the "Three Freedoms"—Economic Freedom, Informational Freedom, and Psychological Freedom. "UBI will give Americans more economic freedom," he says. "Critics of UBI ask: 'Well, how do people earn it?' My argument is that we've earned it collectively, as humanity, by having come up with smart ideas. Like, if you're building a company today, you're not building a company in a vacuum. You're building it on top of all the technology and all the thinking going back to Aristotle. You're not inventing everything from scratch. This is our collective heritage."

Work hard, play by the rules, and you can go from rags to riches and give your family the opportunity for a better and more fulfilling life. That was the old America Dream, the one that's lost credibil-ity because fewer and fewer Americans can actually achieve it. Ac-cording to the new American Dream, we'll each have the freedom to choose and create the life we want for ourselves and our loved ones, according to our deepest values, without ever having to worry about our basic human needs for food, shelter, and security. For future generations of American children, UBI will make possible a world where family, learning, hobbies, service, arts, leisure, and self-actualization aren't in conflict with basic human needs.

A BASIC INCOME FOR ALL

To DATE IN the United States, there hasn't been much scholarly discussion or peer-reviewed economic analysis of UBI. Also, as my economist and policy maker friends keep reminding me: "Andy, you're an organizer. You don't have a PhD in either statistics or economics." That said, the numbers I use below are drawn from the best available research and provide a solid framework for understanding and evaluating my evolving plan. I encourage scholars, economists, and others to do the rigorous work that will be needed to fully vet and develop these ideas.

I propose instituting an unconditional universal basic income (UBI) of $1,000 per month for all adults between the ages of eighteen and sixty-four and for all seniors who do not receive at least $1,000 per month in Social Security payments.

Using the 2015 Federal Guidelines for Poverty as a guide, an income floor of $12,000 per year (and $24,000 for a two-parent family) is sufficient for most Americans to maintain a minimum standard of living. There are solid arguments for including some level of benefits for children, and also for phasing in the UBI program, and I will address these later. However, the starting place for my plan and any debate about it is a UBI of $12,000 per adult per year. I recognize that my plan will cost between $1.75 trillion and $2.5 trillion per year in government spending, and that funding the plan will most likely require:

1. Ending many of the current 126 welfare programs that cost the Federal government $700 billion and state governments $300 billion a year;
2. Making adjustments in long-term retirement policy for future generations without changing Social Security for those who have already been contributing to the system;
3. Creating a new and more cost-effective-non-employer-based healthcare system;

4. Some redirection of government spending and taxation expenditures; and
5. Increased revenue from new sources.

However, as I demonstrate later in this chapter, we have more than enough resources as a nation to finance a UBI at the $12,000 per adult per year level I propose.

My major goal in this book is to raise awareness about how the emerging technologies are impacting jobs, work, and the economy as it is being experienced by the vast majority of American families. Another is to begin having an honest, thoughtful, solution-based exchange of ideas about UBI and America's future. A conversation of this nature can only take place if the participants are open to making trade-offs and to building a broad coalition from across the political spectrum. If our discussion devolves into a left/right debate, it will be impossible to build public support for UBI or make any progress in the areas of funding and implementation. As I've learned in twenty-five years of trying to make big changes in Washington, most politicians' second choice if their own favorite proposal is not supported is to do nothing—a recipe for political gridlock. There is only one antidote to gridlock—a willingness to compromise.

The good news is that people from different places, perspectives, and motivations tend to arrive at the same destination when it comes to UBI. Consider this hypothetical exchange I've staged between Charles Murray, the libertarian political scientist, who self-identifies as a conservative, and the Reverend Martin Luther King, Jr., a liberal, using their own words. Note how the very different paths they take lead them to the same conclusion about UBI.

Murray: "America's population is wealthier than any in history. Every year, the American government redistributes more than a trillion dollars of wealth to provide for retirement, healthcare, and the alleviation of poverty. [And yet we] still have millions of people without comfortable retirements, without adequate healthcare, and living in poverty."

King: "The government believed it could lift up the poor by attacking the root causes of their impoverishment one by one—by providing better housing, better education, and better support for families."

Murray: "Only a government can spend so much money so ineffectually."

King: "The programs of the past all have another common failing—they are indirect. Each seeks to solve poverty by first solving something else."

Murray: "The solution is to give the money [now allocated by government on a slew of programs] to people."

King: "I am now convinced that the simplest approach will prove to be the most effective—the solution to poverty is to abolish it directly by a now widely discussed measure: the guaranteed income."

King wanted to end poverty. Murray wants to do the same thing, but his other (perhaps main) agenda is to get rid of that slew of costly and ineffective welfare programs. The two men could easily get sidetracked into dueling over the nature of big versus small government, or the value and effectiveness of particular programs. But in this hypothetical debate, using actual words that express their deepest wishes, they come to the same conclusion: give poor people cash.

What do I mean by making trade-offs?

Progressives and liberals will need to understand that they won't get the level of basic income they might want by adding to the 126 existing welfare programs; instead, they'll be required to cash out programs.

Conservatives and libertarians need to understand that they can't create an adequate anti-poverty program by simply cashing out welfare programs; they'll be required to find new revenues to fund UBI.

Once the participants state their willingness to make trade-offs, we can discuss whether the monthly disbursement for UBI should be $1,000 (as I'm proposing) or some other number. We can also discuss regional variations in the cost of living, and whether there should be grants or special programs for children, seniors, incarcerated people, disabled veterans, and new immigrants.

For example, one plan that advocates a UBI of $12,000 per year per adult also calls for a grant of $4,000 per year to each US citizen below the age of eighteen. This addition to the program would cost the federal government another $296 billion per year. Of course I like the idea of directly helping young people, but I worry that this extra element complicates the program—just think of all the issues that come up when you try to get your mind around giving $4,000 to a ten-year-old—and also it risks alienating potential supporters of UBI who may come away with the false impression that UBI is just another welfare program. Still, I'd be willing to hear more about this approach and how it can be funded.

Once we've settled on the total universe of UBI recipients and also a final monthly disbursement number, we'll be able to compute the total cost of the program and discuss the trade-offs we'd each be willing to make in order to fund the program.

STRANGE BEDFELLOWS IN
SEARCH OF COMMON GROUND

I'M A PROGRESSIVE who is willing to cash out a large number of the anti-poverty programs my liberal and progressive colleagues support. Perhaps that's why my ideological opposite, the libertarian social scientist Michael Tanner, is willing to talk about UBI with me. We both chuckle at the irony: Here I am, an avowed enemy of the far-right Koch brothers, entering the doors of the modern glass building that houses the Cato Institute, the libertarian think tank founded forty years earlier as the Charles Koch Foundation, where Tanner is a Senior Fellow.

In researching UBI, I've marveled at how Tanner and his fellow libertarians approach UBI with an intellectual curiosity and ferocity that dwarfs almost anything I've encountered from most of their conservative brethren or my fellow progressives. I am particularly intrigued because Tanner was one of the architects of the campaign to privatize Social Security. A decade ago, he argued in favor of taking payroll tax money that now goes into the Social Security trust funds and investing it instead in private investment accounts—a policy that President George W. Bush pursued unsuccessfully during his second term. I was very much against that idea: under the guise of giving Americans more say in investing for their future, it made retirees extremely vulnerable to downturns in the stock market. In 2010, as a member of the Simpson-Bowles Commission, I sought to reform Social Security through a different mechanism—improving benefits and increasing the number of Americans who could receive them. These ideas were included in the Commission's final report, which ultimately didn't get a hearing in Congress.

So Tanner and I couldn't be stranger bedfellows. And like so many odd couplings in the past—Milton Friedman and John Kenneth Galbraith, Richard M. Nixon, and Daniel Patrick Moynihan—we like many of the same things about UBI: its simplicity, its transparency, and its potential to end poverty and give a boost to the middle class.

"So what's the problem with UBI?" I ask Tanner.

"Affordability," he says.

The August 2014 issue of *Cato Unbound-A Journal of Debate* featured a series of policy papers on UBI. The consensus of the experts was that a national UBI would cost the federal government between $2 trillion and $3 trillion, depending of the size of the grant and the number of Americans covered. Cashing out every existing anti-poverty program would raise $1 trillion in annual revenues for UBI, leaving the government with a shortfall of between $1 trillion and $2 trillion to fund the program.

How would Tanner close the UBI funding gap?

In addition to cashing out the 126 anti-poverty programs, he says he would consider eliminating all of the federal government's other income-transfer programs—including Social Security, Medicaid, and Medicare—and raise approximately an additional $1.4 trillion. "My point is you're not going to have money to do a universal basic income as long as there's a big sucking sound at the other end of revenues from Social Security and Medicare. To afford UBI," he says, "you'll need to find a way to fold Social Security and Medicare into UBI and significantly raise taxes."

I share Tanner's concern about UBI's cost, but I do not agree that funding UBI will require doing away with Social Security and Medicare; we can fund it in other ways that don't put Americans at economic risk. My position got clarified for me during my conversation with Albert Wenger, who is one of the growing number of venture capitalists, technologists, and young entrepreneurs who see value in a universal basic income. At a recent TED talk about UBI, Wenger told the audience: "As a VC, I like the fact that a lot of the political establishment is ignoring or dismissing this idea. Because what we see in startups is that the most powerful, innovative ideas are ones truly dismissed by the incumbents." He said that a minimum income would allow us to "embrace automation rather than be afraid of it." And, he added, it would let more of us participate in the era of "digital abundance"—a phrase I really love.

When we meet privately, Wenger tells me that he likes what he calls "the math relative to GDP" of my proposal for a disbursement of $1,000 per month. Multiplying an annual UBI of $12,000 by 234 million (the number of adults over eighteen in the US), he gets a total cost of $2.7 trillion, around 15 percent of the current GDP of $18 trillion a year, a reasonable number for a wealthy country to pay so we have a strong economy and military and keep the deficit under control. In other words, a UBI of $12,000 per person per year wouldn't put the nation out of business. It would allow America to be competitive, defend itself, and provide a floor that keeps its citizens out of poverty.

To fund UBI at that number, Wenger says he would cash out food stamps, EITC, worker's compensation, unemployment insurance, a number of other income transfer programs, and Social Security. "I've only done a very rough calculation—I haven't really sharpened the pencil yet—but that should get you there," he says. He wouldn't reduce Medicare benefits—"that would really anger seniors," he says. Nor would he levy additional taxes on the rich for, I presume, the same reason he wouldn't want to get seniors riled up. More taxes on the wealthy would get them pissed off and jeopardize support for UBI.

THE SOCIAL SECURITY QUESTION

AGAIN, I DON'T agree with the proposal to cash out Social Security. And here is why: Social Security is funded by an investment that working people and their employers have made in good faith for the employee's future well-being. A UBI disbursement of $1,000 a month is a lot less money than most Social Security recipients receive. The federal government shouldn't shortchange Americans on the ROI from money they've worked so hard to earn.

From my experience with Simpson-Bowles, I think a rational starting place for funding UBI is to not touch the Social Security investment of anyone who has already contributed to the trust fund. At the same time, we need to be very thoughtful if we're proposing any long-term changes to the Social Security system, particularly as they might apply to younger generations who've yet to contribute into the system. Also, it's imperative that we acknowledge the gap in Social Security funding that will occur when new members of the labor force aren't required to pay into the system.

Everyone on Simpson-Bowles struggled hard and emotionally with the question of Social Security reform. I wonder aloud why Wenger thinks that his proposal to eliminate Social Security would do anything more than doom UBI politically. I ask him the same question that stymied us during Simpson-Bowles: "When Social Security ceases, where will the government find the money it needs to redeem its promise to the hundreds of millions of Americans who've already paid into the system?"

Wenger smiles, confident that policy makers will be able to come up with an appropriate stopgap measure that enables the federal government to transition from Social Security to UBI.

"You'll never get that far," I tell him from hard-earned experience. By then, the policymakers will have forgotten about UBI and taken their habitual sides in the entitlement wars.

"That's why I don't like talking too specifically about how I'd fund UBI," he says. "There are two main constituencies for UBI—people who believe we need a safety net for everyone, and people who believe in smaller government. The last thing you want to do is drive a wedge between them. If you want anything to actually happen with UBI, you need to build a very broad tent for the idea."

I agree: if you dive straight into the weeds and offer too many specifics, people will stop focusing on what they like as a whole about the idea—and the idea will go nowhere.

Still, I'm convinced that we should take Social Security and Medicare completely off the table when we discuss UBI, not because they're so controversial, but because they are so crucially important to the well-being of millions of Americans. We need to fix major problems in these programs; we'd like each of these programs to cost less and achieve better outcomes. The way to do that is to address them on their own terms, and not in the context of UBI.

WILL UBI BE INFLATIONARY?

A BIG CONCERN that comes up in my conversations with economists and policy makers is that UBI will be inflationary. If people get a basic income, there's a fear that companies will need to raise compensation levels to attract people who will want to work at low-wage jobs. Also, by giving people more cash to spend on consumer goods, some critics say that UBI will raise demand—and prices—for everything from food to housing, putting a middle-class lifestyle out of reach for more Americans.

Wenger argues that UBI's impact will, in fact, be deflationary. First, there shouldn't be any reason to print additional money. The money for a basic income would be existing money already circulating through the economic system. Hence, the value of each dollar will not have changed, it will simply be transferred from one place to another. Second, he says, we're already living in a deflationary world because of technology, which is making everything cheaper, a point on which he and I are in agreement. Consumer durables have been getting cheaper since the mid-1990s on a quality-adjusted basis. And even healthcare and education, the services that have been getting more expensive in recent years, are bound to get cheaper in the near future because of the efficiencies gained by electronic medical records and massive open online courses (MOOCs).

SHOULD UBI BE PHASED IN?

ANOTHER ISSUE THAT warrants discussion is whether UBI should be launched at full value (at $1,000 per month) or phased in. Many people believe that the latter is the more fiscally and politically prudent approach. To take Wenger's temperature on the issue, I ask: "If the government didn't have the money to launch UBI at $1,000 per person per month, what would you rather do: find new taxes to fund the program, or lower the amount to something more affordable?"

"I'd lower the amount. In fact, I'd lower it anyway—whatever the case," Wenger answers. When he was young, he tells me, he was "a political absolutist" and always wanted "to go to the max." But now, he says, "maybe a good theory of change with UBI is to first get everybody to $200. Then once the infrastructure is in place, we go, 'Let's dismantle more programs and go up to $400 per month per person.'" After that, he'd dismantle even more welfare programs and take the disbursement level to $600 per month. And so on, until he reached $1,000 per month by eliminating even more programs along the way. "I think that's the more pragmatic route to take," Wegner says.

"Would you eliminate the minimum wage if we had UBI?" I ask.

"Absolutely," he says. "If everybody had $1,000 a month, I think you could completely do away with the minimum wage, because people would have more control and choice in the work they do. For example, if a job you love pays only $8 an hour, you might choose to keep it instead of taking a job for $15 an hour that really sucks."

I agree that a fully functioning UBI program would make the idea of a minimum wage less necessary. What I don't ask Wenger— because I'm afraid of getting us too far into the weeds—is how he'd deal with the continued need for a minimum wage while the monthly UBI disbursement was being raised from $200 to $400 to $1,000, a process that might take months or even years. If the minimum wage was eliminated at the start of a phased-in UBI program, millions of American families would lose the income floor that helps them get by and get ahead. I can see us devising a formula that phases out the minimum wage as UBI is getting phased in. But wouldn't any such process complicate matters and raise the chances of people falling through the cracks?

Ah, the weeds. See how easy it is to get caught in them. But there is one issue I really can't ignore: Wenger's continued reluctance to tax the rich, even the very, very rich, or the obscenely rich, as part of the overall solution to funding UBI. Most economists see the necessity of levying new taxes in any UBI funding scheme. Is Wenger's reluctance a matter of ideology, self-interest, or simply a fear of upsetting the apple cart?

"Personally," he says, "I believe in the taxation of wealth and high incomes—mine included. And I'd happily pay even more in taxes if I felt that it was going to go directly to the people as opposed to some machine that is out of control," by which he means government.

Michael Tanner offers a similar sentiment. Like most of his Cato colleagues, he isn't opposed to additional taxes on higher incomes but, he tells me, "I'm only willing to consider them if they're part of an overall tax reform and not seen strictly as a 'soak the rich' tax."

(Note to my progressive colleagues: If you want to get anywhere in the fight for UBI, keep your "soak the rich" rhetoric to a minimum. Better yet, nix it.)

I share one of my biggest concerns with Tanner—whether we can keep our elected leaders from lowering the floor once it's been raised. "What happens when there's a new president, with new priorities, or a new Congress that says 'you get less this year for UBI because we need more for defense and more for a space flight to Mars.' How do we protect UBI from those pressures?"

"There's always going to be some other demand on the money," he says. "The best way to protect the money is to build a broad constituency for UBI. The more people you involve in UBI, the less Congress will be willing or able to take from it."

It reminds me of something Peter Barnes told me: "There are two reasons Social Security endures: It's virtually universal, and people feel ownership of it. They put their own money into the program, feel they have a genuine right to it, and if anyone suggests taking away that right, they'll scream." That's one reason it's important to keep UBI simple, universal, and out of the annual budget debates.

Tanner says he's especially concerned about pressure that might come from politicians to keep adding to the disbursement number. "We start with giving everybody $12,000 a year because it's the best number," he says. "Then, next year, someone comes back and says, 'No, it should be $15,000,' and the number keeps going up. Or a newly elected president wants to prove that he's more compassionate than the last guy by pushing to give every American adult a basic income of $2,000 per month."

To keep that from happening, I tell him, it might be necessary in the initial bill to specify that Congress needs a super majority of 75

to 90 percent to change the UBI disbursement level. The most op-
portune time to propose such a mechanism is when there's a political
consensus for UBI. After the hard work of reaching the consensus,
Congress will want to put the policy in place for the long term. And
once Americans receive their first disbursement check and like what
UBI gives them the freedom to do, they'll never want UBI to be taken
away from them.

Tanner is generally a fan of UBI. He sees it as superior to "our current complex, expensive, ineffective welfare system." He likes it as a
simple, transparent anti-poverty effort "that treats recipients like
adults, and has a better set of incentives (than most anti-poverty programs) when it comes to work, marriage, and savings." But he's far
from full-throated in his support of UBI. "What sounds good in theory tends to break down when one looks at questions of implementation," he writes. "As strong as the argument in favor of a guaranteed
income may be, there are simply too many unanswered questions to
rush forward." He urges the following incremental steps: "Consolidate existing welfare programs, move from in-kind to cash benefits,
increase transparency, and gather additional data. This would allow us
to reap some of the gains from a universal income without the risks."

In theory, I'm not against this go-slow incremental approach as
long as we are improving everyone's living standards. But my inclina-
tion, more often than not, is all-or-nothing. Step-by-step approaches
end up raising more concerns and resistance than they either soothe
or squelch. For example, throughout the political fight for health care
reform, each incremental step we took stoked fears that our true aim
was to foist a debt-swelling universal healthcare system on the American people. When we'd propose a step-by-step plan—for example:
1) extend health care coverage to children; 2) implement electronic
medical records; 3) allow fifty-five-year-olds to buy into Medicare—
each step would stiffen our opponents' resolve to resist our efforts.
I'd be afraid of stoking similar fears in the process of trying to phase
in UBI. I'd rather pass one piece of legislation. Then, once we have
a broad consensus on the basic principles and framework for UBI,
and certainly on the disbursement number and category of people
covered, I could envision an incremental or phased-in approach if it
really appeared to be the best way to move forward.

A MENU OF FUNDING POSSIBILITIES

As NOTED ABOVE, my estimate is that it will cost the federal government between $1.75 trillion and $2.5 trillion to create an income floor of $12,000 per year for all 18-to-64-year-olds and for all seniors receiving less than a $1,000 a month in Social Security. Our nation can afford a UBI program at this level. The following items comprise a menu of viable funding options:

A. Cash out all or some number of the 126 welfare programs that currently cost $1 trillion a year. For example, we can make a major down payment on funding UBI by eliminating food stamps ($76 billion), housing assistance ($49 billion), and EITC ($82 billion).

B. Raise revenue by eliminating all or some of the federal government's $1.2 trillion in tax expenditures. (A tax expenditure is when the government spends revenue through the tax code—for example, by giving a deduction off taxable income—rather than through the regular budget.) As a general principle, tax expenditures disproportionately benefit higher earners who take deductions on their income tax for mortgage interest, accelerated depreciation, pension contributions and earnings, investment expenses, interest on state and local bonds, preferential treatment of capital gains, charitable contributions, foreign taxes, employer-sponsored health insurance, and state and local taxes. Raising revenues for UBI by doing away with these deductions requires a disciplined process for deciding which to retain and which to eliminate. For example, when Simpson-Bowles was seeking to balance the federal budget, the chairmen of the Commission directed us to eliminate every tax expenditure except the credits for children, earned income, and foreign taxes. If we wanted to reinstate any other tax break, we had to find another revenue source to replace it. I'm not suggesting that we follow the chairmen's precise dictates, but that we are similarly disciplined in our approach as we eliminate tax expenditures.

C. I would strongly consider levying a value added tax (VAT) of 5 to 10 percent on the consumption of goods and services, with all the revenue going to the funding of UBI. Currently there are 160 countries in the world that use this highly effective sales tax to generate revenue. (In some countries VATs are also levied on business services—e.g., legal and accounting.) Columbia Law School professor Michael Graetz, an expert on national and international tax law, recently did a major analysis of VAT for the Pew Foundation and Tax Policy Center. Extrapolating on his proposal, I calculate that a VAT of 5 to 10 percent on consumer goods (at an estimated base of $13 trillion) would generate between $650 billion and $1.3 trillion in revenues for UBI. Mark Walker, a philosophy professor at New Mexico State University who is on the board of the Institute of Ethics and Emerging Technologies, proposes a plan for an annual $11,400 basic income paid to everyone ages 18 through 64 through the adoption of a 14 percent VAT. Despite this new tax, Walker calculates that "anyone making between $0 and $80,000 would be monetarily better off" because of his basic income proposal. There's a crossover point, where people would pay more in VAT than they'd earn in basic income, but, according to Walker, 90 percent of the population has a net personal income that falls below that crossover point, meaning they would be getting more in basic income than they'd be paying in the 14 percent VAT.

D. I would implement the widely supported Financial Transaction Tax (FTT)—also known as the Robin Hood Tax, Tobin Tax, and Speculation Tax (as the left likes to call it). The FTT is being implemented by a number of member states in the European Union, but it is not a new idea here in the United States. From 1914 to 1966, there was a federal tax on stock sales of 0.1 percent at issuance and 0.04 percent on transfer. Dean Baker of the Center for Economic Policy and Research estimates that an FTT of 0.25 percent on each side of a stock trade could produce over $150 billion a year.

E. And, as I noted earlier in this chapter, I am intrigued by Peter Barnes' proposal for raising revenue on the Alaska Permanent Fund model by charging corporations a fee for using and/or abusing our "common wealth"—the property and resources that belong to all of us, including water, air, the electromagnetic spectrum, Big Data, and intellectual property. Barnes believes that he could raise enough revenue through this mechanism to fund a basic income of $5,000 per person per year. "And we could obtain it through common ownership sources," he says.

F. I would also consider a wealth tax (also called a net worth tax), which is a levy on the total value of personal assets, including

housing and real estate, cash, bank deposits, money funds, stocks, etc., as championed by Thomas Piketty in his book *Capital in the 21st Century.* In September of 2015, American household wealth reached a record total of $85.7 trillion. If a 1.5 percent flat tax was levied on all personal assets over $1 million, conservatively it would generate over $600 billion in new revenue. How would wealthy people respond to this new wealth tax? First, to state the obvious, no one really likes to pay more taxes. But 1.5 percent is a relatively low amount to pay, especially after a $1 million exemption, and this particular tax would go toward funding a UBI that benefits all Americans, including you and your family members. In other words, it's not simply a matter of taking from the rich to give to the poor. Also, the fact that UBI eliminates welfare programs and makes government more efficient may be seen as a plus by many wealthier Americans, or at least make the tax seem less onerous than, for example, higher taxes on their income.

G. **In addition to cashing out welfare programs and coming up with new revenues to fund UBI, we can look at the expenditure side of the federal budget ledger** and consider significantly trimming the military budget ($600 billion), farm subsidies ($20 billion), or subsidies to oil and gas companies ($30+ billion) to fund UBI.

It's important to reiterate that this a menu of funding options. Some combination of the seven options listed above will raise sufficient revenue to offset the costs of a universal basic income of $1,000 per person per month.

The bottom line is if there is a will, there is a series of choices, in addition to ending current welfare programs, that could end poverty, stimulate consumer purchasing, reduce government, allow for individual choice, and respond to the eventual elimination of middle-class jobs as technology accelerates.

It is especially important that UBI keep pace with inflation, so that the recipients don't lose purchasing power, as they have with the federal minimum wage. Since 2009, when Congress raised it to $7.25 per hour, the federal minimum wage has lost 8.1 percent of its purchasing power to inflation. We can't allow UBI to erode as politicians fight year after year over whether to raise the disbursement number. Options include indexing UBI to the consumer price index (CPI) or to the GDP per capita. I like the latter idea—adjusting the UBI disbursement number to productivity—because it will mean that the gains of society will accrue more widely for every American citizen, and not just the few, at a time when advances in technology will continue decreasing the need for human labor.

UBI is far from a perfect solution to all the economic challenges we face. But, in offering it, I remember what British Prime Minister Winston Churchill famously said about our system of governance as a whole: "Democracy is the worst form of government, except for all those other forms that have been tried from time to time."

And, with Churchill front of mind, I offer this battle plan to get Americans invested in and charged up about UBI.

A BATTLE PLAN FOR A UNIVERSAL BASIC INCOME

WITH A UNIVERSAL basic income, we can raise the floor high enough to end poverty for the first time in our country while making a thoughtful pivot towards an economy that can still make the dreams of most Americans come true.

Of course, UBI is no political slam-dunk. While I am confident that the continued loss of good jobs to technology will move public sentiment toward a basic income, implementing UBI will require creative and energetic organizing. While Switzerland and the UK are engaged in active debates about universal basic incomes, in the US there has been only limited interest and little formal organizing around the issue. The center of action has been the US Basic Income Guarantee Network (USBIG), comprised mainly of social scientists who are engaged in basic income research. To date, progressives have been channeling their organizing energy into the Occupy movement, Fight for $15, and other campaigns to help freelancers and restaurant, fast food, and domestic workers. My hope is that some of this energy will shift to UBI.

The 2015 World Summit on Technological Unemployment drew Joseph Stiglitz, Larry Summers, and Robert Reich as speakers and participants—a sign, as Dylan sang, that "the times they are a changin'" and that technological unemployment is becoming a mainstream concern. Reich's recent statements about UBI have been a shot in the arm to proponents.

Also, there is a small but dedicated group of young scholars and activists who have embraced UBI as their cause. Scott Santens, a thirty-seven-year-old writer and UBI advocate in New Orleans, deserves special mention. Selling a t-shirt with the logo: "Basic Income is Not Left or Right. It's Forward," Santens crowdfunded a basic income for himself of $1,111 per month so that he could devote all his time and energy to advocating for a basic income. He is, in effect, a one-man clearinghouse for people all over the world who are engaging with the idea. "Without an income floor set at the poverty level as a bare minimum, I believe poverty and inequality will continue to grow, the middle classes will continue to shrink, and the livelihoods of all but the top fifth of society will continue to slip away," he has written. Santens moderates the basic income community on Reddit, the social networking and news website, where he's helped it grow from less than 2,000 to over 30,000 subscribers.

In drawing up my plan for building a UBI movement, I seek input from Natalie Foster, one of the most creative organizers I know. She is the co-founder of Rebuild the Dream, a platform for people-driven change, and Peers, the world's largest independent community for the sharing economy. She also has had major organizing successes for the Sierra Club, the Obama campaign, and MoveOn.org.

What would she do to get a national UBI movement off the ground?

"If work will look different and there will be big shifts," Foster says, "then I believe it would behoove us all to take very seriously a policy that gives people an equal starting place and the economic security to do the kind of work they want to do in the world. In Silicon Valley, we like to say: 'Entrepreneurs aren't riskier or smarter than you. They're just people who had some padding from which to take a risk.' Bill Gates, Donald Trump, they all came from wealthy families. They had some padding if they failed. But just imagine if everyone in America had some of that padding. If everyone had a chance to start their own business and do the work they feel called to do."

To get UBI off the ground, Foster proposes having a national conversation that gets people imagining what life could be like if every single American had an equal starting point. "Also, we should collectively imagine the new ways we might organize work and life that don't involve working fifteen hours a day, or going from gig to gig for relatively little money," she says. Foster would like to see people all over America "meeting and connecting around UBI" in lunchtime conversations and book clubs.

She mentions the Townsend Clubs of the 1930s as a historical model. On September 30, 1930, Dr. Francis Townsend sent a letter to the editor of the *Long Beach Press-Telegram* with a plan to end the Depression. Townsend, a physician, proposed that the government send every US citizen a check for $200 a month in reward for a lifetime of work. (Townsend suggested that the stipend be funded by a 2 percent national sales tax.) He claimed that the stipend would end elderly poverty and stimulate the spending needed to get the Depression-era economy moving again.

Townsend Clubs sprang up all over the country in support of the idea. By 1935, there were 7,000 Townsend Clubs with 2.2 million members and 56 percent of Americans were in favor of Townsend's idea. The avalanche of support for Townsend's plan was an important factor in President Roosevelt's decision to establish Social Security that year.

Foster believes that UBI is about to have "its Townsend Club moment"—not simply in the US, but throughout the world. "I've had calls from Finland and other European countries about UBI. And the tech sector here has become interested in building a version of universal basic income on top of the block chain—the ledger that is the supporting technology underlying bitcoin. They're imagining something that is not state-based or run by a government. There are all kinds of interesting versions of UBI being conjured up, and people are really starting to engage with the idea."

As I've noted earlier in this book, this is also what I call "the Vietnam moment" for UBI. During the Vietnam era, the selective service draft mobilized parents from every walk of life to be vocal anti-war activists. Once their own children could be drafted to fight and die, many parents began questioning whether President Johnson had any justification for sending troops there. The draft also mobilized young people: Vietnam did not fit into their college and career plans; nor did the idea of killing people or getting killed in a far-off land.

A similar dynamic has been playing out since the 2008 recession. Before the recession, middle-class Americans and the nation's elite could sit on the sidelines as globalization threatened mainly blue-collar industrial jobs. Since the recession, white-collar jobs have been eliminated—a trend that will continue with advances in robotics, AI, and software. With college becoming prohibitively expensive, middle-class parents are feeling more anxious about their own and their children's future, which should make them and their children more receptive to and even enthusiastic about UBI.

If I had access to a lot of money, like I did at SEIU, I would launch a huge public-awareness advertising campaign for UBI. You'd see those three letters on billboards all across America with a question mark at the end, and with an asterisk leading people to a website explaining what those three big letters stand for. I'd like those letters to show up on websites, TV commercials, t-shirts, everywhere, so that people will be able to discover for themselves that UBI is a form of Social Security for every American over the age of eighteen, giving you and your loved ones more security, bargaining power, and flexibility as the economy keeps changing, and more freedom and resources to achieve your personal American Dream.

And then, of course, there are the targeted messages: UBI offers conservatives a vehicle for eliminating welfare programs and shrinking government; it gives consumers the purchasing power they need to buy products and services; it provides businesses with customers who have enough purchasing power to buy their products; it gives young people more financial security and independence; it relieves parents of the anxiety they may be having about the job prospects of their twenty-something children; it helps progressives fulfill their dream of ending poverty; and it restores poor Americans' dignity and hope. And, for all these reasons, UBI has the potential to fuel a sustained bipartisan effort—what we haven't seen in years in the nation's capital.

Here's my own dream: to help build a movement so broad and bipartisan that we can collect enough online signatures to run Basic Income Party candidates for all 535 seats in the 2020 Congressional primary elections. There are twenty-three states that allow for a citizens' initiative process, whereby citizens can draft a legislative bill or constitutional amendment. They then propose the bill or amendment by petition. If the petition receives sufficient popular support, the measure is then placed on the ballot and can be enacted into law by a direct vote of citizens. My goal is to get enough support to put either a constitutional amendment for UBI or a demand for the state's congressional delegation to support UBI on the ballot in these twenty-three states.

It's easy to imagine other opportunities for organizing on behalf of UBI. Here are some that immediately come to mind:

- Tailor the successful no tax pledge of Grover Norquist to basic income, holding politicians accountable to the pledge in primaries, and working to defeat those who turn away from their promise in the general election.
- Leverage Kickstarter and set a goal of raising $50 million to campaign in Iowa and Nevada and $50 million more in New Hampshire and South Carolina to draft an independent candidate to run for president in 2020 or 2024 for the Basic Income Party. We would copy the tactics of the group No Labels and qualify the Basic Income Party on every state presidential ballot. By raising a real war chest ($100 million) in donations, big and small, we could ensure that our candidate achieves the necessary minimum requirements to qualify for the debates. To have a major candidate for president articulating the need for a basic income would catapult our issue and stimulate a national debate.
- Build a significant social media presence by setting a goal of ten million "likes" on Facebook or one million followers on Twitter, an online version of the Townsend Clubs. When we hit that number, ask businesses for support and do patch-through calls and email campaigns encouraging consumers to not spend their money with businesses that oppose UBI. In a world where change is vastly accelerated by the proliferation of smartphones, tablets, instant information, and twenty-four-hour news cycles, what one day seemed impossible can rapidly become quite mainstream. If you need proof, look to marriage equality, NSA monitoring, repealing three-strike laws, and the legalization of marijuana.
- Organize a tax strike, gaining the pledge of five million people to refuse to pay a higher tax rate than Warren Buffett pays until

Congress votes on a basic income package to ensure greater
security and less inequality.

- Engage with religious leaders and persuade them to follow the
direction of Pope Francis to push to end poverty with simulta-
neous interfaith Saturday-Sunday multi-denominational "End
Poverty" prayer services. Encourage religious leaders to support guaranteed family incomes and set up sessions where supporters can sign up, stand up, and give up some of their income
to the campaign.

- Enlist a charismatic leader, actor, athlete, businessperson, or a
number of them in the cause, particularly to help us crystallize
the jobs problem and convey UBI's importance as a solution.
Again, Pope Francis comes to mind. As I said to Diane Farrell:
"We need a truth teller. Someone who will tell us what's really
going on with the economy. Someone like the Pope." At first
she laughed at my suggestion, but then she said: "Actually, he's
a great example of someone in an unbelievably short amount
of time who has been able to shift a conversation that was stagnant for two thousand years" by speaking truth to power.

In one of our many talks about UBI, Natalie Foster asks me about
timing: "When do you think UBI will be politically feasible—in ten
years, fifteen years, or is it thirty years away?"

I tell her that I think she's way off, and that UBI will begin gaining
traction by 2020. Why? Because Americans are already tuning in to
the fact that technology will displace massive numbers of jobs while
fundamentally changing the nature of work.

By way of comparison, it took the issue of same-sex marriage
nearly nineteen years to gain the traction it needed to gain protection
under federal law. In 1996, Democratic President Bill Clinton signed
the Defense of Marriage Act (DOMA), which slowed progress on the
issue. DOMA defined marriage for federal purposes as the union of
one man and one woman, and it allowed states to refuse to recognize
same-sex marriages granted under the laws of other states. Yet, by
2014, polls showed that nearly 60 percent of the American people
supported same-sex marriage, including President Obama, who had
evolved in his thinking from opposition to support. And on June 26,

2015, the US Supreme Court ruled that states cannot prohibit the issuing of marriage licenses to same-sex couples, or deny recognition of lawfully performed out-of-state marriage licenses to same-sex couples.

"I think UBI is going to come far faster than same-sex marriage," I tell Foster. "I'm not saying tomorrow, but in a few years, not ten or twenty. That's why I think that someone should run as a presidential candidate on this issue in 2020 or 2024 when the nation will be ready for the message that a basic income is probably the easiest and most transparent solution for improving the lives of our families."

Meanwhile, the seeds of a movement are being born. Inspired by the Alaska Permanent Fund, a group of activists in Oregon are planning for a referendum to place a cap on carbon emissions, with the revenue used to provide a dividend to each Oregonian. In October 2015, a group of us (including several of the people interviewed for this book) met in San Francisco to plot a US strategy for UBI.

As I told this group, it's important not to be distracted by positive economic trends or by temporary improvements in the economy—for example, the significantly lower oil prices of 2014 and 2015 that seemed to proclaim energy independence for America. (And then oil prices rose up, then fell, then leveled off again. We're making progress on energy independence, but it remains very far from a done deal.) It's also important to keep ourselves from being lulled into inactivity by the economic promises of our presidential candidates, whose silence in the face of potential future job loss has been deafening.

The American people, hoping for the best, may hitch their dreams to the next promising jobs report, then lurch from crisis to crisis. If so, our leaders will keep serving up twentieth-century solutions for our twenty-first-century problems. The alternative is: we can look to the future and try to understand it. And, through a national conversation now, build support for an idea whose time has come.

"What's the worst-case scenario for America if our leaders don't begin planning for technological unemployment?" Foster asks.

Half-joking, I answer: "We'll begin to look like Panem, the country in the *Hunger Games* trilogy, where a wealthy elite in the nation's gilded Capitol rules over the impoverished masses, who live at a safe distance, in twelve regional enclaves. And yes, once a year, two children in each enclave will compete in the gilded Capitol for the scraps of the privileged few."

"Really?" she asks.

"No." But I do fear a divided America where the wealthiest 1 percent live in gated communities while an increasing number of their fellow citizens live in ghettos filled with needless despair. We had a taste of that in the 1960s when the disempowered demonstrated and rioted in the streets, and the privileged and powerful feared that their children could, like Patty Hearst or Somali pirate victims, be kidnapped and held for ransom. If a scenario like that returns to America—and I pray it doesn't—Natalie Foster and I will be out in the streets, wearing one of Scott Santens t-shirts.

Better yet, we'll be wearing a t-shirt of our own design. On the back it will say: "It's really not that complicated." On the front it will proclaim: "Basic Income." Why? Because, as the t-shirt suggests, the answer to poverty and economic insecurity is really not that complicated: give people cash.

There's no turning back. We live in an era of fundamental economic change. Technology is transforming work and the workplace. This can be thrilling and empowering but also alienating and scary. At times it feels that we have no say in our future. But we do! If you believe, as I do, that our economy's problems are structural, and that technology is very likely going to make decent-paying jobs harder to find, if you believe that our children and grandchildren deserve a more secure livelihood and an opportunity to achieve their dreams, then I invite you to join in a national conversation to raise the floor and shape the future of jobs, work, and the American Dream, with UBI as our guiding star.

JOIN THE CONVERSATION #RAISINGTHEFLOOR

THE FOLLOWING QUESTIONS will get you thinking about your values and aspirations for both yourself and your fellow Americans. My hope is that you continue the conversation about raising the floor for all US citizens at your workplace, around the dinner table, online, and at school—and that you feel compelled to play an active role in shaping our nation's future.

1. Do you believe that human beings have a fundamental right to a basic income? If so, do you think people should get a basic income whether they work or not?

2. Do you agree with Steven Berkenfeld's assessment that the transition to the future of work will be "a mess" and very painful for most American families? Will it be painful for your family? If so, how?

3. Are you concerned about the status of the benefits that used to come routinely with a full-time job and paycheck, including unemployment insurance, workers' compensation, and job training? How would you compensate for the loss of those benefits in your own life?

4. Work as it exists now is actually three things: the means by which the economy produces goods; the means by which people earn income; the central activity that lends meaning or purpose to most

people's lives. Can you envision a world where the above conditions are no longer true? What are your major concerns about such a scenario? What excites you about that possibility?

5. Do you think work, in its current form, does a good job of delivering the central tenets of "well-being," most notably purpose, meaning, identity, fulfillment, creativity, and autonomy? Are there differences by economic class and race?

6. Do you worry about social unrest if enough people who want to work can't find jobs anymore?

7. Do you agree with Charles Murray and the Rev. Martin Luther King, Jr., that the best way to end poverty is to give cash directly to poor people and not indirectly through welfare programs?

8. If asked the trillion-dollar question, what would you choose for America: a guaranteed job for every adult, or a guaranteed basic income? Why?

9. The old American Dream was "work hard and play by the rules and you'll be able to move up in your life and lifestyle and give your children a better future." That dream has become much harder to achieve for lower- and middle-income Americans. Do you think we need a new American Dream? If so, would the American Dream you propose be more, less, or equally rooted in the historical Protestant ethic of hard work? What would be your American Dream's core values?

10. Before we can talk about a guaranteed basic income, Dorian Warren thinks we need to have another conversation—about the nature and value of work. Do you agree with him?

11. Make a list of all the types of work you can think of, both paid and unpaid. Are there types of work that seem less valuable to you and to society than other types of work? Put a check mark by all the types of work you do in the course of a typical week. Put another check mark by the types you deem most essential. For which of these tasks and jobs do people tend to get paid? Is technology changing the nature of any of this work? If you were paid a basic income, which work would you either need or choose to keep doing, and why?

12. Do you think America is capable of adapting to a world with far fewer jobs? Currently, most jobless people don't 'take advantage'

of their downtime, instead they watch TV, browse the Internet, or sleep. Are we capable of such a drastic cultural leap?

13. "The Paradox of Work" has been described as the phenomenon in which most people report that they wish they weren't at work when they are working and yet, they report feeling better and less anxious at work than when not working. Why do you think this is so? How would this change in a world with less work?

14. In a world with far fewer jobs, where will people find satisfaction in their daily lives? Where will they derive pride?

15. Do you share Dorian Warren's view that technology gives us an opportunity to reclaim leisure?

16. Consider your friends, loved ones, and yourself, as well as human nature in general. Will a guaranteed basic income make Americans lazy? Or will it help them focus their talents and energies on activities that give meaning to their lives?

17. Do you agree with Albert Wenger that we are living in a deflationary world of decreasing prices? Is technology making the products and services you use more affordable? Are you concerned that UBI will raise the price of real estate? Or do you think, as Wenger does, that it will give you and other Americans more freedom and the wherewithal to live in a more affordable town or city?

18. Wenger says that UBI should be phased in over several years, beginning with a monthly disbursement of $200 per citizen. He suggests eliminating more and more government programs along the way to fund a target disbursement of $1,000 per month. Do you agree with his basic premise that UBI needs to be phased in so that Americans can become acclimated to the idea? What would be your own proposed route to UBI?

19. Does my hypothetical proposal of a UBI of $1,000 per month for every adult seem right to you? Make a list of your basic needs—rent, food, transportation, and healthcare. Would $1,000 for each of your adult family members per month cover them? If not, how much money would you need to live at a subsistence level? If you took healthcare out of the equation, would it work for you then? Would you propose a different monthly disbursement amount?

20. Which, if any, of these taxes would you support to help fund UBI? A value-added tax, Thomas Piketty's wealth tax on assets,

personal and corporate tax reform, a carbon tax on the content of fuels.

21. Do you agree with Thomas Paine and Peter Barnes that part of the basic income should be funded by a fee for the commercial use and/or abuse of the "natural inheritance" of the human race, also known as our common wealth—i.e., air, water, and the electromagnetic spectrum?

22. Do you agree with Carl Camden that citizens need to fulfill certain obligations of citizenship in order to receive a basic income? If so, what should those obligations be? If people are required to do something socially beneficial, does that inhibit the potential of UBI to give us more choices in how we live our lives or does it open up new pathways for enriching our lives and communities? Are you more or less likely to support a guaranteed basic income if it requires a service component?

ACKNOWLEDGMENTS

To the Members and Leaders of SEIU whose compassion, hard work, and dreams shaped my life.

To my incredible Mother, my own family, my beach house family, and my partner Jennifer—all of your love and friendship make me feel supported everyday.

To my wonderful son Matt, who keeps me grounded, to Kaitlyn his new lovely wife, and to sassy Cassie Sue my daughter who lives forever in my heart.

To my partners in this adventure: Lee Kravitz, a superb writer and collaborator who made my story come to life; Ryan Johnson, who was my thought partner and guide; John Mahaney, whose wisdom shaped the whole process; Elizabeth Kaplan, my agent and advisor, and Ronald Perelman whose faith in me and generosity was a gift.

And to a future where dreams, like mine, still come true!

NOTES

INTRODUCTION

3   *CE 2.0 is "a collaboration . . . "* https://www.media.mit.edu/

4   *Machover, who co-created the popular Guitar Hero . . .* Machover, Tod; "Hyperinstruments/Opera(Orchestra) of Future. http://opera.media.mit.edu/

5   *"In 3.5 seconds . . . "* Herr, Hugh; "The new bionics that let us run, climb and dance"; 2004; TED Talk; https://www.ted.com/talks/hugh_herr_the_new_bionics_that_let_us_run_climb_and_dance?language=en

7   *Kayser shows us a video . . .* http://arts.mit.edu/mel-chin-saharan-sand-dollar/2013

9   *Buffalo Springfield . . .* https://en.wikipedia.org/wiki/For_What_It%27s_Worth_(Buffalo_Springfield_song)

10 *They aren't thinking about the forty-seven million Americans . . .* Current Population Survey (CPS); Annual Social and Economic Supplement; 2015; (ASEC); https://www.census.gov/hhes/www/poverty/about/overview/

CHAPTER 1

11 *"You'd probably be bored, too . . . "* Labor Union Report, RedState; "The Exit Interview: Andy Stern changed America forever . . . and he's bored"; 2010; http://www.redstate.com/diary/laborunionreport/2010/04/15/the-exit-interview-andy-stern-changed-america-foreverand-hes-bored/

12 *My goal at SEIU . . .* Bai, Matt; "The New BOSS"; 2005; http://www.nytimes.com/2005/01/30/magazine/the-new-boss.html?_r=1.

14   *I called the labor movement* . . . Klein, Erza; "SEIU president offers a look ahead before stepping down"; 2010; http://www.washingtonpost .com/wp-dyn/content/article/2010/04/17/AR2010041702554.html

15   *Today private sector union membership is* . . . Economic News Release; Bureau of Labor Statistics, US Department of Labor; 2015; http://www .bls.gov/news.release/union2.nr0.htm

15   *"To a remarkable extent* . . . " Gordon, Colin; "Low-Wage Work and Wage Theft in Iowa"; 2015; http://www.iowapolicyproject.org/

16   *As illustrated in the chart* . . . Gordon, Colin; "Union decline and rising inequality in two charts". Economic Policy Institute; 2012; http://www .epi.org/blog/union-decline-rising-inequality-charts/

16   *In a speech he gave at the Greater Omaha Chamber of Conference in 2007* . . . Bernanke, Ben; "The Level and Distribution of Economic Well-Being"; 2014; http://www.federalreserve.gov/newsevents/speech /bernanke20070206a.htm; Greater Omaha Chamber of Commerce

16   *Why? Because as unions weaken* . . . Florence, & Osorio, Carolina; "Power from the People"; 2015; IMF; http://www.imf.org/external /pubs/ft/fandd/2015/03/jaumotte.htm

17   *"Strong unions have helped reduce* . . . " Stiglitz, Joseph; "The Price of Inequality: How Today's Divided Society Endangers Our Future"; Norton & Company; 2012.

19   *"Can This Man Save Labor?"* Bernstein, Aaron; "Can This Man Save Labor?"; 2014; Bloomberg Business; http://www.bloomberg.com/bw /stories/2004-09-12/can-this-man-save-labor

20   *"I stand here knowing that my story* . . . " Speech by Barack Obama, Candidate for U.S. Senate in Illinois; 2004; the Democratic National Convention; Boston, MA

21   "You can't overemphasize how important . . . " Walk a Day in My Shoes; Barack Obama/Pauline Beck; 2007; SEIU; https://www.youtube.com /watch?v=miUS7WnMgBw

21   *"Our Congressmen have to know* . . . " Ruff, Bob & Costello, Carol; 2010. "Lobbying for Your Health: 'War rooms' push for legislation"; CNN; http://am.blogs.cnn.com/2010/01/05/lobbying-for-your-health-war -rooms-push-for-legislation/

22   *"The House should pass* . . . " Stern, Andy; "A Path Forward: It's Time to Pass Health Insurance Reform"; 2011; Huffington Post; http://www .huffingtonpost.com/andy-stern/a-path-forward-its-time-t_b_429902 .html

22   *We were instructed to identify policies* . . . "About the National Commission on Fiscal Responsibility and Reform"; 2015; Fiscal Commission .gov. https://www.fiscalcommission.gov/about/

CHAPTER 2

24   *The summer after I left the presidency* . . . Grove, Andy; "Andy Grove: How America Can Create Jobs"; 2010; *Business Week*; http://www .bloomberg.com/bw/magazine/content/10_28/b4186048358596.htm

25   *About a year later I recalled* . . . Andy, Stern. "China's Superior Economic Model"; 2011; *WSJ*; http://www.wsj.com/articles/SB1000142405 297020463090457705649002451980

26   *He tells the story of Intel's rise* . . . Grove, Andy; Only the Paranoid Survive; How to Exploit the Crisis Points that Challenge Every Company and Career; Doubleday; 1996.

26   *Grove sets the scene in 1985* . . . Ibid.

28   *Strategic Inflection Point (n)—* . . . Ibid.
     "Americans are coming to realize . . . " Stiglitz, Joseph; Equal Opportunity Our National Myth; *New York Times*; 2013

30   *Figure "The Great Decoupling of Wages and Jobs from Growth"* McAfee, Andrew; Census Bureau, Bureau of Labor Statistics; 2011.
     "Almost two-thirds of American households . . . " Tankersley, Jim "The 21st century has been terrible for working Americans"; 2015; *Washington Post*; https://www.washingtonpost.com/news/wonk /wp/2015/03/06/the-21st-century-has-been-terrible-for-working -americans/

32   *In their book* Race Against the Machine . . . McAfee and Brynjolfsson, Erik; *Race Against The Machine: How the Digital Revolution Is Accelerating Innovation, Driving Productivity, and Irreversibly Transforming Employment and the Economy*; Digital Frontier Press; 2011.

33   *according to two separate polls* . . . Fox News Poll: Voters say US still in recession, glad they know Snowden secrets; 2014; http://www.foxnews .com/politics/interactive/2014/01/22/fox-news-poll-voters-say-us -still-in-recession-glad-know-snowden-secrets/ Dan, Weil; "Survey: Three Out Of Four Americans Feel Like Recession Continues"; 2014; The Public Religion Research Institute. http://www.newsmax.com /Finance/Survey-Americans-Financial-Shape-Recession/2014/09/24 /id/596710/

33   *British economist Alan Manning coined the term* CentrePiece; Lovely and Lousy Jobs; 2013; http://cep.lse.ac.uk/pubs/download/cp398.pdf

36   *Only 40 percent of Americans* . . . Great Jobs, Great Lives; The Gallup-Purdue Index Report; 2014; https://www.luminafoundation.org/files /resources/galluppurdueindex-report-2014.pdf

36   *That is a decline of 27 percent* . . . http://www.bls.gov/data/inflation _calculator.htm

36   *according to the 46th annual PDK-Gallup poll* . . . PDK/Gallup Polls; 2014; http://pdkintl.org/programs-resources/poll/

36   *That's a marked turnaround from the 42nd annual poll* . . . Dywer, Liz; "A Shockingly Low Percentage of Americans Believe a College Education Is Important"; 2014; http://www.takepart.com/article/2014/09/18 /americans-no-longer-believe-college-education-very-important

37   *To make matters worse* . . . Middle Class in America; 2014; U.S. Department Of Commerce Economics and Statistics. http://www.esa.doc .gov/sites/default/files/middleclassreport.pdf

37   *Genius Bar techies at Apple* . . . Segal, David; "Apple's Retail Army, Long on Loyalty but Short on Pay"; 2012; *New York Times*; http://www.ny-times.com/2012/06/24/business/apple-store-workers-loyal -but-short-on-pay.html?%20_r=1

39   *according to the Bureau of Labor Statistics* . . . Brett, Michael. "Occupational employment projections to 2020"; 2012; Office of Occupational Statistics and Employment Projections at the Bureau of Labor Statistics; http://www.bls.gov/opub/mlr/2012/01/art5full.pdf

38   *My earlier book* . . . Stern, Andy; *A Country That Work: Getting America Back on Track*; Free Press; 2012

39   *"Now it's synonymous with economic anxiety."* Luhby, Tami; Why America's Middle Class is Losing Ground; CNN Money; 2013

39   *Grove calls it a "10X force"* . . . Grove, Andy; *Only the Paranoid Survive; How to Exploit the Crisis Points That Challenge Every Company*; Doubleday; 1996

40   *A November 25, 2013 Washington Post-Miller Center poll* . . . Washington Post-Miller Center; Poll on the American Dream; 2013; http:// millercenter.org/ridingthetiger/washington-post-miller-center-poll -on-the-american-dream-released

41   *That we are at a strategic inflection point* . . . Piketty, Thomas; *Capital in the Twenty-First Century*; Belknap Press;

42   *The richest one percent* . . . Kristof, Nicholas; "An Idiot's Guide to Inequality"; 2014; *New York Times*

42   *The wealthiest 160,000 families* . . . Matthews, Chris; "Wealth inequality in America; It is worse than you think"; *Fortune*; 2014

42   *The richest 85 people* . . . "The 85 Richest People In The World Have As Much Wealth As The Poorest 3.5 Billion"; *Forbes*; 2014; http://www .forbes.com/sites/laurashin/2014/01/23/the-85-richest-people-in-the -world-have-as-much-wealth-as-the-3-5-billion-poorest/

42   *If you are born poor* . . . Matthews, Chris; "The Myth of the 1% and the 99%"; *Fortune*; 2015; http://fortune.com/2015/03/02/economic -inequality-myth-1-percent-wealth/

43   *During his talk at the Graduate Center* . . . Piketty, Thomas; *Capital in the Twenty-First Century*; Belknap Press; 2014

45   *a whopping 93 percent* . . . Noah, Tim; "The One Percent Bounce Back"; The New Republic; 2012; https://newrepublic.com/article/101369 /the-one-percent-bounce-back

46   *In his book,* The Price of Inequality . . . Stiglitz, Joseph; *The Price of Inequality: How Today's Divided Society Endangers Our Future*; W. W. Norton & Company; 2013

48   *"One of the most convincing empirical findings . . . "* Fernholz, Tim; "Ten ways to Fight Inequality Without Piketty's Wealth Tax"; *Quartz*; 2014; http://qz.com/201695/ten-ways-to-fight-inequality-without -pikettys-wealth-tax/

48   *In his review of Piketty's book* . . . Summers, Lawrence; "The Inequality Puzzle: Piketty Book Review"; 2013; http://larrysummers.com/2014 /05/14/piketty-book-review-the-inequality-puzzle/

49   *In his closing remarks* . . . Roosevelt, Theodore; "New Nationalism Address"; 1910; Commonwealth Club; Osawatomie, Kansas

CHAPTER 3

53   *Sooner or later most* . . . Kurzweil, Ray; "How my predictions are faring—an update by Ray Kurzweil"; 2010. http://www.kurzweilai.net /how-my-predictions-are-faring-an-update-by-ray-kurzweil

54   *Schwab's is one of* . . . https://intelligent.schwab.com/

54   *And a new firm called Robinhood* . . . Bhatt, Baiju; "Robinhood Brings Stock Trading to Millennials"; 2015; *WSJ* http://www.wsj.com/video /robinhood-brings-stock-trading-to-millennials/19778928-DA21 -457F-997B-8CFA952727A3.html

54   *Contour Crafting is using* . . . Agarwal, Rohit; "3D Printing Concrete: A 2,500-Square-Foot House in 20 Hours"; 2015 https://www.linkedin .com/pulse/3d-printing-concrete-2500-square-foot-house-20-hours -rohit-agarwal?trk=prof-post&trkSplashRedir=true&forceNo Splash=true

54   *Lowe's, the hardware chain* . . . King, Rachel; "Newest Workers for Lowe's: Robots"; *Wall Street Journal*; 2014; http://www.wsj.com/articles /newest-workers-for-lowes-robots-1414468866

54   *A new 72-room hotel* . . . Plaugic, Lizzie; "A high-tech hotel opening in Japan will be staffed by multilingual robots"; 2015; *The Verge*; http:// www.theverge.com/2015/2/8/8000665/robot-h-japan-huis-ten-bosch

55   *Momentum Machines, in San Francisco* . . . "Robots Advance: Automation in Burger Flipping and Beyond"; 2015; KWHS Wharton

School; http://kwhs.wharton.upenn.edu/2015/08/robots-advance
-automation-in-burger-flipping-and-beyond/

55   *A robo-journalist helped* . . . Oremus, Will "The First News Report on
the L.A. Earthquake Was Written by a Robot"; 2014; *Slate Magazine*;
http://www.slate.com/blogs/future_tense/2014/03/17/quakebot_los_
angeles_times_robot_journalist_writes_article_on_la_earthquake.html

55   *90 percent of all news articles* . . . Loosvelt, Derek; "The One Job Robots
Can't Do (Yet)"; 2015; *Vault* Blog; http://www.vault.com/blog/job
-search/the-one-job-robots-cant-do-yet/

55   *A robot bartender* . . . McShane, Sveta. "Robot Bartender to Set Sail On
Cutting-Edge Royal Caribbean Cruise Ship"; 2014; *Singularity Hub*;
http://singularityhub.com/2014/09/10/robot-bartender-to-set-sail-on
-cutting-edge-royal-caribbean-cruise-ship/

55   *About 150 hospitals* . . . "The invisible unarmed"; 2014; *The Economist*;
http://www.economist.com/news/special-report/21599526-best
-robot-technology-unseen-invisible-unarmed

55   *A company called True Companion* . . . http://www.truecompanion
.com/home.html

56   *2015 was a banner year for robot* . . . Gresser, Edward; "200,000 new
robots go to work each year"; *Progressive Economy*; 2015; http://www
.progressive-economy.org/trade_facts/200000-new-robots-go-to-work
-each-year/

56   *But now a computer charts* . . . McKinley, Jesse; "With Farm Robotics,
the Cows Decide When It's Milking Time"; 2014; *New York Times*.
http://www.nytimes.com/2014/04/23/nyregion/with-farm-robotics
-the-cows-decide-when-its-milking-time.html?_r=0

56   *There are more than 25 companies* . . . "The cost effectiveness and advantages of Robotic Surgery"; *Robotenomics*; 2013 http://robotenomics
.com/2014/06/05/the-cost-effectiveness-and-advantages-of-robotic
-surgery/

56   *The Defense Advanced Research Projects Agency* . . . Mok, Kimberley;
"DARPA Tech Treats Disease with Electricity, Light, Sound, and Mag-
netic Fields"; 2015; http://thenewstack.io/darpa-tech-will-treat-disease
-electricity-light-sound-magnetic-fields/

56   *The SensiumVitals patch* . . . Pennic, Fred; "New Disposable Wearable
Patch Measures Vital Signs Every 2 Mins"; 2015; HIT: http://hit
consultant.net/2015/09/30/disposable-wearable-patch-measures
-vital-signs-every-2-mins/

56   *Super-thin and super-strong* . . . Bilton, Nick; "Bend It, Charge It, Dunk
It: Graphene, the Material of Tomorrow"; 2014; *New York Times*; http://
bits.blogs.nytimes.com/2014/04/13/bend-it-charge-it-dunk-it
-graphene-the-material-of-tomorrow/

57   *AliveCor's new heart monitor . . .* "Study Results from Cleveland Clinic's iTransmit Study Published in Heart Rhythm Journal". 2015. http://www.alivecor.com/press/press-releases/study-results-from-cleveland-clinics-itransmit-study-published-in-heart-rhythm-journal

57   *Not according to Ray Kurzweil . . .* Kurzweil, Ray; *The Age of Spiritual Machines*: Penguin Books; January 1, 2000.

59   *In September 2013, I read a study . . .* Frey, Carl Benedikt and Osborne, Michael A; "The Future Of Employment: How Susceptible Are Jobs To Computerisation?"; 2013; Oxford Martin School, Programme on the Impacts of Future Technology, University of Oxford, Oxford.

67   *He noted an article in* USA Today . . . Krantz, Matt. 2014. "Companies' stocks soar after slashing workforce"; 2014; *USA Today Money*; http://americasmarkets.usatoday.com/2014/05/07/companies-shares-soar-after-slashing-workers/

68   *He quotes Terry Gou . . .* Blodget, Henry; "CEO OF APPLE PARTNER FOXCONN: 'Managing One Million Animals Gives Me A Headache'" http://www.businessinsider.com/foxconn-animals-2012-1; 2012; *Business Insider*

71   *As of 2014, Frey wrote . . .* Frey, Carl Benedikt and Osborne, Michael A; "The Future Of Employment: How Susceptible Are Jobs To Computerisation?"; 2013; Oxford Martin School, Programme on the Impacts of Future Technology, University of Oxford, Oxford http://www.oxfordmartin.ox.ac.uk/downloads/academic/The_Future_of_Employment.pdf

71   *Juliano Pinto, a 29-year-old paraplegic . . .* Martins, Alejandra and Rincon, Paul; "Paraplegic in robotic suit kicks off World Cup"; 2014; BBC News; http://www.bbc.com/news/science-environment-27812218

72   *As a benchmark, here are some of Kurzweil's predictions . . .* Diamandis, Peter; "Ray Kurzweil's Mind-Boggling Predictions for the Next 25 Years"; 2015; *Singularity Hub*; http://singularityhub.com/2015/01/26/ray-kurzweils-mind-boggling-predictions-for-the-next-25-years/

72   "As humans, we are biased to think linearly." http://singularityhub.com/

CHAPTER 4

76   *In 2006, the GAO estimated . . .* Employment Arrangements; Report to the Ranking Minority Member, Committee on Health, Education, Labor, and Pensions, US Senate; 2006; GAO: http://www.gao.gov/new.items/d06656.pdf

76   *A 2015 survey . . .* Horowitz, Sara, and Rosati, Fabio; "53 million Americans are freelancing, new survey finds"; 2015; *Freelancers Union Blog*;

https://www.freelancersunion.org/blog/dispatches/2014/09/04/53million/

77   *According to a 2015 report* . . . "ILO warns of widespread insecurity in the global labor market"; World Employment and Social Outlook; 2015; ILO; http://www.ilo.org/global/about-the-ilo/newsroom/news/WCMS_368252/lang—en/index.htm

85   *A survey of 1,055 millennials* . . . Wagner, Jacob; "New Study Reveals Millennials' Most Ridiculous, Shocking Job Expectations"; 2015; *NEXTSHARK*; http://nextshark.com/new-study-reveals-millennials-most-ridiculous-shocking-job-expectations/

CHAPTER 5

100   *But, in New Orleans* . . . Davis, Aaron; "U.S. paying a premium to cover storm-damaged roofs"; 2005; Knight Ridder Newspapers; http://www.mcclatchydc.com/incoming/article24450391.html

102   *But instead, the students found themselves* . . . "Leveling The Playing Field: Reforming The H2b Program To Protect Guest workers And U.S Workers"; 2012; National Guestworker Alliance, and 87. Pennsylvania State University, Dickinson School of Law's Center for Immigrants' Right; http://www.guestworkeralliance.org/wp-content/uploads/2012/06/Leveling-the-Playing-Field-final.pdf

103   *The strike was front-page news* . . . Preston, Julia; "Foreign Students in Work Visa Program Stage Walkout at Plant"; *New York Times*; 2011; http://www.nytimes.com/2011/08/18/us/18immig.html?_r=0

103   *The* New York Times *reported that the Walt Disney Company* . . . Preston, Julia; "Pink Slips at Disney. But First, Training Foreign Replacements"; 2015; *New York Times*; http://www.nytimes.com/2015/06/04/us/last-task-after-layoff-at-disney-train-foreign-replacements.html?_r=0

106   *Sometimes, there's a thin line between* . . . https://www.topcoder.com/

109   *As she wrote in her inaugural letter* . . . Vincent, James; "Amazon's Mechanical Turkers want to be recognized as 'actual human beings'" 2014; *The Verge*; http://www.theverge.com/2014/12/4/7331777/amazon-mechanical-turk-workforce-digital-labor

110   *Over the next few years* . . . Ipeirotis, Panagiotis; Analyzing the Mechanical Turk Marketplace; 2010; NYU; https://archive.nyu.edu/bitstream/2451/29801/4/CeDER-10-04.pdf

114   *as evidenced in the title of her bestselling book* . . . Poo, Ai-Jen; *The Age of Dignity; Preparing for the Elder Boom*; The New Press; 2015

116   *In 2007, DWU and 11 other organizations* . . . http://www.domesticworkers.org/

117   *To improve employee-employer communication* . . . http:/domestic employers.org/qa/

CHAPTER 6

125   *And first and second generation* . . . Bellman, Eric; "The Real Reason Indian-Americans Were Celebrating at Modi's Speech in Madison Square Garden"; *Wall Street Journal*; 2014 http://blogs.wsj.com/india realtime/2014/09/29/the-real-reason-indian-americans-were -celebrating-at-modis-speech-in-madison-square-garden/

126   *That means when it equalizes* . . . McCarthy, Niall; The Country with the Most Engineering Graduates (Infographic); 2015; *Forbes* magazine; http://www.forbes.com/sites/niallmccarthy/2015/06/09/the -countries-with-the-most-engineering-graduates-infographic/

127   *According to* New Yorker *writer John Cassidy* . . . Cassidy, John; College Calculus: New Yorker; 2015; http://www.newyorker.com/magazine /2015/09/07/college-calculus

127   *In his new book, Will College Pay Off* . . . Cappelli, Peter; Will College Pay Off?; Public Affairs; 2015.

127   *As Michael S. Teitelbaum wrote* . . . Teitelbaum, Michael; "The Myth of the Science and Engineering Shortage"; 2014; *The Atlantic* http://www .theatlantic.com/education/archive/2014/03/the-myth-of-the-science -and-engineering-shortage/284359/

132   *Despite all the government assistance programs* . . . Porter, Eduardo. 2015. "Electing to Ignore the Poorest of the Poor"; *NYT* http://www .nytimes.com/2015/11/18/business/economy/electing-to-ignore-the -poorest-of-the-poor.html?emc=eta1&_r=0

132   *That's the equivalent of* . . . Ibid. Porter, Eduardo; "Electing to Ignore the Poorest of the Poor"; 2015; *New York Times* http://www.nytimes .com/2015/11/18/business/economy/electing-to-ignore-the-poorest -of-the-poor.html?emc=eta1&_r=0

139   *After the 1963 March on Washington* . . . Rustin, Bayard.; "The Meaning of the March on Washington" 1963; *Liberation*; http://www.crmvet .org/info/mowrust.htm

CHAPTER 7

145   *I was at the Full Frame Film Festival* . . . http://thehandthatfeedsfilm .com/

146   *Healthcare reform, in contrast* . . . http://www.gpo.gov/fdsys/pkg /PLAW-111publ148/pdf/PLAW-111publ148.pdf; 2010; GPO

146   *As of March 2015 . . .* "ObamaCare Enrollment Numbers"; 2015;
      ObamaCare Facts; http://obamacarefacts.com/sign-ups/obamacare
      -enrollment-numbers/

149   *They would cite very reputable scholars . . .* Edsall, Thomas; "No More
      Industrial Revolutions?"; 2012; *New York Times*; http://campaignstops
      .blogs.nytimes.com/2012/10/15/no-more-industrial-revolutions/
              According to Robert Gordon, an economist at Northwestern Uni-
      versity and author of a report on technological unemployment for the
      National Bureau of Economic Research, "The greatest innovations are
      behind us, with little prospect for transformative change along the
      lines of the three previous industrial revolutions . . . "
              In an article in the *Wall Street Journal*, reporter Tim Aeppel credits
      MIT economist David Autor as having " . . . the non-alarmist view" on
      automation, "The 50-year-old believes automation has hurt the job
      market—but in a more targeted way than most pessimists think. He
      also doesn't see the automation wave killing a wider array of jobs as
      quickly as many predict."

149   *My assumptions were summed up . . .* Thompson, Derek; "A World With-
      out Work"; *The Atlantic*; 2015; http://www.theatlantic.com/magazine
      /archive/2015/07/world-without-work/395294/

150   *"Until a few years ago . . . "* Summers, Lawrence; Economic Possibilities
      of Our Children; NBER Reporter; 2013; http://www.nber.org/reporter
      /2013number4/2013no4.pdf

150   *The web-based instrument was fielded . . .* Smith, Aaron and Anderson,
      Janna; "AI, Robotics, and the Future of Jobs"; Pew Research Center;
      2014; http://www.pewinternet.org/2014/08/06/future-of-jobs/

151   *"Computers are so dexterous . . . "* McAfee, Andrew and Brynjolfsson,
      Erik; *The Second Machine Age*; W. W. Norton & Company; 2014.

152   *"But the possibility seems significant . . . "* Ibid. Thompson, Derek; "A
      World Without Work"; *The Atlantic*; 2015; http://www.theatlantic.com
      /magazine/archive/2015/07/world-without-work/395294/

154   *And real earnings for college graduates . . .* Shierholz, Heidi and Mishel,
      Larry; *A Decade of Flat Wages*; Economic Policy Institute; 2013; http://
      www.epi.org/publication/a-decade-of-flat-wages-the-key-barrier
      -to-shared-prosperity-and-a-rising-middle-class/;

154   *As of this writing in early 2016 . . .* Neff, Blake; College Enrollment
      Dropped Over 2% Last Year; The Daily Caller Foundation: 2015; http://
      dailycaller.com/2015/05/14/college-enrollment-dropped-over
      -2-percent-last-year/

155   *McAfee and Brynjolffson,* The Second Machine Age . . . .; W. W. Norton
      & Company; 2014

155   *As McAfee noted in a presentation* . . . McAfee, Andrew; *60 Minutes,* "How Many Jobs?"; 2013; http://andrewmcafee.org/2013/01/mcafee-60-minutes-jobs-amazon-apple-facebook-google/

155   *The American Recovery and Reinvestment Act of 2009* . . . American Recovery and Reinvestment Act of 2009; Public Law 111-5; 111th Congress; http://www.gpo.gov/fdsys/pkg/PLAW-111publ5/html/PLAW-111publ5.htm

156   *President Franklin Roosevelt's Works Progress Administration (WPA)* . . . . Works Progress Administration: Executive Order Franklin D. Roosevelt; 1936

157   *We can overcome this hurdle* . . . Rubin, Richard; "U.S. Companies Are Stashing $2.1 Trillion Overseas to Avoid Taxes"; 2015; *Bloomberg-Business*; http://www.bloomberg.com/news/articles/2015-03-04/u-s-companies-are-stashing-2-1-trillion-overseas-to-avoid-taxes

157   *With a modest initial investment* . . . US Chamber, AFL-CIO Urge Infrastructure Bank: US Chamber of Commerce Press Release: 2015; https://www.uschamber.com/press-release/us-chamber-afl-cio-urge-infrastructure-bank

157   *While Senator Warner suggested.* Ibid

158   *In 2012 Carl Camden, the CEO of Kelley Services* . . . Stern, Andy and Camden, Carl; "Why we need to raise the minimum wage"; Los Angeles Times; 2013; http://articles.latimes.com/2013/mar/10/opinion/la-oe-stern-camden-why-we-should-raise-the-minimum-20130310

159   *Under current law* . . . "Policy Basics: The Earned Income Tax Credit"; 2015; Center for Budget and Policy Priorities. http://www.cbpp.org/research/federal-tax/policy-basics-the-earned-income-tax-credit

161   *Innovation and the hope* . . . Frey, Carl Benedikt and Osborne, Michael A. "The Future Of Employment: How Susceptible Are Jobs To Computerisation?"; Oxford Martin School, Programme on the Impacts of Future Technology, University of Oxford; 2013

161   *Digital progress has surprised* . . . McAfee, Andrew, and Brynjolfsson, Erik; "Jobs, Productivity and the Great Decoupling"; 2012; *New York Times*; http://www.nytimes.com/2012/12/12/opinion/global/jobs-productivity-and-the-great-decoupling.html

162   *"All of the above abilities* . . . ." Edsall, Thomas B.; "The Hollowing Out"; *New York Times*; 2012; http://campaignstops.blogs.nytimes.com/2012/07/08/the-future-of-joblessness/

163   *"Andy Grove offered this more prodding guidance* . . . ." Grove, Andy; *Only the Paranoid Survive; How to Exploit the Crisis Points that Challenge Every Company and Career*; Doubleday; 1996

166   *At first the notion of "money for nothing,"* . . . Dire Straits; Money for
       Nothing: 1985;https://www.google.com/search?client=safari&rls=en&
       q=money+for+nothing+dire+straits&ie=UTF-8&oe=UTF-8

166   *But the more I researched UBI* . . . Page 214

166   *As measured by hours spent in the workplace* . . . Miller, Claire Cain;
       "The 24/7 Work Culture's Toll on Families and Gender Equality"; The
       Upshot; *New York Times*; 2015; http://www.nytimes.com/2015/05/31
       /upshot/the-24-7-work-cultures-toll-on-families-and-gender-equality
       .html

167   *Technology also means* . . . Whittle, Jon; "How Technology Blurs the
       Lines Between Work and Home Life"; 2015; http://www.epsrc.ac.uk
       /blog/articles/how-technology-blurs-the-lines-between-work-and
       -home-life/

167   *Work has been at the center* . . . Rule of St. Benedict; https://en.wikipedia
       .org/wiki/Pray_and_work

168   *The German sociologist Max Weber* . . . Weber, Max; *The Protestant Ethic
       and the Spirit of Capitalism*; 1992; Routledge Taylor & Francis Group.

168   *In 1900, Americans spent* . . . Will, George F.; Review of Brink Lindsay's
       *The Age of Abundance: How Prosperity Transformed America's Politics
       and Culture*; 2007; New York Times Sunday Book Review; http://www
       .nytimes.com/2007/06/10/books/review/Will-t.html?pagewanted
       =all&_r=0

169   *The literature I began to read* . . . Skidelsky, Robert and Skidelsky, Ed-
       ward; "In Praise of Leisure; The Chronicle of Higher Education"; 2012;
       http://chronicle.com/article/In-Praise-of-Leisure/132251/

169   *"Economic Possibilities for Our Grandchildren* . . . *"* Keynes, John May-
       nard; Essays in Persuasion; London: Macmillan; 1931

169   *As the French economist Philippe Van Parijs* . . . Parijs, Philippe Van; *A
       Basic Income for All*; Boston Review 2000; http://new.bostonreview
       .net/BR25.5/vanparijs.html

CHAPTER 8

172   *The first major proponent* . . . Paine, Thomas; *Agrarian Justice*; 1797;
       https://en.wikipedia.org/wiki/Agrarian_Justice

172   *His proposal was never adopted* . . . Barnes, Peter; *With Liberty and Div-
       idends for All*; Berret-Koehler; 2014

173   *In his 1918 book Roads to Freedom* . . . Russell, Bertrand; *Roads to Free-
       dom*; H. Holt; New York; 1919

173   *As Article 25 states* . . . UN Declaration of Human Rights; General As-
       sembly Resolution 217A; 1948

174   *It was in the United States that basic income* . . . Friedman, Milton; Capitalism and Freedom; University of Chicago Press; 1962

174   *Another libertarian* . . . Shearmur, Jeremy; Hayek and After; Routledge; 1996

174   *In response, more than 1,000 economists* . . . Caputo, Richard; *Basic Income Guarantee and Politics*; Palgrave Macmillan; 2012

175   *King expressed his reasons* . . . King, Dr. Martin Luther; *Where Do We Go From Here; Chaos or Community*; Beacon Press 1967, 2010

176   *Supporters credit it with making Alaska* . . . http://www.apfc.org/home/Content/aboutFund/aboutPermFund.cfm

177   *In their 1999 book* . . . Ackerman, Bruce and Alstott, Anne, *The Stakeholder Society*; Yale University Press; 2000

177   *In his 2006 book* . . . Murray, Charles; *In Our Hands: A Plan to End the Welfare State*; AEI Press; 2006

178   *In his 2014 book* . . . Barnes, Peter; *With Liberty and Dividends for All*; Berret-Koehler; 2014

179   *It also improved parenting quality.* Akee, Randall K.Q., Copeland, William E., Keeler, Gordon, and Costello, Elizabeth J.; "Parents' Incomes and Children's Outcomes"; A Quasi-Experiment; HHPMC US National Library of Medicine; 2010

179   *"Before the casino opened . . . ."* Velasquez-Manoff, Moises, What Happens When the Poor Receive a Stipend;? *New York Times* "Opionator"; 2014; http://opinionator.blogs.nytimes.com/2014/01/18/what-happens-when-the-poor-receive-a-stipend/

180   *During the five-year experiment* . . . Forget, Evelyn L; "The Town with No Poverty"; University of Manitoba; 2011; http://public.econ.duke.edu/~erw/197/forget-cea%20(2).pdf

180   *There were several other findings* . . . Ibid; Forget; University of Manitoba

181   *In July of 2015 it was reported* . . . Namibia: Government 'strongly considering' basic income: BIEN News; 2015; http://www.basicincome.org/news/2015/07/namibia-government-strongly-considering-basic-income/

181   *The Dutch city of Utrecht* . . . Brett, Luke; "Keeping an eye on Utrecht's Basic Income experiment"; http://www.capx.co/keeping-an-eye-on-utrechts-basic-income-experiment/CAPX;

181   *Switzerland will hold a nationwide* . . . BIEN Basic Income News; 2014; http://www.basicincome.org/news/2014/08/switerland-government-reacts-negatively-to-ubi-proposal/

181   *According to a recent poll, 69 percent of Finns support* . . . http://www.vox.com/2015/12/8/9872554/finlnd-basic-income-experiment

182   *A plank in the Liberty Party's platform reads* . . . Policy Resolution 100:
       "Priority Resolution: Creating a Basic Annual Income to be Designed
       and Implemented for a Fair Economy"; Liberal; 2015

182   *In a major report on basic income* . . . "Creative Citizen, Creative State:
       the principled and pragmatic case for a Basic Income" https://www
       .thersa.org/discover/publications-and-articles/reports/basic-income

186   *Tanner, a libertarian, says that the first ten years* . . . www.newyorker
       .com/news/john-cassidy/how-the-war-on-poverty-succeeded-in
       -four-charts

       It is important to note that while Tanner's conclusions regarding
       the effectiveness of anti-poverty programs is correct if you simply ac-
       cept the official measure of poverty, there is substantial and convincing
       research to suggest that that measure has failed to accurately portray
       the improvements in poverty over time. The official poverty measure is
       considered by many experts and academics to be extremely outdated
       and crude, in that it bases its measure of poverty exclusively on the cost
       of food. More recent and sophisticated measures of poverty, which in-
       clude food, clothing, shelter (rent/mortgage), utilities, medical ex-
       penses, and child care, and which also acknowledge the fact that
       poverty is relative to the income levels of other people in your state and
       country (poverty in sub-Saharan Africa is different from poverty in
       America) suggest that we have made significant improvements in our
       fight against poverty over the years. A recent study from Columbia
       University, which created the new metric and studied how poverty has
       shifted since 1967 suggested that, "Our estimates . . . show that histori-
       cal trends in poverty have been more favorable—and that government
       programs have played a larger role—than [previous] estimates sug-
       gest . . . Government programs today are cutting poverty nearly in half
       (from 29% to 16%) while in 1967 they only cut poverty by about one
       percentage point." In other words, we HAVE made progress through
       our existing social welfare programs, despite Tanner's (and many other
       Republicans') assertions. That being said, we have a long way to go and
       there are many questions about the design of our current social safety
       net and whether it can hold up to the 21st century.

188   *Capitalists can always walk away* . . . Carter, Timothy Roscoe; "One
       Minute Case for Basic Income"; BIEN; 2014; http://www.basicincome
       .org/bien/pdf/montreal2014/BIEN2014_Carter.pdf

189   *Every extra dollar going* . . . Anderson Sarah; "Wall Street Bonuses and
       the Minimum Wage"; Institute for Policy Studies; 2014

190   *And this is a key advantage* . . . Groth, Aimee; "Entrepreneurs don't
       have a special gene for risk—they come from families with money";

Quartz; 2015; http://qz.com/455109/entrepreneurs-dont-have-a -special-gene-for-risk-they-come-from-families-with-money/

191   *Finally, many people seem to not believe that the policies . . .* Etzioni, Amitai; "It's Economic Insecurity, Stupid"; Huff Post Politics; 2014

191   *On his radio show, Nader compared . . .* Ralph Nader Radio Hour; http://ralphnaderradiohour.com/category/auto-safety/

191   *Vinod Khosla, the founder. . . .* Khosla, Vinod; Fireside Chat with Google Co-founders Larry Page and Sergey Bring; 2014; http://www .khoslaventures.com/fireside-chat-with-google-co-founders-larry -page-and-sergey-brin

192   *In an article he wrote for* Vice . . . .Schneider, Nathan; "Why the Tech Elite Is Getting Behind Universal Basic Income;" *Vice*; 2015; http:// www.vice.com/read/something-for-everyone-0000546-v22n1

192   *"After one speaker enumerated . . . ."* Ibid

192   *Netscape creator Marc Andreessen . . . ."* Roose, Kevin; "In Conversation with Mark Andreessen"; *New York Magazine*; 2014 http:// nymag.com/daily/intelligencer/2014/10/marc-andreessen-in -conversation.html

192   *Others include . . .* Piston, Federico; *Robots Will Steal Your Job, But That's Ok: how to survive the economic collapse and be happy*; CreateSpace Independent Publishing Platform; 2012

192   *written a novella called* Manna . . . Brain, Marshall; *Manna: Two Visions of Humanity's Future*; BYG Publishing, Inc.; 2012

192   *Former U.S. Labor Secretary Robert Reich . . . .* Reich, Robert; *Saving Capitalism: For the Many, Not the Few*: Knopf First Edition; 2015

196   *"In a January 2016 interview with the Swiss newspaper Blick, . . . "* http://www.blick.ch/news/wirtschaft/wef-gruender-klaus-schwab -ueber-die-vierte-industrielle-revolution-in-der-schweiz-fallen -200000-buerojobs-weg-id4538228.html

201   *Using the 2015 Federal Guidelines for Poverty . . .* Federal Register; https://www.federalregister.gov/articles/2015/01/22/2015-01120 /annual-update-of-the-hhs-poverty-guidelines

202   *"America's population is wealthier . . . "* Ibid. Murray, Charles; *In Our Hands: A Plan to End the Welfare State*; AEI Press; 2006

203   *"I am now convinced . . . "* Ibid. King, Dr. Martin Luther; *Where Do We Go From Here; Chaos or Community*; Beacon Press 1967, 2010

203   *"For example, one plan that advocates a UBI of $12,000 per year . . . "* Santens, Scott; "Why Should We Support the Idea of Universal Basic Income?"; Huff Post Politics; 2015

205   *These ideas were included in the Commission's final report . . .* National Commission on Fiscal responsibility and Reform: Moment Of Truth;

2010; https://www.fiscalcommission.gov/sites/fiscalcommission.gov /files/documents/TheMomentofTruth12_1_2010.pdf

205   *The August 2014 issue* . . . Zwolinski, Matt, Huemer, Michael, Manzi, Jim, and Frank, Robert H.; "The Basic Income and the Welfare State"; Cato Unbound: 2014; http://www.cato-unbound.org/issues/august -2014/basic-income-welfare-state

205   *At a recent TED talk about UBI* . . . Wenger, Albert; "A BIG idea, a bot idea—How smart policy will advance tech"; | TEDxNewYork; 2015; https://www.youtube.com/watch?v=t8qo7pzH_NM

212   *Cash out all or some number* . . . Safety New Programs; Federal Safety Net; 2015; http://federalsafetynet.com/safety-net-programs.html

213   *90 percent of the population has a net personal income* . . . Walker, Mark; "BIG and Technological Unemployment: "Chicken Little Versus the Economists"; Journal of Evolution and Technology; 2014

213   *an FTT of 0.25 percent on each side* . . . Baker, Dean, Pollin Robert, McArthur, Travis, and Sherman, Matt, "The Potential Revenue from Financial Transactions Taxes," *Center for Economic and Policy Research*, 2009; http://www.cepr.net/documents/publications/ftt-revenue-2009 -12.pdf

214   *In September of 2015* . . . Zumbrun, Josh, "US Household Wealth Set Record in 2nd Quarter," *The Wall Street Journal*; 2015; http://www .wsj.com/articles/u-s-household-wealth-hit-record-in-second -quarter-1442593339

214   *trim the military budget* . . . "Policy Basics:Where Do Our Federal Dollars Go," Center for Budget and Policy Priorities, 2015; http://www .cbpp.org/research/policy-basics-where-do-our-federal-tax-dollars-go

214   *farm subsidies* . . . "Milking Taxpayer," *The Economist*; 2015; http:// www.economist.com/news/united-states/21643191-crop-prices-fall -farmers-grow-subsidies-instead-milking-taxpayers

214   *oil and gas companies* . . . Weissman, Jordan, "America's Most Obvious Tax Reform Idea: Kill the Oil and Gas Subsidies," *The Atlantic*; 2013; http://www.theatlantic.com/business/archive/2013/03/americas -most-obvious-tax-reform-idea-kill-the-oil-and-gas-subsidies /274121/

215   *"Democracy is the worst form of government* . . . " Churchill, Winston S.; Speech in the House of Commons, November 11, 1947)

216   *I believe poverty and inequality* . . . Santens, Scott; Patreon; 2015; https://www.patreon.com/scottsantens?ty=h

216   *They had some padding if they failed* . . . .Smith, Ned, "The Sad Truth About the American Dream" *BusinessNewsDaily*; 2012

       In his study of inequality around the world, Fabian Pfeffler, a sociologist at the University of Michigan Institute of Social Research, found that parental wealth has an influence above and beyond the three factors that sociologists and economists traditionally consider in research on social mobility: parental education, income and occupation. His research is based on data on two generations of families in the U.S. and a comparison with similar data from Germany and Sweden.

217   *She mentions the Townsend Clubs* . . . Townsend, Dr. Francis; Social Welfare History Project; http://www.socialwelfarehistory.com/eras /great-depression/townsend-dr-francis/

INDEX

ANDY STERN, formerly president of the 2.2–million-member Service Employees International Union and a member of the Simpson-Bowles Commission, is now the Ronald O. Perelman Senior Fellow at Columbia University's Richman Center. His work with the SEIU was widely credited for helping to elect President Barack Obama in 2008 and to secure the historic passage of the 2010 Health Care Reform Act. Stern has been named a "top power player" by both *Fortune* and *Washingtonian Magazine*, and has been profiled by *60 Minutes*, Bill Moyers, Charlie Rose, *Business Week*, and the *New York Times Magazine*.

PublicAffairs is a publishing house founded in 1997. It is a tribute to the standards, values, and flair of three persons who have served as mentors to countless reporters, writers, editors, and book people of all kinds, including me.

I. F. STONE, proprietor of *I. F. Stone's Weekly*, combined a commitment to the First Amendment with entrepreneurial zeal and reporting skill and became one of the great independent journalists in American history. At the age of eighty, Izzy published *The Trial of Socrates*, which was a national bestseller. He wrote the book after he taught himself ancient Greek.

BENJAMIN C. BRADLEE was for nearly thirty years the charismatic editorial leader of *The Washington Post*. It was Ben who gave the *Post* the range and courage to pursue such historic issues as Watergate. He supported his reporters with a tenacity that made them fearless and it is no accident that so many became authors of influential, best-selling books.

ROBERT L. BERNSTEIN, the chief executive of Random House for more than a quarter century, guided one of the nation's premier publishing houses. Bob was personally responsible for many books of political dissent and argument that challenged tyranny around the globe. He is also the founder and longtime chair of Human Rights Watch, one of the most respected human rights organizations in the world.

·   ·   ·

For fifty years, the banner of Public Affairs Press was carried by its owner Morris B. Schnapper, who published Gandhi, Nasser, Toynbee, Truman, and about 1,500 other authors. In 1983, Schnapper was described by *The Washington Post* as "a redoubtable gadfly." His legacy will endure in the books to come.

Peter Osnos, *Founder and Editor-at-Large*